Food Policy
Old and New

Food Policy
Old and New

Edited by
Simon Maxwell and Rachel Slater

Published by Blackwell Publishing
9600 Garsington Road, Oxford OX4 2DK, UK
350 Main Street, Malden, MA 02148-5018, USA
550 Swanston Street, Carlton South, Melbourne, Victoria 3053, Australia

First published 2003 as *Development Policy Review* Theme Issue 21(5-6) by Blackwell Publishing Ltd

Library of Congress Cataloging-in-Publication Data has been Applied for

A catalogue record for this title is available from the British Library

ISBN 1-4051-2602-7 (paperback)

The publisher's policy is to use permanent paper from mills that operate a sustainable forestry policy, and
which has been manufactured from pulp processed using acid-free and elementary chlorine-free
practices. Furthermore, the publisher ensures that the text paper and cover board
used have met acceptable environmental accreditation standards.

For further information on
Blackwell Publishing, visit our website:
http://www.blackwellpublishing.com

Cover photo: Arusha, Tanzania by Charles Mindel
Cover design: Graeme Crowley

Contents

Figures

Tables

Boxes

Acronyms

ACP	African, Caribbean and Pacific
AEZs	Agricultural Export Zones
AHP	Anti-Hunger Programme
AoA	Agreement on Agriculture
AP	Andhra Pradesh
ATTP	Africa Trade and Poverty Programme
AusAID	Australian Agency for International Development
BC	Backward Castes
BSE	Bovine Spongiform Encephalopathy (or Mad Cow Disease)
CAP	Common Agricultural Policy
CBI (neths)	Center for the Promotion of Imports from Developing Countries
CDC	Centers for Disease Control and Prevention
CGIAR	Consultative Group on International Agricultural Research
CHNS	China Health and Nutrition Study
CIDA	Canadian International Development Agency
CN	Combined Nomenclature
COAG	Committee on Agriculture
CODEX	Codex Alimentarius Commission
CPBS	Cartagena Protocol on Bio-Safety
DAC	Development Assistance Committee
DALYs	Disability Adjusted Life Years
DECTA	Developing Countries Trade Agency
DR-NCDs	diet-related non-communicable diseases
EBA	Everything but Arms
ECHO	European Union's Humanitarian Office
EPOS	Electronic Point of Sale
EU	European Union
FAC	Food Aid Convention
FAO	Food and Agriculture Organization
FAOSTAT	FAO Statistical Databases
FFE	Food for Education Programme
FFV	fresh fruit and vegetables
FIELD	Foundation for International Environmental Law and Development
FIVIMS	Food Insecurity and Vulnerability Information Mapping System
FMD	foot and mouth disease
FSA	Food Standard Agency
GATT	General Agreement on Tariffs and Trades

GDP	Gross Domestic Product
GM	genetically modified
GMOs	Genetically Modified Organisms
GNP	Gross National Product
GoAP	Government of Andhra Pradesh
GVCs	global-value or commodity chains
ICRISAT	International Crops Research Institute for the Semi-Arid Tropics
IDC	International Development Committee
IEFR	International Emergency Food Reserve
IFA	Immediate Response Account
IFAD	International Fund for Agricultural Development
IFAT	International Fair Trade Association
IFC	International Finance Corporation
IFPRI	International Food Policy Research Institute
ILO	International Labour Organization
INTERFAIS	International Food Aid Information System
LDCs	Least Developed Countries
LIFDCs	Low-Income Food Deficit Countries
LSAFP	Large-Scale Advanced Farm Project
MINs	Marchés d'Intérêt Nationale
MRL	EU Minimum Residue Level
NCDs	non-communicable diseases
NGO	Non-governmental Organisation
NR-NCDs	nutrition-related non-communicable diseases
NSS	National Sample Survey
OC	other Castes
ODA	Official Development Assistance
OECD	Organisation for Economic Co-operation and Development
PRRO	Protracted Relief and Rehabilitation Operations
PRSP	Poverty Reduction strategy paper
PVOs	private and voluntary organisations
R&D	Research and Development
rBST	recombinant Bovine Somatotropin
SACU	Southern African Customs Union
SADC	Southern African Development Community
SC	Scheduled Castes
SPS	Sanitary and Phytosanitary
ST	Scheduled Tribes
TRIPs	Trade Related Intellectual Property Rights
UN	United Nations

UNCTAD	United Nations Conference on Trade and Development
UNDP	United Nations Development Programme
UNEP	United Nations Environmental Programme
UNHCR	United Nations High Commissioner for Refugees
UNICEF	United Nations Children's Fund
UNIDO	United National Industrial Development Organisation
USAID	United States Agency for International Development
USDA	United States Department of Agriculture
VCJD	variant Creutzfeldt-Jakob Disease,
WFC	World Food Council
WFP	World Food Programme
WFS	World Food Summit (1996)
WFS-fyl	World Food Summit five years later (2002)
WHO	World Health Organization
WTO	World Trade Organization

About the Overseas Development Institute

The Overseas Development Institute (ODI) is Britain's leading independent think-tank on international development and humanitarian issues. Our mission is to inspire and inform policy and practice which lead to the reduction of poverty, the alleviation of suffering and the achievement of sustainable livelihoods in developing countries. We do this by locking together high-quality applied research, practical policy advice, and policy-focused dissemination and debate. We work with partners in the public and private sectors, in both developing and developed countries.

The Overseas Development Institute's work centres on four research and policy programmes: the Humanitarian Policy Group, the International Economic Development Group, the Poverty and Public Policy Group, and the Rural Policy and Environment Group.

A list of ODI's free and priced publications can be obtained by contacting the Publications Office, ODI, 111 Westminster Bridge Rd, London, SE1 7JD, UK; Phone 00 44 (0) 20 7922 0300; Fax 00 44 (0) 20 7922 0399; E-mail: publications@odi.org.uk; Web: http://www.odi.org.uk/

Notes on Contributors

Dr Edward J. Clay, a Senior Research Associate at ODI, has extensively researched and written on food security and natural disasters, as well as advising many international agencies and governments on food aid policy. He was formerly Director of the Relief and Development Institute, London and a Fellow of the Institute of Development Studies at the University of Sussex. Edward Clay and Olav Stokke of NUPI jointly edited *Food Aid and Human Security* published by F. Cass in 2000 for EADI.

Priya Deshingkar is a Research Fellow at the Overseas Development Institute. She has a multidisciplinary background and was first trained as an agricultural scientist at the Indian Agricultural Research Institute and then studied Economics at Sussex before completing a DPhil at the Institute of Development Studies, University of Sussex on the entitlements of the poor to biomass resources. Her research interests include agriculture, rural development and poverty. She recently led a three year DFID-funded policy study in Andhra Pradesh, India which involved village-level research on various aspects of rural livelihoods. Usha Kulkarni, Sreenivas Rao and Laxman Rao worked as Research Officers on this project and were responsible for collecting qualitative and quantitative data from six villages over a period of 18 months.

Elizabeth Dowler is a registered public health nutritionist and a Senior Lecturer in the Department of Sociology at the University of Warwick, where she works on food and nutrition as social policy issues. She has carried out research and consultancy in many parts of the world, and now works on food and inequality, policy support for local initiatives and consumer perspectives of the food chain and risk, in the UK and the rest of Europe. She is a member of the Food Ethics Council. Among recent publications are: *Poverty Bites: Food, Health and Poor Families* (2001) London: CPAG; (ed. with Jones Finer) *The Welfare of Food: Rights and Responsibilities in a Changing World* (2003) Oxford: Blackwells; (ed. with Mosley) *Poverty and Social Exclusion in North and South* (2003) London: Routledge; and contributions to Dora and Wilson (eds) *Engaging with Public Concerns over Safe Food: Lessons from BSE/CJD for Health and Risk Communication Strategies* (forthcoming) WHO: Geneva.

Peter Gibbon is Senior Researcher in Trade and Development at the Danish Institute for International Studies (formerly Centre for Development Research). Between 1999 and 2003 he led a research programme on 'Globalisation and Economic Restructuring in Africa'. He is now preparing a new programme on 'Standards and Developing Country Agro-food Exports'.

Lawrence J. Haddad joined IFPRI as a research fellow in 1990 and since 1994 has been director of the Food Consumption and Nutrition Division. His overall research focus is on the design and impact of policies and programmes to reduce poverty and malnutrition. His research interests include the nutrition and poverty consequences of gender differences in access to resources; how decisions are made within families and the role of individual status; the links between agriculture, poverty, and nutrition; the role of social capital in protecting income levels and promoting income growth; the role of community participation in the performance of poverty programs; the implications of the human rights movement for food policy research; and the challenges faced by households and policymakers in areas of the developing world where rapid urbanisation is contributing to growing poverty and malnutrition. Before joining IFPRI he was a lecturer in quantitative development economics at the University of Warwick.

Hartwig de Haen is currently the Assistant Director-General and head of the Economic and Social Department of the Food and Agriculture Organization of the United Nations (FAO). Before joining FAO, he worked as a Research Associate at Michigan State, USA, and at the University of Bonn, Germany. He was Professor of Agricultural Economics at the University of Göttingen, Germany, where he has also served as Dean of the Faculty of Agriculture and Director of the Interdisciplinary Center for Agriculture and the Environment. His applied research comprised agricultural policy issues in Europe as well as in various countries of Asia, Near East and Africa. He received his Ph.D. in Agricultural Economics from the University of Göttingen and has published various books and articles in the fields of production economics, development economics, agricultural policy and environmental economics.

Tim Lang is Professor of Food Policy at City University's Institute of Health Sciences in London. He specialises in how policy affects the shape of the food supply chain, what people eat and the social, health and civic outcomes. He is chair of Sustain, the UK NGO alliance, and a Fellow of the Faculty of Public Health and a Vice-President of the Chartered Institute of Environmental Health. He is a member of the UK government's Defra Horizon Scanning Team, advising the Chief Scientist and is an advisor to the Commons Health Committee Inquiry into Obesity 2003-4.

Simon Maxwell has been Director of the Overseas Development Institute since 1997. Before that, he worked for the UN Development Programme in Kenya and India, for the British aid programme as an agricultural economist in Bolivia, and for some sixteen years at the Institute of Development Studies, University of Sussex, latterly as Programme Manager for Poverty, Food Security and the Environment. He has worked on food policy for over thirty years, in academic and non-academic contexts, and in both developing and developed countries. He has advised many national and international agencies in this field; and has published extensively on food security, food policy, food planning, food aid, food rights, food safety nets, food production, and related topics.

Erik Millstone is Reader in Science Policy at the University of Sussex. His research has focused on the role of scientific evidence and expertise in public policy-making, especially on issues of food and chemical safety. His publications include: (with P. van Zwanenberg) *BSE: Risk, Science and Governance* (2004) Oxford: Oxford University Press; C. Dora et al. *Engaging with Public Concerns (over Safe Food): Lessons from BSE/CJD to Health and Risk Communication Strategies* (2004) Geneva: WHO; (ed. with T. Lang) *The Atlas of Food: Who Eats What, Where and Why* (2003) London: Earthscan, and New York: Penguin Books; and (with P. van Zwanenberg) (2002) 'The

Evolution of Food Safety Policy-making Institutions in the UK, EU and Codex Alimentarius', *Social Policy and Administration* 36 (6): 593-609.

Sheila Page has been a Research Fellow, Overseas Development Institute, London, since 1982. Previously she was at Queen Elizabeth House, Oxford, 1972, and the National Institute of Economic and Social Research, 1972-82. Her current research interests include how and why developing countries participate in international negotiations and regional trading arrangements among developing countries and between developing countries and developed. Her publications include *Developing Countries in GATT/WTO Negotiations* (2002), *Regionalism among Developing Countries* (2000), *World Commodity Prices: Still a Problem for Developing Countries? How Developing Countries Trade* (1994), *World Trade Reform: Do Developing Countries Gain or Lose?* (1994), and *Trade, Finance and Developing Countries* (1989).

Prabhu Pingali is the Director of the Agricultural and Development Economics Division of the Food and Agriculture Organization of the United Nations. He is also the President of the International Association of Agricultural Economists (IAAE) and co-chairs the Millennium Ecosystem Assessment Panel's working group on Future Scenarios. An Indian national, he earned a Ph.D. in Economics from North Carolina State University in 1982 and has over twenty years of experience in assessing the extent and impact of technical change in developing country agriculture in Asia, Africa and Latin America. He has authored six books and dozens of refereed journal articles and book chapters on technological change, productivity growth and resource management issues in Asia, Africa and Latin America and has received several international awards for his work.

Barry M. Popkin, Ph.D., an economist, is Professor of Nutrition at UNC-CH where he heads the Division of Nutrition Epidemiology in the School of Public Health. His research focuses on dynamic changes in diet, physical activity and inactivity and body composition and the factors responsible for these changes as well as some consequences and program and policy options for change. Much of his work on the nutrition transition focuses on the rapid changes in obesity. He is actively involved in research in the US and a number of other countries around the world, involving detailed longitudinal studies and large-scale survey research. He serves on several scientific advisory organisations including Chair, the Nutrition Transition Committee for the International Union for the Nutritional Sciences and has published more than 210 journal articles along with other book chapters and books.

Rachel Slater is a Research Fellow at the Overseas Development Institute, London. Her doctoral and post-doctoral work focused on urban and rural livelihoods in South Africa, including social research on food and agriculture issues in low-income urban areas. Her current research interests include food security and food policy, and livelihoods diversification. She has also worked in India, Lesotho, Mozambique and Zambia.

Prakash Shetty is Chief, Nutrition Planning, Assessment and Evaluation Service, Food and Nutrition Division of the Food and Agriculture Organization of the UN in Rome

Before joining FAO, he was Professor of Human Nutrition at the London School of Hygiene and Tropical Medicine (London University). Since 1994 he has been Head of the Public Health Nutrition Unit, Department of Epidemiology and Population Health at the London School. As Commonwealth Medical Scholar, he was awarded his Ph.D. in 1980 from Cambridge University while researching at the MRC Dunn Nutrition Laboratory. He was appointed Professor and Chairman of the Department of Physiology at St Johns Medical College in Bangalore and established a Nutrition Research Centre of which he was the Director with research interests in energy and protein metabolism. He has served on the Editorial Boards of several international journals and on the scientific advisory committees of funding agencies and charities.

Kostas Stamoulis is Service Chief, Agricultural Sector in Economic Development Service in FAO Headquarters in Rome. Before joining FAO, he taught Agricultural Economics at the University of Illinois in Urbana Champaign. He has many years of experience in research and analysis of the role of agriculture in growth and poverty reduction; the effects of stabilisation on agricultural performance; the role of the non-farm rural sector on growth and food security and the impact of urbanisation and globalisation on the structure of food markets and small farmers. He is the representative of FAO in the Hunger Task Force of the Millennium project. A national of Greece, he has a Ph.D. in Agricultural and Resource Economics from the University of California at Berkeley.

Dr Christopher Stevens is an economist with over 25 years' professional experience specialising in international trade policy affecting developing countries. His principal interests on which he has written extensively are: the agenda for multilateral trade and trade-related policy in the new century (including dispute settlement, SPS, and 'new' issues such as TRIPs and services trade); trade preference agreements (especially those of the EU) and related issues (for example, rules of origin and WTO provisions); and the external dimensions of food security and export promotion of high-value agriculture. His main geographical focus is Southern and Eastern Africa, the Caribbean and the Mediterranean. He has also worked on the Andean region and the former Soviet Union.

Patrick van Zwanenberg was a Research Fellow at the Science and Technology Policy Research Unit, Sussex University until 2003. He trained initially in natural science before taking postgraduate degrees in science policy. He has been researching the science and politics of bovine spongiform encephalopathy for the last four years and is co-author, with Erik Millstone, of *BSE: Risk, Science and Governance* (2004) Oxford: Oxford University Press.

Preface

The papers in this volume first appeared in a theme issue of the ODI Journal, *Development Policy Review*, published with financial support from the UK Department of International Development in September 2003. As editors, and to use an appropriate metaphor, we make no apology for a second bite of the cherry. The issues are important, and we think the papers are of a quality which easily merits publication in book form. We hope that they will thereby – hereby – reach a wider audience.

We are frequently asked whether what we have termed the new food policy really matters in the poorest countries. Is obesity really a marker of poverty in countries where many face death by starvation? Is the supermarket revolution really the most important food problem in largely self-provisioning peasant societies? Do we really think that quality and safety standards for horticulture exports are the dominant force shaping local markets in poor countries? Well, no, of course not. But that's not quite the point. Our argument is not that traditional food security concerns are suddenly invalid, nor that the new agenda now dominates everywhere. We are trying to make a more subtle point, that food systems are changing, sometimes more quickly and sometimes more slowly – and that these changes are sometimes beneficial for the poor and sometimes not. It would be wrong to underestimate the eventual impact. As we know from much other work, changes introduced by supermarkets or by international trading companies have a habit of spreading fast through both production and marketing systems, and of generating substantial restructuring as they do so.

In preparing the original volume, we were struck by the relative abundance of literature describing change, but the relative lack of literature evaluating change. We tried to think about this problem in writing our editorial, but we think there is much more to do in this area. The new food policy challenges us to work more closely with regulatory and competition authorities, with environmental assessors, and with poverty planners. The old food policy – food security policy – was always concerned with the links between food and other fields, for example social protection. The links now need to be wider.

We hope this book will promote that kind of widening in food policy. We would like to thank DfID once more, and all those who have contributed. The list includes the authors, but also our Associate Editor, Margaret Cornell, the Production Co-ordinator of *DPR*, Tammie O'Neil, and the Marketing Officer for the book, Jane Northey. Special thanks also to David Sunderland, who was Simon Maxwell's Personal Assistant during the time this work was carried out.

SM
RS
December 2003

Chapter 1
Food Policy Old and New

Simon Maxwell and Rachel Slater

The character of the food system and the nature of food policy are both changing, as urbanisation, technical change and the industrialisation of the food system transform the way food is produced, marketed and consumed in developing countries. This overview presents an evaluation framework and explores new policy options. Some issues feature more prominently in richer, more urbanised, more industrialised developing countries, but the new food policy agenda is relevant in all countries – and it is in the poorest countries where challenges are set to emerge most rapidly. The agenda is more one of 'food policy' than 'food security': developing countries need both, but particularly a greater engagement with the new food policy.

1   Introduction

Remember 'food policy'? It is what some of us used to do before we discovered 'food security'. The very term 'food policy' induces nostalgia for the 1970s and early 1980s: the first meetings of the World Food Council (following the World Food Conference in 1974), the establishment of the International Food Policy Research Institute (in 1975), and of the journal *Food Policy* (1976), the World Bank Staff Working Paper by Clay and others (1981), the path-breaking book by Timmer, Falcon and Pearson (1981).[1]

The emphasis on food policy in developing countries was necessary. It was not just that the world food crisis of 1972-4 had triggered new interest in the availability of and access to food, especially at global and national levels. It was also that policy-makers had begun to appreciate the interdependence between supply- and demand-side issues, and the value of applying especially economic analysis to the links. Thus, Timmer and his colleagues dealt separately with the production, marketing and consumption of food, but then in a more holistic manner with what they termed 'macro food policy'. Those concerned with nutrition had already become familiar with integrated planning (Joy, 1973). Timmer, Falcon and Pearson reminded us that

> where the food system is headed, of course, is the key question. Developing an intuitive understanding of the critical pressures on the system at any particular time is the artistic part of analysis, but having a framework of how issues are connected is the starting point for the craft (1981: 262) ... [However] no country has put the pieces together. (ibid: 269)

---

1. By contrast, the well-known reader edited by J. Price Gittinger and others came somewhat later (Gittinger et al., 1987). For a chronology of food-related initiatives, particularly relating to Africa, see Maxwell (2001a: 22-3).

It was not long before the 'putting together' began, stimulated, for example, by the European Union's 1981 Plan of Action to Combat Hunger in the World and by its pilot programme of food strategies in Kenya, Zambia, Rwanda and Mali.

The 'food policy' discourse was short-lived, however. Amartya Sen (1981) is usually credited with shifting the discourse towards entitlement and access. In fact, similar ideas, perhaps less elegantly expressed, could be found in the nutrition literature (for example, Berg, 1973; Levinson, 1974; Kielman et al., 1977), and, indeed, in the contributions in food policy to the debate about safety nets (see for example, Timmer et al., 1981: 269ff). Whatever the source, the primary concern of the international discourse did shift quite rapidly, from food supply to food demand. Entitlement, vulnerability and risk became the new watchwords: this was the emergent language of food security.

The idea of 'food security' has predominated since the early 1980s.[2] From Sen, it was a short step to Reutlinger (1985), to Reutlinger and van Holst Pellekaan (World Bank, 1986), and eventually to Drèze and Sen (1989). Donors developed an enthusiasm for national food security planning (Maxwell, 1990), partly as a 'proxy for poverty planning' during the darkest years of structural adjustment (Hindle, 1990). The International Conference on Nutrition (1992), the World Food Summit (1996) and WFS-five years later (2002) cemented the consensus. A reduction in under-nutrition even made it into the Millennium Development Goals.[3] The core concept of food security evolved over time, but was commonly taken to include both supply and access, also safety, and, in some cases, cultural suitability (Box 1.1). These ideas were also reflected in the debate about the right to food (for example, Eide, 1996).

Box 1.1: Definitions of food security

'A basket of food, nutritionally adequate, culturally acceptable, procured in keeping with human dignity and enduring over time' (Oshaug, 1985).

'Access by all people at all times to enough food for an active, healthy life' (World Bank, 1986).

'A country and people are food secure when their food system operates efficiently in such a way as to remove the fear that there will not be enough to eat' (Maxwell, 1988).

'Food security exists when all people, at all times, have physical and economic access to sufficient, safe and nutritious food to meet their dietary needs and food preferences for an active and healthy life' (FAO, 1996).

Meanwhile, however, other issues began to infiltrate. They included a concern for the commercialisation and industrialisation of food systems, a stronger focus on the institutional actors in food trade, including supermarkets (see Reardon and Berdegué, 2002; Weatherspoon and Reardon, 2003), warnings about the environmental consequences of new technologies (including salinisation, pesticides, and the risk of

---

2. For a history, see Maxwell (1996, 2001a).
3. See www.undp.org/mdg/goalsandindicators.html

mono-cropping, as well as more recent worries about GMOs), and issues to do with health, including problems of food safety and the growth of nutrition-related illnesses, especially heart disease and diabetes. Often, these issues were picked up outside the mainstream (Lappé and Collins, 1977; Tudge, 1977; Bernstein et al., 1990; Hewitt de Alcantara, 1993; Tansey and Worsley, 1995), or mainly in developed countries (Leather, 1996; Riches, 1997; Dowler et al., 2001; Dowler and Jones Finer, 2002; Schlosser, 2001; Nestle, 2002). Perhaps, to those primarily concerned with famine and severe under-nutrition in the very poorest countries, they seemed superfluous.

Not so. The core message of this volume is that what we term the 'new food policy' cannot be ignored, even by the poorest countries.[4] The world food system, described only a few years ago, by Gaull and Goldberg (1993), as 'emerging', is no longer quite the chrysalis it once was. The pace of change is accelerating.[5] The challenges are daunting. They are immediate. And they need to be on the agenda of policy-makers throughout the developing world. A preoccupation with food security is no longer sufficient. It is necessary to rediscover food policy.

In the pages that follow, we explore why this should be so. With the aid of our contributors, we track the changes, ask why they matter, and begin to map what might be done. We conclude that developing countries need both 'food security' and 'food policy' – including a more vigorous engagement than has so far been the case with the new agenda.

2   What are the issues?

The changing character of the food system, and the changing nature of food policy, are summarised in schematic form in Table 1.1.[6] Few countries, if any, will conform exactly to the 'old' or 'new' characterisations: most are in between, but are also moving along a continuum from old to new. The changes have many causes. The chapters in this volume identify drivers in many sectors: urbanisation, technical change, income growth, lifestyle changes, mass media and advertising, and changes in relative prices. There are three main sets of issues: (i) the character of the food system; (ii) the effects on the human population; and (iii) the actors and agendas of food policy.

2.1 The food system

The collected papers offer a vivid picture of a global food system undergoing transformation – as Lang observes, 'a revolution in the nature of the food supply chain ... characterised by unprecedented changes in how food is produced, distributed, consumed and controlled'. We should not judge the transformation, at least not yet; but we should certainly observe.

The transformation has many features. In Table 1.1, we point particularly to the industrialisation and globalisation of the food system. The food system can no longer be

---

4. Critics will say that we should have reached this conclusion long ago. Probably. Indeed, many of the contributors to this volume did so.

5. As Popkin (in this volume) demonstrates, for example, with reference to the nutrition transition.

6. An earlier version of this table appeared in EC *Courier* No. 197, March-April 2003.

Table 1.1: Food policy old and new

		Food policy 'old'	Food policy 'new'
1	Population	Mostly rural	Mostly urban
2	Rural jobs	Mostly agricultural	Mostly non-agricultural
3	Employment in the food sector	Mostly in food production and primary marketing	Mostly in food manufacturing and retail
4	Actors in food marketing	Grain traders	Food companies
5	Supply chains	Short – small number of food miles	Long – large number of food miles
6	Typical food preparation	Mostly food cooked at home	High proportion of pre-prepared meals, food eaten out
7	Typical food	Basic staples, unbranded	Processed food, branded products More animal products in the diet
8	Packaging	Low	High
9	Purchased food bought in	Local stalls or shops, open markets	Supermarkets
10	Food safety issues	Pesticide poisoning of field workers Toxins associated with poor storage	Pesticide residues in food Adulteration Bio-safety issues in processed foods (salmonella, listeriosis)
11	Nutrition problems	Under-nutrition	Chronic dietary diseases (obesity, heart disease, diabetes)
12	Nutrient issues	Micronutrients	Fat Sugar
13	Food-insecure	'Peasants'	Urban and rural poor
14	Main sources of national food shocks	Poor rainfall and other production shocks	International price and other trade problems
15	Main sources of household food shocks	Poor rainfall and other production shocks	Income shocks causing food poverty
16	Remedies for household food shortage	Safety nets, food-based relief	Social protection, income transfers
17	Fora for food policy	Ministries of agriculture, relief/rehabilitation, health	Ministries of trade and industry, consumer affairs Food activist groups, NGOs
18	Focus of food policy	Agricultural technology, parastatal reform, supplementary feeding, food for work	Competition and rent-seeking in the value chain, industrial structure in the retail sector, futures markets, waste management, advertising, health education, food safety
19	Key international institutions	FAO, WFP, UNICEF, WHO, CGIAR	FAO, UNIDO, ILO, WHO, WTO

understood simply as a way of moving basic commodities from farm to (often local) plate. Today, food is increasingly produced by commercial growers, feeding long and sophisticated supply chains which market often processed and branded products to mainly urban consumers. Many people work in the food industry, but few of them are farmers or farm workers: in developed countries, as few as one in ten (Tansey and Worsley, 1995).

The papers document the transformation, in both developed and developing countries. Lang, in particular, lists thirteen changes, ranging from how food is grown and animals reared, to the mass marketing of food brands and the concentration of power in food manufacturing and marketing. The top ten food manufacturers in the world, he tells us, have a combined turnover of around $225 billion; the top thirty retailers a combined turnover of $930 billion. Concentration, he believes

> is strongly linked to power, and the concentration of power over the food system is now remarkable, whether one looks nationally, regionally or globally. A web of contractual relationships turns the farmer into a contractor, providing the labour and often some capital, but never owning the product as it moves through the supply chain.

Lang's description of the food chain will be familiar to those who have tackled the ideas in *Fast Food Nation* (Schlosser, 2001). They find an echo here in the chapters by Gibbon and Deshingkar et al., who describe the operation of horticultural value chains in Africa and India respectively. What Gibbon describes as 'the central reference point' for work in this area is the study by Dolan and Humphrey (2001) on horticulture in Kenya, but there is now much other research on the growth of contractual arrangements between supermarkets and growers, often through intermediary 'category managers' and specialised importers.[7]

Supermarkets play a key role, and not just as purchasers of exotic products for export to the North. Pioneering work by Reardon and others, some of it published in *Development Policy Review* 20 (4), documents the growing importance of supermarkets in developing countries: in Latin America, for example, supermarkets controlled 50-60% of food marketing in 2000 (Reardon and Berdegué, 2002: 371; Reardon et al., 2002, 2003). The share is smaller in Africa, but is growing: in South Africa, supermarkets control 55% of food retailing (Weatherspoon and Reardon, 2003). The same pattern is found in India: Deshingkar and her colleagues describe the growth of the FoodWorld chain, and the future plans of large business houses like Tata. Many supermarket chains in developing countries are now multinational: for example, the South African chain, Shoprite, has 64 outlets in 13 countries outside South Africa itself (Weatherspoon and Reardon, 2003). Wherever supermarkets enter the market, the supply chain is greatly changed, driven by issues like quality standards and traceability, as well as by the need to deliver large quantities to tight schedules.

Supermarkets are inevitably involved in the business of 'selling' food, part of what Dowler describes here as a 'dominant policy framework for food [favouring] consumer and individual choice rather than public health and citizenship'. There has been much debate about the proliferation of new food products and the role of advertising: Marion

---

7. For example, see the articles in Gereffi and Kaplinsky (2001).

Nestle's recent book, for example, reports that 11,037 new food products were brought to market in the US in 1998 (Nestle, 2002). Advertising plays a big part in shaping food preferences, as Dowler and Lang both observe.

We should note that the food system is changing, even for those who do not shop in supermarkets. Urbanisation has a lot to do with this. As Haddad observes

> The urban environment is ... marked by a greater physical distance between places of work and of residence, and by smaller household sizes. In this environment, where time is scarcer, at least for those gainfully employed, and where the fixed costs of food preparation are higher in smaller families, more food tends to be purchased outside the home, even for poor households.

The data support this conclusion. Haddad cites data showing that rich and poor households acquire significant shares of calories outside the home, often in the form of 'street foods', with the share often being higher for the poor. Thus, Dan Maxwell established in Accra that the poorest quintile acquired 31% of calorie intake away from home; Tinker has similar findings in Bangladesh and the Philippines (both cited in Haddad).

Finally, it is important to note that globalisation and changing food preferences, especially the growing demand for livestock products, have a large impact on food trade. De Haen and his colleagues make this point: they note that the main growth in production in developing countries will be of livestock products, oilseeds and livestock feed; nevertheless, the current agricultural trade surpluses of developing countries will shrink and turn into substantial deficits. This will have political as well as economic repercussions (Brown and Kane, 1994).

2.2 Diet and social impacts

People are not unaffected by the changes in the food system. Many are very directly affected by changes on the production side: Gibbon, Deshingkar et al. and Page and Slater all discuss the impact on small producers, who generally face a much more difficult trading environment as a result of higher standards and the scale, quality, traceability and timeliness requirements of commercial supply chains. Retailers are also affected: in Argentina, 64,198 small shops went out of business from 1984 to 1993; in Chile, 5240 small shops closed from 1991 to 1995 (Reardon and Berdegué, 2002: 374). At the same time, some benefit: street foods can provide a good source of employment, especially for women, and can be useful for the poor who lack the facilities to cook (FAO, 2002a). Similarly, freeing up women's reproductive labour in the home enables them to spend more time on remunerative activities.

Large numbers are affected by changes in diet associated with higher income, changing lifestyles and the pressures of living with a market-driven retail sector. Popkin has famously described this as the 'nutrition transition', and it is a major theme of the papers here. Popkin's thesis is that

> Modern societies seem to be converging on a diet high in saturated fats, sugar and refined foods and low in fibre – often termed the 'Western diet' – and on lifestyles

characterised by lower levels of activity. These changes are reflected in nutritional outcomes, such as changes in average stature, body composition and morbidity.

Popkin's own chapter provides a definitive account of dietary shifts and resultant health problems. The key changes are increases in the consumption of edible oil, caloric sweeteners (mainly sugar), and animal source foods. In China, for example, overall per capita consumption of cereals fell by about a fifth during the 1990s, with a particularly marked fall in consumption of coarse grains like millet and sorghum. Meanwhile, the consumption of animal products rose sharply, among the poor as well as the rich (though more for the rich). And the share of energy from fat, mainly vegetable oil, rose by nearly 50%.

These changes are occurring throughout the world, and at progressively lower levels of income. They have serious health implications, for the poor as well as the rich. Popkin assembles data on obesity, diabetes and heart disease, all of which are increasing rapidly in developing countries. He shows that overweight in countries as diverse as Mexico, Egypt and South Africa is equal to or greater than in the US, and points out that the rate of increase in Asia, North Africa and Latin America is two to five times greater than in the US. Obesity is frequently a marker of poverty and is associated with a poor quality diet. The health costs are substantial. The cost of diet-related non-communicable diseases will soon equal or exceed the costs of under-nutrition in developing countries: by 2025 in the cases of China and India.

Other papers provide corroborating evidence. Lang reviews the health costs of changes in diet, and makes the important point that the costs are leading insurance industries and Finance Ministries to take an unaccustomed interest in issues like obesity. Dowler makes similar points. She cites data suggesting that the UK National Health Service could save £30 billion a year by 2022 if 'the population ate better, was less obese, smoked less, and took more physical activity'.

Dowler extends the argument by emphasising the social costs of the new food economy. Writing about the UK, she focuses particularly on the social exclusion associated with not being able to buy the foods that are advertised and available in supermarkets, particularly for families with children:

> For those who live on tight budgets, there is continual anxiety over whether or not their children can or will exhibit the sophistication required to resist the persuasiveness of advertisements, and the need to ensure that their children are not victimised because they do not eat the latest 'fashionable' food.

Finally, it is important to note the issue of food safety. This is not a 'new' issue in itself, and there have always been problems with adulteration and food quality. However, new problems arise in the rapidly growing cities of developing countries: in Ghana, Tomlins and his colleagues found that street-food vendors had limited access to clean potable water, that 69% of them handled food with their bare hands, and that only about 41% washed their hands before or after handling food (Tomlins et al., 2001).

More generally, there are many food safety problems associated with the industrialised food system. As the FAO argues, the

> public generally perceives agricultural residues, pesticides and veterinary drugs as the major sources of health risks, but they are not. In Europe, for example, they account for just 0.5 per cent of food-borne illnesses. More common, and possibly increasing in frequency, is contamination by bacteria, protozoa, parasites, viruses and fungi or their toxins, introduced during food handling. (FAO, 2002b)

In industrialised countries, up to 30% of people suffer from food-borne illnesses every year (see Lang, this volume). The incidence of food-borne disease may be 300 to 350 times higher than the number of reported cases worldwide. An estimated 70% of the approximately 1.5 million annual cases of diarrhoea in the world are caused by biological contamination in foods (FAO, 2002b).

As Lang notes, referring, *inter alia*, to mad cow disease, concerns over food safety have become an important driver of reform of food policy.

2.3 Food policy

The new global food system requires a new food policy, and there is progress towards this, albeit uneven. Many of the papers in this volume document new initiatives, ranging from community nutrition projects to international initiatives on issues like obesity. However, there are also issues in the wider food economy.

Much attention has been focused on trade policy, as a factor shaping livelihoods as well as access to food. Stevens is our guide here. He points out that 'patterns of agricultural trade are changing so fast that the effects are likely to be powerful in the medium term'. The priorities are counter-intuitive, however, because a complex pattern of trade policy rents plays out differently for different products. Writing about Africa, Stevens distinguishes between traditional products (such as beverages) that are exported to a relatively undifferentiated liberal world market, other traditional exports (such as beef and sugar) that are exported to heavily protected markets, and non-traditional products (like horticulture). Paradoxically, he concludes that

> Africa's greatest gains from exporting to Europe have been in the products that appear at first glance to be the most heavily protected and to receive the least generous preferences.

Beef and sugar are prime examples. Stevens foresees serious threats ahead for Africa, not least in the area of standards: more rigorous safety requirements, new areas of health concern, and new forms of monitoring. This is also a theme taken up by de Haen et al., including with respect to the Codex Alimentarius Commission, the joint FAO/WHO body concerned with food safety.

International regulation plays an important part in other areas, also. Millstone and van Zwanenberg explore biosafety issues, analysing the extent to which developing countries can find room for manoeuvre within the rules of the World Trade Organization and the Cartagena Protocol on Biosafety. They examine two cases in detail, the beef hormones dispute between the US and the European Union, and the parallel dispute about rBST, a hormone which increases milk yields. They are cautious about the role of science, but do conclude that there is scope for the exercise of discretion by developing countries. The Codex Alimentarius again has a role to play.[8]

International regulation matters because the risks to food security, whether climatic, environmental, political or economic, are more easily transmitted between countries in a more globalised food system. Lang writes eloquently of a food system in which 'slack (has) been so cleverly taken out of the system that if something (goes) wrong , it (does) so catastrophically'. The risks are no longer local, nor principally climatic.

New actors are then drawn in. Historically, food policy has been the preserve of Ministries of Agriculture, with a supporting role played by Ministries of Health and, in some countries, departments dealing with drought relief and rehabilitation. Increasingly, however, food policy is becoming the concern of Ministries of Trade and Industry, Ministries of the Environment, and competition authorities. It is notable, for example, that the EU, and many of its Member States, have created independent Food Standards Agencies, and that competition authorities have taken an interest in food retailing (Competition Commission, 2001). The same is true internationally: as de Haen and his colleagues document for FAO, the new food policy is driving change in the organisation's work programme.

3   Do the changes matter?

'Do the changes matter?' is an evaluation question, and this points to the need for an evaluation framework. However, the construction of a framework is not straightforward.

We might start with the general issues used in evaluation, deriving from the logical framework approach to project and programme planning (Figure 1.1): sustainability, relevance, impact, effectiveness and efficiency (Norwegian Ministry of Foreign Affairs, 1993). But what do these words mean – in the context of food policy – and are there other factors to take into account?

Efficiency is a good place to start, since this has precise economic content: in terms of production function, technical efficiency describes a position in which output is maximised for a given level of inputs, and allocative efficiency describes a position in which the output mix correctly reflects prices.[9] The term 'economic efficiency' is sometimes used to describe a situation in which both technical and allocative efficiency have been achieved. Note that efficiency can be assessed from the point of view of private actors, using market prices, or from the point of view of society as a whole, correcting for price distortions and externalities (for example, environmental costs). As one of us observed in 1991, expanding on the definition that a food system should be 'efficient' (as well as equitable), this means that

> all stages in the food chain, from production to final consumption, should be efficient in
> a social-welfare sense. Production policies should take account of dynamic comparative
> advantage; marketing margins should provide no more than normal profits in the long
> term; and consumer prices should reflect real scarcity values. (Maxwell, 1991: 16)

---

8. For decisions taken on this topic in July 2003, see www.fao.org/english/newsroom/news/2003/20363-en.html

9. See Ellis, 1993: 67ff for a succinct definition of these terms.

Figure 1.1: An evaluation model for analysing development assistance

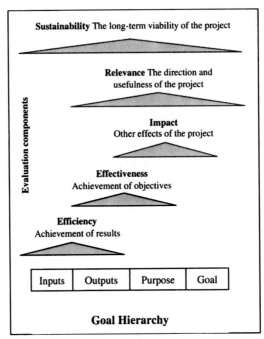

Source: Norwegian Ministry of Foreign Affairs (1993).

Beyond efficiency, the evaluation framework points to impact and sustainability. The impact of the food system is perhaps best approached in terms of welfare, and here there are valuable lessons to be learnt from the literature on poverty. This is no longer thought of in terms of income alone, but has many other dimensions. Again, Amartya Sen has been very influential, through his work on human capability and human development (ODI, 2001).

For example, the livelihoods perspective, much favoured by aid agencies working on rural development (Hussein, 2002), features income as an objective, but also reduced vulnerability, more sustainable use of the natural resource base, and stronger 'voice'. More generally, the poverty framework adopted by aid agencies, in a set of guidelines agreed in 2001 by the Development Assistance Committee of the OECD, identifies thirteen facets of poverty, grouped into five clusters: economic, human, socio-cultural, political, and protective. In this model, reproduced in Figure 1.2, gender and environment are cross-cutting issues.

Equity is not specifically mentioned in the DAC model, but of course is frequently discussed in the context of poverty reduction, for both instrumental and intrinsic reasons (Killick, 2002; McKay, 2002; Naschold, 2002). It is particularly relevant to remember Townsend's definition of poverty as

the lack of the resources to obtain the types of diet, participate in the activities and have the living conditions and amenities which are customary, or at least widely encouraged and/or approved, in the societies to which they belong. (Townsend, 1979: 21)

Figure 1.2: Interactive dimensions of poverty and well-being

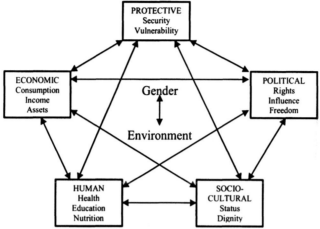

Source: DAC (2001).

Dowler is one who has written extensively on the interpretation of this definition for the understanding of food poverty in the UK, as an element of social exclusion (for example, Dowler, 1998, and in this volume). The definition of food security by one of us, reproduced in Box 1.1, which refers to the subjective nature of food poverty, is also relevant: the shift from objective to more subjective indicators of food shortage has been identified as a major shift in thinking about food security (Maxwell, 1996), and has become a recurrent analytic theme (Radimer et al., 1992; Gordon et al., 2000; Bickel et al., 2000). Dowler reminds us that

> in the general public's mind, food is more than a bundle of nutrients: it represents an expression of who a person is, where they belong, and what they are worth, and is a focus for social exchange.

Sustainability is the other issue present in the initial framework, and has been a long-standing feature of the debate on food and agriculture, at least since the publication of *Silent Spring* in 1962 (Carson, 1962). Concerns have multiplied around Green Revolution technologies and the environmental cost of 'food miles' (Tansey and Worsley, 1995). In a recent review, Pretty and Hine cite the environmental costs of British agriculture at £2.3 billion p.a., or £208/hectare (Pretty and Hine, 2000).

Finally, it is worth referring back to the other definitions of food security in Box 1.1, to remind ourselves of the importance particularly of food safety – certainly a dominant issue in recent discussion about food policy in the North (Millstone and van Zwanenberg, 2002; Draper and Green, 2002; Lang, Millstone and van Zwanenberg, and de Haen et al., all in this volume).

Can all these different themes be integrated? As Barling et al. (2002) have suggested, 'joined up food policy' is certainly needed, and can be thought of using what they describe as an 'ecological public health model'. In this connection, they refer approvingly to a WHO-Europe initiative on 'Better Health through Safe Food and Good Nutrition', which links food safety, nutrition and sustainability (WHO-Europe, 2000). This looks plausible, but misses some of the efficiency (and equity) arguments advanced earlier, and also the democratisation aspects, which, as it happens, those same authors strongly advocate (see, for example, Lang in this volume).

It looks, then, as though we need a new list of evaluation criteria. This is attempted in Table 1.2, which draws together the points from the previous discussion. There are no fewer than 19 criteria against which a food system can be judged.

Table 1.2: Criteria for a food system

A food system can be judged by whether it:		
• is technically efficient in social prices; • is allocatively efficient in social prices; • leads to increased consumption by the poor; • leads to increased asset-holding by the poor; • is good for health;	• is good for nutrition; • supports higher standards of education; • enables people to have status; • enables people to have dignity; • enables people to have rights; • enables people to have influence; • underpins freedom;	• offers security; • reduces vulnerability; • is good for environmental sustainability; • promotes gender equality; • promotes equality in general; • promotes social inclusion.

The very number of criteria, and their diverse character, immediately illustrate a challenge of aggregation in evaluating food systems, whether globally or locally. Some of the criteria are economic and financial, so that it might be possible to hope for a quantitative summary, using money as a *numéraire*. Others, however, are qualititative, and some are subjective. No single cost-benefit analysis is likely to be possible, even with heroic assumptions about valuation, weighting and time preference. As an alternative, the way forward may be to use multiple-criteria tables, as has been done before in evaluating food policy interventions (Huddleston, 1990; Maxwell, 1990).

Sadly, we do not feel strong enough at this point to evaluate the world food system – or even any local part of it – using a formal, multiple criteria approach. We are not that ambitious. Instead, we note that most of the topics identified in Table 1.2 are dealt with in one way or another in the contributions to this volume. We can identify seven major themes.

First, it is important not to be dismissive of technical and organisational changes which increase the productivity and efficiency of the food system. The many actors in the world food system, including farmers, have been astonishingly successful in increasing the supply and diversity of food, whilst simultaneously reducing prices. Lang is correct to talk of a 'cornucopia', at least in aggregate terms, for which we owe much to the kinds of innovations he lists (from the Chorleywood process for baking bread to the use of satellite tracking of lorries delivering food to supermarket distribution centres). Innovations shift the production function outwards and help improve both technical and allocative efficiency. They have included the Green Revolution, which, despite much criticism, turned out to be good for poor people (Mellor, 1976; Lipton with Longhurst, 1989), and they have the capacity to deliver much more, including the hoped-for 'Doubly Green Revolution' (Conway, 1997). This is no time to be Luddite about technical change.

Second, however, and at the same time, there do need to be significant concerns about both the technical and allocative efficiency of the food system, when the costs and benefits are expressed in social prices, and when all externalities are taken into account. Market failure is ever present (Haddad in this volume), and there is at least circumstantial evidence of oligopoly, monopsony and rent-seeking in the food system. Lang's analysis of concentration in input supply and marketing does not prove uncompetitiveness, but it certainly, as he observes, raises questions about power along the global supply chain, and about the scope for regulation by single states.[10] This, of course, is a major theme of value global chain analysis, of which there has been a good deal especially in the horticulture sector (Dolan and Humphrey, 2001; Gereffi and Kaplinsky, 2001). It is also a theme of Stevens' work on trade policy rents across a range of commodities: there are many costs associated with the current policy stance, and not all of them are reflected in budget allocations.

Third, health externalities need to feature in the social analysis, if not in the market calculation. The figures cited for the health costs of poor diet are remarkable, as Popkin, Lang and Dowler emphasise, among others.

Fourth, environmental externalities also need to feature, both on and off the farm. Pretty and Hine's estimates of the environmental cost of British agriculture, cited earlier, provide a powerful reminder. Water is another focus of concern, as de Haen et al. demonstrate.[11]

Fifth, the income distribution effects of changes in the food system need to be kept under review. In the wider literature, for example about the Green Revolution, or about agricultural growth more widely, the consensus is that increases in output tend to benefit the poor, because they are small farmers themselves, or work on farms, or buy food the price of which is falling (Lipton with Longhurst, 1989; Irz et al., 2001). In the papers in this volume, the focus is more on the difficulties faced by the poor: as producers (Gibbon, Page and Slater, Deshingkar et al., de Haen et al.); as traders (especially poor African countries – Stevens); and as consumers (Dowler, Haddad, de Haen et al.).

Sixth, policy-making and regulation are problematic. This is partly a familiar problem of how to deal with a cross-cutting issue (Lang, Dowler, Haddad), but it arises particularly in relation to 'new' topics like biotechnology (Millstone and van Zwanenberg, de Haen et al.), and to other issues that cut across national borders (Lang, Stevens). Self-regulation by the food industry will certainly be insufficient.

Finally, the process of improving policy is also problematic. Public pressure for change is beginning to mount (Haddad, Lang), but there is a limit to piecemeal adaptation (Clay).

---

10. An enquiry into the competitiveness of the UK supermarket sector, conducted by the Competition Commission in 2001, found that the industry 'is currently broadly competitive and that, overall, excessive prices are not being charged, nor excessive profits earned'.

11. See also ODI (2002).

4   What might be done?

There is a process answer to the question of what needs to be done about food policy, and an answer about substance. The mainstream answer to the process question is easy, and is the same as in the 1970s: prepare a food strategy. We have, however, learned a good deal since the 1970s, about how to prepare food and nutrition strategies – in particular, about how to avoid over-loading such strategies with analysis, designing excessively complex organisational structures, and planning in such detail as to make implementation impossible (Field, 1987; Berg, 1987; Maxwell, 1997, 2001b). The main lessons are summarised in Box 1.2, emphasising a process approach of learning by doing and constant iteration between planning and practice. Clay (in this volume) effectively provides a case study of the method in action, illustrating the gradual adaptation to changing circumstances of the World Food Programme. He emphasises, however, that adaptation has limits: at a certain point, it is necessary to grapple with the fundamental reformulation of what policy is about, and with the reconstruction of institutions. In the case of the WFP, he argues, this point has now been reached.

Box 1.2: Lessons of food security planning

- On planning:
  - o   set clear, short-term goals and work towards them; focus on the task;
  - o   train the team to work together, with training in communication, conflict resolution and multi-disciplinary skills;
  - o   build team cohesion, through collaborative fieldwork, participative leadership;
  - o   stay close to the customer, build in participation.

- On implementation:
  - o   build in a bias to action; start small and grow;
  - o   take risks and innovate; embrace error;
  - o   downgrade overt integration – integrated planning but independent implementation.

- On evaluation and public relations:
  - o   constant iteration between planning, execution and evaluation; be flexible;
  - o   monitor progress; be publicly accountable for targets;
  - o   raise the profile of the topic; raise consciousness.

Source: Maxwell (2001b: 315).

The currently most popular form of strategy planning is for poverty reduction, through the mechanism of Poverty Reduction Strategy Papers. These have much to learn from past experience in the food and nutrition sectors (Maxwell, 1998a), but have also contributed new insights, especially about the value of participation and the importance of political processes (Booth, 2003). As Booth reminds us, 'politics matter'.

This theme is again taken up in the papers in this volume. Lang, for example, identifies public pressure as one of the main drivers of policy change in the food arena, reflecting concerns about health, but also about the state of the planet. Food activism has an honourable history and is growing fast.[12]

Haddad explores in more detail the 'triggers' for public action. Drawing on the work of Kersh and Morone, and taking the issue of obesity as an example, he identifies seven triggers, including social disapproval, mass movements, and interest-group action. Only three of the seven triggers have been tripped so far. Haddad concludes that

> such constructs help us to remember that evidence is only one ingredient in the formulation and implementation of public health policy.

This is especially true because the evidence itself is often unreliable: science does not provide the certainty that policy-makers might hope for. Millstone and van Zwanenberg provide evidence on this point, using the case of genetic modification. They describe the state of scientific knowledge as 'rudimentary', and the scientific debate as 'fractious', and conclude that

> the assumption (that science might settle ... regulatory disputes) is seriously undermined by the fact that our scientific understanding of the risks that GM crops and seeds might pose is chronically uncertain, incomplete and contested.

What, then, can be done? The papers are actually rich in prescription, ranging from ideas well outside the narrow remit of food policy (for example, Popkin's thoughts on urban design and the connectivity of streets, designed to encourage higher levels of physical activity), to those which are very precisely about food (for example, Haddad's ideas about how to increase the price, and thereby reduce the attraction, of unhealthy diet options). The proposals made in the papers relate to both the public and the private sectors, to international as well as national policy, and to all aspects of the production, marketing and demand for food. Table 1.3 summarises some of the policy ideas contained in the various papers.

There are various ways of classifying the proposals, various entry points for more detailed analysis. For example, Lang identifies a key choice between regulation and self-regulation:

> An important duality has emerged. On the one side, we find a state system of regulations, on the other a system of self-regulation, largely driven by the major forces in supply chain management, the food retailers in particular.

Examples of self-regulation are found in the area of standards, for example in horticulture (Page and Slater). However, Lang is sceptical about the potential of self-regulation to deliver a food system that meets the multiple criteria listed in the previous section. This is largely, he argues, because of the interconnectedness of food policy.

Haddad takes a different route, focusing on public intervention, and distinguishing interventions on the demand and supply sides. His supply-side list includes technology,

---

12. See, for example, the Food Commission in the UK (www.foodcomm.org.uk), the NGO consortium which works together in the UK Food Group (www.ukfg.org.uk), and the food sovereignty movement (www.forumfoodsovereignty.org and www.peoplesfoodsovereignty.org).

Table 1.3: Policies for a new food policy: an initial list

- Learn how to increase consumption of fruit and vegetables and high fibre products (Popkin)
- Modify the physical environment to enhance physical activity (Popkin)
- More investment in technology to deliver high-productivity, low-cost vegetables and fruits and low-fat livestock products to poorer consumers (Haddad)
- Eliminate price incentives on growing high-fat foods and relax quantity restrictions on growing healthier foods (Haddad)
- Evaluate food trade policy from a health perspective (Haddad)
- Impose tougher standards on the fat content of food away from home and in schools (Haddad)
- Reduce malnutrition *in utero* (Haddad)
- Increase the relative price of unhealthy choices (Haddad)
- Clearer information about product contents (Haddad)
- Better awareness about consequences of poor diet (Haddad, de Haen et al.)
- Promote healthy eating and dietary change (Dowler, de Haen et al.)
- Local food projects (Dowler)
- Set state benefits at realistic levels (Dowler)
- Trade regulation at EU level (Gibbon)
- Regulation by exporting countries (Gibbon)
- Regulation of markets within developed countries (Gibbon)
- New production and marketing arrangements at local level that support small and marginal farmers(Deshingkar et al.)
- Direct foreign investment enabling small producers to keep in touch with tastes and standards in foreign markets (Page and Slater)
- Large direct private buyers providing partial access to production and technology advantages via technical advice and training (Page and Slater)
- Initiatives by developing country producers where there is no external private or public sector intervention (Page and Slater)
- Alternative trading companies offer inputs into production and organisation (Page and Slater)
- Establish export promotion agencies as the first point of contact for new exporters (Page and Slater)
- Establish import promotion agencies to encourage trade from developing to developed countries (Page and Slater)
- Use aid programmes to analyse the poverty reduction effects from trade and developed policies that maximise these effects (Page and Slater)
- Target technical research towards new export opportunities (Page and Slater)
- Encourage agencies promoting small production not just for export but also for local markets (Page and Slater, Deshingkar et al.)
- Better scientific risk assessment (Millstone and van Zwanenberg)
- Regional co-operation on biosafety (Millstone and van Zwanenberg)
- Better food security analysis of trade policy (Stevens)
- Better understanding of standards (Stevens)
- Better advocacy and monitoring (de Haen et al.)
- Promoting sustainable intensification (de Haen et al.)
- Strengthen Codex Alimentarius (de Haen et al.)
- Rethink the role of international food aid (Clay)

prices, standards, and a variety of nutrition interventions. His demand-side list again includes pricing, but also adds labelling and information/education. There are some intriguing ideas here. For example, in the US, a policy-induced increase in meat prices is shown to have some positive effects on diet, such as a reduction in fat and cholesterol intake, but also some negative effects, such as a reduction in iron and calcium. By contrast, an increase in the price of edible oil has much more generally favourable effects. Haddad does note, however, that 'in a developing country context, edible oil is often used to increase the energy density of infant diets' – and that the policy may therefore not be transferable.

Other papers explore particular aspects of policy. Thus, Gibbon reviews the potential of three types of public regulation designed to help small producers. Deshingkar et al. identify three forms of collaboration by farmers that can help small producers. Page and Slater assess nine ways in which the obstacles to market access by small producers can be overcome.

Some of these policies are more promising than others. Gibbon is probably the least sanguine. He concludes from his review of market regulation options that WTO rules, EU competition regulations, and structural adjustment practice all militate against intervention:

> unfortunately, at least from the viewpoint of small-scale producers, regulation in all the forms mentioned has become difficult to maintain and virtually impossible to (re-)introduce.

Others are more optimistic. The village-level interventions identified by Deshingkar and her colleagues, for example labour-water exchange arrangements and group leasing of land, have sprung up of their own accord in response to market opportunities for the sale of exotic vegetable crops, like asparagus and baby sweetcorn. The interventions identified by Page and Slater are mostly at a national level. They include sub-contracting by the private sector, farmers' organisations, fair trade arrangements, and trade promotion agencies. There are many examples of success.

An important stream of recommendations concerns the international level. Thus, Stevens takes a characteristically careful and pragmatic look at current trade issues, and identifies key threats to developing countries, especially in Africa, from the erosion of preferences, higher import costs, and changes in standards. These are not, it needs to be emphasised, the places where most observers focus their attention. Stevens argues that debate about liberalisation of Northern agriculture is

> largely irrelevant as a practical policy concern, since we are not about to see anything resembling liberal trade in OECD agriculture, despite the much-heralded 'reforms' to the Common Agricultural Policy (CAP) and the on-going agricultural reforms in the WTO Doha Round.

In a similar vein, Clay examines in detail the evolution of the global food aid regime, and argues strongly that a fundamental review is needed. He wonders whether a crisis is needed to trigger change – and whether such a crisis has now arrived, because of the increasing dependence of the WFP on US food aid. Lang would probably agree with the general thesis: his description of changes in UK food policy corresponds to a crisis-driven model, including health crises.

5   Conclusion

The papers in this volume make powerful points about the scale and speed of changes in the global food system. We have argued that these changes matter, and that new policies and new policy processes are required to deal with them. But are the issues of equal salience everywhere? Is this really a rich or middle-income country problem? One of us has written about 'comparisons, convergence and connections' between developed and developing countries (Maxwell, 1998b). Do we have connections and convergence, or merely interesting comparisons?

There are certainly issues which feature more prominently in richer, more urbanised or more industrialised developing countries. For example, Millstone and van Zwanenberg make a distinction between the bulk of developing countries and those few, like Argentina, China and Cuba, which have deliberately set out to foster a domestic industry dealing with GM crops and food. Similarly, the urbanisation issues will, for now, feature much more strongly in countries which are already highly urbanised than in those which are not: the salt and fat content of street foods is likely to matter much more in Zambia, say (39.8% urbanised in 2001), than in Ethiopia (15.9% urbanised in 2001) (UNDP, 2003).

However, there are also grounds for arguing that the new food policy agenda is relevant in some degree to all countries, and to a high degree in very many. This is for four reasons.

First, all countries engage in food trade, as both importers and exporters. All countries therefore need to be aware of the way in which global value chains are evolving, to review negotiating strategies, and to consider the regulatory environment and institutional structure within which trade takes place. Stevens, Page and Slater, Gibbon, and de Haen et al. are all eloquent on this point. There is much in the wider literature, for example on the WTO, to back them up (Morrissey, 2002); also on the opportunities for improved negotiation by developing countries (Page, 2003).

Second, the domestic food systems of the developing world are evolving rapidly. The best evidence on this comes from the extensive work on supermarkets by Reardon and his colleagues, in Latin America and Africa. Even in India, a laggard in this transformation, as Deshingkar et al. show, the supply chain is beginning to undergo the kinds of revolutionary changes seen elsewhere.

Third, the diet-related changes in nutrition and health are pervasive, and become visible at progressively lower levels of per capita GDP. Popkin's data are particularly persuasive here: in 1962, countries reliant on fat for 20% of energy had an average per capita income of US$1475; by 1990, the income figure had halved, to only US$750 per capita. At the same time, overweight and obesity are increasing rapidly in the poorest countries, and the rate of change is higher in poorer countries than in rich ones. In general, Popkin tells us, obesity is associated with poverty, both between countries, and, importantly, within countries.

Fourth, the capacity to make food policy is probably weakest in just those poorest countries where the new challenges are emerging most rapidly. As various papers in this volume make clear, food policy-making is difficult because of the number of sectors involved. It is also expensive. Millstone and van Zwanenberg cite the budget of the UK's new Food Standards Agency as £115 million in 2001-2, covering a staff of nearly 600 people, and the budget of the new European Food Safety Authority as over £25m. in its first year, with an initial staff of 250. For developing countries, they point out, the scarcity of expertise and financial resources is likely to be a 'significant constraint'. Of course, these numbers are trivial compared to the cost of getting policy wrong: the recent foot and mouth crisis in the UK is estimated to have cost around £6 billion (Anderson, 2002).

The obvious conclusion is to strengthen both policy-making and policy in all countries. There will be country-specific choices to make about priorities and sequencing. There is also scope for collaboration, however. Millstone and van Zwenenberg make this point explicitly with reference to biotechnology, but it is more general. A particular role needs to be played by international institutions, as Clay reminds us in the case of food aid, and de Haen and his colleagues for other topics. 'Food Policy New' is growing in importance. Developing countries and their international partners will not want to be taken by surprise.

Chapter 2
Food Industrialisation and Food Power: Implications for Food Governance

Tim Lang

Food supply chains of developed countries industrialised in the second half of the twentieth century, with significant implications for developing countries over policy priorities, the ensuing external costs and the accompanying concentration of market power. Very powerful corporations dominate many sectors. Primary producers are locked into tight specifications and contracts. Consumers may benefit from cheaper food but there are quality implications and health externalities. As consumer confidence has been shaken, new quality agencies have been created. Tensions have emerged about the state's role as facilitator of industrial efficiencies. Food policy is thus torn between the pursuit of productivity and reduced prices and the demand for higher quality, with implications for both producers and consumers in the developing world.

1   Introduction

The twentieth century witnessed a revolution in the nature of the food supply chain, the implications of which are only now being worked through at policy and institutional levels. The period was characterised by unprecedented changes in how food is produced, distributed, consumed and controlled – and by high levels of concentration of market share. After a period in which the state in developed countries actively promoted the restructuring of supply chains in the name of efficiency and output maximisation, adverse public reaction to these changes in the West is now forcing governments to respond differently, taming rather than forcing the pace and scale of change. The state is caught on the horns of a policy dilemma: on the one hand, actively promoting the development of efficient modern food supply chains; on the other hand, having to develop processes of food governance which can respond to and retain public trust in food.

The struggle over the direction of the food supply chain now going on in many developed countries has lessons for the developing world, still heavily focused on trade issues such as market access, the subsidies of the European Union's Common Agricultural Policy and economic protectionism. Important though these issues are, the emergence of another discourse is potentially both more threatening and important for the developing world. A policy choice looms.

This chapter explores the conflict and the choice, drawing mainly on the European experience, and particularly on the British. The UK is interesting not just because it was the first industrial nation and thus the first to sever its people from the land in a systematic and mass manner, but because it has had to grapple with the peculiarities of a post-colonial political transition into a European Member State.

2   Changes in industrial and post-industrial food supply chains

The last half century ushered in a period of unprecedented and rapid change in the food system, whose impact is on a par with that of the so-called Columbian exchange half a millennium ago; or the impact of British nineteenth-century colonialism which used foreign lands both to feed trade and to home populations on a massive scale; or the impact of the internal combustion engine, in particular the tractor, and its substitution for animal traction power; or that of the chemical revolution on soil management. The new era of food supply management has redrawn the spatial as well as the cultural food map.

Developed world consumers have been able to transcend the seasons, with a cornucopia of year-round fruit and vegetables arriving in tightly planned waves from Europe, the Americas, Africa, and Australasia. Although the new food system has new characteristics, explored below, it could not have been ushered in without previous technical and social transformations. In particular, the twentieth-century agricultural revolution drew on patient and much slower transformations in the understanding of chemistry, plants, animals and engineering. In the late nineteenth century, for example, there had been a shift from milling grains using hands, animals, wind and water to the faster steam or electric roller mills. But in the 1960s, another quantum leap was made with the 'Chorleywood process' which allowed bakers to emulate car manufacturers in the organisation of their throughput. The new process whipped bread to rise in a few minutes, where, for the previous four millennia, bakers had had to wait hours. Yeast was added purely for taste.

Among the core characteristics of the twentieth-century revolution in the food supply chain are its integration, control systems and astonishing leaps in productivity, as measured in labour and capital use. The resultant restructuring has included changes in:

- how food is grown – for example, mass use of agrochemicals, hybrid plant breeding;
- how animals are reared – for example, factory farms, intensive livestock rearing, prophylactic use of pharmaceuticals to increase weightgain;
- the emergence of biotechnology – as applied to plants, animals and processing;
- food sourcing – for example, a shift from local to regional and now global supply points, with a blurring of the notion of seasonality and a tendency to monoculture on the farm belying the biodiversity on the supermarket shelf;
- means of processing – for example, use of extrusion technology, fermentation, wholesale use of cosmetic additives to disguise products and yield consistency;
- use of technology to shape quality – the goal of mass production to deliver consistency and regularity (uniformity) is now focused on the development of niche products with 'difference';
- the workforce – for example, a dramatic shedding of labour on developed-world farms but a retention of pools of cheap labour (immigrants) to do the manual tasks such as grading and picking; also a strong push to 24-hour working;

- marketing – a new emphasis on product development, branding and selling has accompanied a dazzling display of apparent choice, with thousands of products vying for attention;
- retailers' role – they have emerged as the main gateways to consumers, using contracts and specifications to gate-keep between primary producers and consumers;
- distribution logistics – for example, use of airfreight, regional distribution systems, 'trunker' (heavy lorry) networks, satellite tracking;
- methods of supply chain management – for example, centralisation of ordering, application of computer technology, application of batch /niche production to mass lines ('flexible specialisation');
- moulding of consumer tastes and markets – for example, mass marketing of brands, the use of product placement methods, huge investments in advertising and marketing and the targeting of particular consumer types;
- level of control over markets – for example, rapid regionalisation and moves towards globalisation, and the emergence of cross-border concentration.

As the twentieth century unfolded, the industrial approach was applied from farm to retailing to food service/catering. A new human geography of food emerged. In developed countries such as the UK, more people now work in catering than in the entire rest of the food supply – though in catering, too, there is now pressure to shed labour and introduce pre-processed products into the kitchen.

Meat production is one sector with many advanced industrial characteristics. It has witnessed the application of factory methods of management, production and control, not just in the meat packing plants of Buenos Aires or Chicago, but in the rearing of animals themselves. This is illustrated by the emergence of huge feedlots where land was cheap (the Americas), or caged poultry and pig production and intensive dairy production units where land and/or weather demanded it. Productivity of animals, land and labour has risen to unprecedented levels. Dairy cattle have been bred to achieve a doubling and trebling of milk output, for instance. This industrial meat production regime is now being transferred to the developing world. The Indian broiler industry, for example, has grown from 31 million birds a year in 1981 to 800 million two decades later (Gold, 2003).

The role of Information Technology is another important new feature. Laser bar codes and Electronic Point of Sale (EPOS) systems in retailing are, to the consumer, the visible end of a sophisticated technological web covering the supply chain (Brown 1997). Computers enable the application of 'just-in-time' distribution systems (which minimise build-up of stocks and allow the application of an Efficient Consumer Response ethos to deliver business-to-business efficiencies), robotic warehouses, satellites for monitoring crops in distant places and the management of shipments and lorry delivery schedules. A retailer with annual sales of £17 billion cannot afford to run out of key food products or it will lose consumer credibility. Computers are central to this industrialised management approach.

By the late twentieth century, such was the tightness of control of the managerial revolution in the food sector, that it had replaced the motor industry as the benchmark for efficiency. Retail management was being offered to other service sectors as varied as hospitals and education as the ideal customer-oriented approach.

3 Redefining the market: the emergence of high levels of concentration

The food sector has been concentrating rapidly. The sectors vary in their dynamics. Land ownership is locked by the fact that land cannot move. Food manufacturers, by contrast, can relocate production outside their parent country, yet still have access to 'home' consumer markets. Thus, and following the creation of the Single European Market in the late 1980s, a company like European giant Unilever was able to rationalise its product mix, recipes and factories, to make maximum use of European scale and transport systems. In the United States, a similar regional market, the market share of the top 20 food manufacturers has doubled since 1967 (Connor, 2003); 100 firms now account for 80% of all value-added in the sector. European levels are not dissimilar to those of the US. Globally, a group of global players with enormous purchasing power has emerged among manufacturers (Table 2.1) and retailers (Table 2.2).

Table 2.1: World top 10 food manufacturers, 2002

Sector rank	Global rank	Company	Country	Market value $m	Turnover ($m)
1	34	Nestle SA	Switzerland	88,112.0	50,615.8
2	62	Unilever	UK & Netherlands	56,394.0	48,505.0
3	201	Kraft Foods	US	21,450.8	33,875.0
4	240	General Mills	US	17,843.9	7,077.7
5	266	Danone	France	16,706.2	12,687.3
6	272	Sara Lee	US	16,304.7	17,747.0
7	305	Heinz (H J)	US	14,539.7	9,430.4
8	311	Cadbury Schweppes	UK	14,202.0	7,898.8
9	325	Kellogg	US	13,685.9	8,853.3
10	347	Conagra Foods	US	13,026.8	27,194.2

Source: Financial Times FT500 (2002).

The situation among retailers is changing particularly rapidly. In the period 1993-9, the aggregate concentration of the top 10 grocery retailers in the EU grew by 24.9%, whereas the market share of the bottom 10 companies in the EU top 50 declined by 72.2%. The larger are getting larger and the small (even though large in relative historical terms) are being squeezed (Dobson, 2003). In Europe, retailers are now concentrating regionally, perhaps due to the fact that home markets were already concentrated.[1] There are some emerging European giants such as Carrefour, Aldi, Tesco and Ahold.[2] The UK's Tesco, for instance, is now structured into three divisions: UK and Ireland, Central Europe and the Far East.

---

1. The share held by the top three firms in EU countries ranges from 40% (Germany, UK) to over 80% (Finland and Ireland). But the largest countries are now poised to emulate the smaller ones (Grievink, 2003).
2. The last was hit by a crisis of fraudulent accounting after falsely claiming $880 m. higher earnings than had happened (Bickerton, 2003).

Table 2.2: World top 30 food retailers, 2002

Rank	Company	Country	Turnover ($m)	No. of Countries	Foreign Sales (%)	Ownership
1	Wal-Mart	US	180,787	10	17	Public
2	Carrefour	France	59,690	26	48	Public
3	Kroger	US	49,000	1	0	Public
4	Metro	Germany	42,733	22	42	Public/family
5	Ahold	NL	41,251	23	83	Public
6	Albertson's	US	36,762	1	0	Public
7	Rewe	Germany	34,685	10	19	Co-operative
8	Ito Yokado (incl. Seven Eleven)	Japan	32,713	19	33	Public
9	Safeway Inc.	US	31,977	3	11	Public
10	Tesco	UK	31,812	9	13	Public
11	Costco	US	31,621	7	19	Public
12	ITM (incl. Spar)	France	30,685	9	36	Co-operative
13	Aldi	Germany	28,796	11	37	Private
14	Edeka (incl. AVA)	Germany	28,775	7	2	Co-operative
15	Sainsbury	UK	25,683	2	16	Public/family
16	Tengelmann (incl. A&P)	Germany	25,148	12	49	Private/family
17	Auchan	France	21,642	14	39	Private/family
18	Leclerc	France	21,468	5	3	Co-operative
19	Daiei	Japan	18,373	1	0	Public
20	Casino	France	17,238	11	24	Public
21	Delhaize	Belgium	16,784	11	84	Public
22	Lidl & Schwartz	Germany	16,092	13	25	Private
23	AEON (formerly Jusco)	Japan	15,060	8	11	Public
24	Publix	US	14,575	1	0	Private
25	Coles Myer	Australia	14,061	2	1	Public
26	Winn Dixie	US	13,698	1	0	Public
27	Loblaws	Canada	13,548	1	0	Public
28	Safeway plc	UK	12,357	2	3	Public
29	Lawson	Japan	11,831	2	1	Public
30	Marks & Spencer	UK	11,692	22	18	Public
	TOTAL		**930,537**			

Source: IGD (2002).

These trends are likely to continue. The Institute of Grocery Distribution, a food sector research institute, predicts that, based on historical growth rates in European turnover for the last five years, the top ten retailers will increase market share from 37 to 60% by 2010. Their combined European grocery turnover will grow from €337.1bn in 2000 to €461.7bn by 2005 and €669.7bn by 2010 (IGD, 2001).

Much current market concentration has occurred not by slow gains due to superiority of product or consumer appeal, but by buy-outs. Mergers and acquisitions have been rife from the 1980s on both sides of the Atlantic, as already large companies snapped up competitors. The results have changed both the architecture of the food supply chain and its public face. For example, a 'national' brand like Kit-Kat (once owned by former Quaker confectioner Rowntree's of York) could be bought by Swiss based Nestlé and turned into a global brand.

Similar trends occur in other sectors. Concentration is probably at its most advanced in agrochemicals, a key infrastructural sector. In the late 1980s, the top 20 firms worldwide accounted for around 90% of sales (Lang and Clutterbuck, 1991). By the late 1990s, this level was held by 10 firms. Today it is just seven (see Table 2.3).

Table 2.3: World top 7 agrochemical companies, 2001

Rank	Company	AgChem Sales 2001 (US$m)
1	Syngenta	5,385
2	Aventis	3,842
3	Monsanto	3,755
4	BASF	3,105
5	Dow	2,612
6	Bayer	2,418
7	DuPont	1,917

Source: Agrow (2002).

There are also strong links between sectors. Chemical companies have diversified into seeds and biotech. In the US, the top four beef packers already controlled around a quarter of the market in the mid-1970s. Today, just 20 feedlots feed half of the cattle in the US and these are directly connected to the four processing firms that control 81% of the beef processing either by direct ownership or through formal contracts (Connor, 2003; Hendrickson et al., 2001).

Concentration is strongly linked to power and the concentration of power over the food system is now remarkable, whether one looks nationally, regionally or globally. A web of contractual relationships turns the farmer into a contractor, providing the labour and often some capital, but never owning the product as it moves through the supply chain. Farmers never make the major management decisions. Table 2.4 gives the level of concentration in the US for each sector held by the top three or four firms in some key meat, cereal, processing and retail sectors.

Rapid concentration throughout the supply chain also has implications for how a 'market' is defined in competition policy. Should a market be defined by consumers' travel-to-shop time, as the UK's Competition Commission suggested when reviewing the UK retail sector in 2000? Is a market national? Or is it a regional entity (for example, European/US)? Or global? Should consumers or regulators decide how to define a market? These questions illustrate policy dilemmas that will shape the governance of food policy in the twenty-first century – and to which developing countries will not be immune.

Table 2.4: Concentration in some US food processing sectors

Sector	Concentration ratio (%)	Companies involved
Beef Packers	81	Tyson (IBP), ConAgra Beef Cos, Cargill (Excel), Farmland National Beef Pkg. Co
Pork Packers	59	Smithfield, Tyson (IBP), ConAgra (Swift), Cargill (Excel)
Pork Production	46	Smithfield Foods, Premium Standard Farms (ContiGroup), Seaboard Corp., Triumph Pork Group (Farmland Managed)
Broilers	50	Tyson Foods, Gold Kist, Pilgrim's Pride, ConAgra
Turkeys	45	Hormel (Jennie-O Turkeys), Butterball (ConAgra), Cargill's Turkeys, Pilgrim's Pride
Animal Feed Plants	25	Land O'Lakes Farmland Feed LLC\Purina Mills, Cargill Animal Nutrition (Nutrena), ADM (Moorman's), J.D., Heiskell & Co
Terminal Grain Handling Facilities	60	Cargill, Cenex Harvest States, ADM, General Mills
Corn Exports	81	Cargill-Continental Grain, ADM, Zen Noh
Soybean Exports	65	Cargill-Continental Grain, ADM, Zen Noh
Flour Milling	61	ADM Milling, ConAgra, Cargill, General Mills
Soybean Crushing	80	ADM, Cargill, Bunge, AGP
Ethanol Production	49	ADM, Minnesota Corn Producers (ADM has 50% Equity Stake), Williams Energy Services, Cargill
Dairy Processors	n/a	Dean Foods (Suiza Foods Corp.), Kraft Foods (Philip Morris), Dairy Farmers of America, Land O'Lakes
Food Retailing	38	Kroger Co., Albertson's, Safeway, Wal-Mart, Ahold

Source: Hendrickson et al. (2001).

4　The role of the state

Government action has often lagged behind technological, managerial and industrial changes in food supply. Traditionally, food policy was addressed in discrete analytical boxes such as 'farming', 'fisheries', 'development', 'health', 'environment', 'transport', 'consumer affairs', etc. But a series of public crises have driven change. A new consciousness began first at the social fringes in the 1970s, with regard to concerns about quality (for example, contaminants, residues, pathogens) and among epidemiologists (for example, about the impact of diet on health). By the 1990s it was mainstream, aided by a series of crises and food scandals in Europe. Slack had been so cleverly taken out of the system that if something went wrong, it did so catastrophically, as was seen with the UK's BSE (1986-) and Foot and Mouth Disease (2001) outbreaks, and with the numerous food safety scandals from the late 1980s.

Governments and food scientists and technologists, as well as the now high-profile market leaders, were increasingly forced onto the defensive, having to justify why, when they had such power and spoke in terms of meeting consumer needs, consumer interests had apparently been somewhat marginalised in pursuit of industrial efficiencies. While companies introduced tougher specifications for suppliers and new traceability controls ('plough to plate'), governments introduced reforms ranging from the creation of food agencies to wholesale shake-ups of ministries. The UK, for instance, set up a Food Standards Agency in 2000, and effectively abolished its Ministry of Agriculture in 2001 (Barling and Lang, 2003). In 2003, the European Union launched a new multi-state European Food Safety Authority.

An important duality has emerged. On the one side, we find a state system of regulations, on the other a system of self-regulation, largely driven by the major forces in supply chain management, the food retailers in particular (Barling and Lang, 2003).

But this state-corporate duality has compounded policy incoherence, because it fails to address a central feature of food policy, its inter-connectedness. The UK has not solved this problem. For example, in the wake of the Foot and Mouth Disease debacle that cost the taxpayer nearly £3 billion, the government set up a Commission into the Future of Farming and Food (Curry, 2002). But in the end, the problem was framed as primarily about cost and efficiency. The problem with UK farming, the report argued, was that it was not efficient enough. Better co-ordination and information flow was essential if the UK food supply chain was to compete with cheap imports. The Commission acknowledged that if consumers wanted improvements in the conservation and environmental aspects of farming (wildlife, biodiversity, land management, reduction of pesticide use, etc.), this had to be paid for. It recommended an *increase* of £500 million in subsidies to engineer the transition to this new policy package of efficiency with environmentalism.

Inter-connectedness means that trust is a central issue in food policy. This is perhaps most clearly seen in times of war or crisis, when food's multi-sectoral impact emerges from the analytical and practical shadows to take centre stage in political life (see for the UK: Beveridge, 1928; Le Gros Clark and Titmus, 1939; Hammond, 1950). Food can have a direct impact on morale. This has been acknowledged by the military for millennia, but with the severance of a majority of people from the land, this factor is now increasingly important in civil society too. The need for a multi-sectoral approach in food policy is also well appreciated in both the study and management of famine and hunger, and other deficiency situations in the development process.

5 The complexity of consumer sovereignty

Focus on the issue of trust reminds us that consumers have played an important part in the evolution of food policy (Marsden et al., 2000). The period of public crises (1980-2000) included concerns about unnecessary use of food additives, the impact of pesticides, weak microbiological standards (particularly for food-borne pathogens), limited labelling and the role of diet in degenerative diseases such as heart disease, diabetes and some cancers. Consumer scepticism is rife (Gabriel and Lang, 1995). By the end of the last century, the nature of production, distribution and consumption, even cooking, was being subjected to considerable scrutiny and was sparking debate in most developed economies (Lang, 1996).

The relationship between industry and consumers is complex, however. Rhetoric suggests that the food supply chain is consumer-led, but this phrase disguises more complex impetuses. Consumers, as most observers note, are at the heart of the battles not just for global brands (Grievink, 2003), but for minds. The top 20 food brands in the UK spend over £105 million a year on marketing (*Marketing*, 2002). While the UK Government spends around £5 million on healthy eating advice, Coca-Cola alone spends £27 million in the UK yearly. It spends $1.4 bn on advertising worldwide, as does McDonalds (Ad-Brands, 2003).

Kinsey (2003) has argued that the old supply-demand chain is now a loop, where intelligence is gathered about consumers but shaped by supply requirements coming back up the supply chain. US and European food sectors have for a decade espoused a management goal known as 'Efficient Consumer Response', the purpose of which is improved co-ordination and waste reduction. The old policy framework which pursued regularity and risk reduction as farmers struggled against the vagaries of nature is now being replaced by a battle over marketing. The product innovation and quality controller for one of Britain's top five retailers informed this author: '...sometimes we have to do things before the customer even knows what they want'.

Table 2.5: Economic costs of diet- and exercise-related health problems, US

Disease	Direct costs US$ bn (medical expenditures)	Indirect costs US$ bn (productivity losses)	Total costs US$ bn
Heart disease	97.9	77.4	175.3
Stroke	28.3	15.0	43.3
Arthritis	20.9	62.9	83.8
Osteoporosis	n/a	14.9	14.9
Breast cancer	8.3	7.8	16.1
Colon cancer	8.1	n/a	8.1
Prostate cancer	5.9	n/a	5.9
Gall bladder disease	6.7	0.6	7.3
Diabetes	45.0	55.0	100.0
Obesity	55.7	51.4	107.1
Total			561.8

Note: Costs are expressed in constant 1998 US$, using the Consumer Price Index.
Source: Kenkel and Manning (1999).

Advertising expenditure is not the only additional cost borne by consumers when purchasing. While the relative price of food might have dropped in many societies, health costs associated with diet have risen dramatically compared with the 1940s. Life expectancy has risen, of course, but so has evidence about the impact of diet-related diseases like cancers, heart disease and diabetes from which consumers die prematurely. Political attention for the last decade has been on food safety but the real crisis comes from food's role in degenerative diseases. The World Health Organization's

Table 2.6: Growth of expenditure on health, 1990-2000

	Real per capita growth rates, 1990-2000 (%)		Health spending as % of GDP		
	Health Spending	GDP	1990	1998	2000
Australia	3.1	2.4	7.8	8.5	8.3
Austria	3.1	1.8	7.1	8.0	8.0
Belgium	3.5	1.8	7.4	8.5	8.7
Canada	1.8	1.7	9.0	9.1	9.1
Czech Republic	3.9	0.1	5.0	7.1	7.2
Denmark	1.7	1.9	8.5	8.4	8.3
Finland	0.1	1.8	7.9	6.9	6.6
France	2.3	1.4	8.6	9.3	9.5
Germany	2.2	0.2	8.7	10.6	10.6
Greece	2.8	1.9	7.5	8.7	8.3
Hungary[a]	2.0	2.7	7.1	6.9	6.8
Iceland	2.9	1.6	7.9	8.3	8.9
Ireland	6.6	6.4	6.6	6.8	6.7
Italy	1.4	1.4	8.0	7.7	8.1
Japan	3.9	1.1	5.9	7.1	7.8
Korea	7.4	5.1	4.8	5.1	5.9
Luxembourg[b]	3.7	4.5	6.1	5.8	6.0
Mexico	3.7	1.6	4.4	5.3	5.4
Netherlands	2.4	2.3	8.0	8.1	8.1
New Zealand	2.9	1.5	6.9	7.9	8.0
Norway	3.5	2.8	7.8	8.5	7.5
Poland[b]	4.8	3.5	5.3	6.4	6.2
Portugal	5.3	2.4	6.2	8.3	8.2
Slovak Republic	..	4.0	..	5.9	5.9
Spain	3.9	2.4	6.6	7.6	7.7
Switzerland	2.5	0.2	8.5	10.6	10.7
United Kingdom	3.8	1.9	6.0	6.8	7.3
United States	3.2	2.3	11.9	12.9	13.0
OECD Average[c,d]	**3.3**	**2.2**	**7.2**	**8.0**	**8.0**
EU Average	**3.1**	**2.3**	**7.4**	**8.0**	**8.0**

Notes: a) 1991-2000; b) 1990-9; c) Excludes the Slovak Republic because of missing 1990 estimates; d) unweighted averages. No recent estimates available for Sweden and Turkey.
Source: OECD Health Data (2002: 1). Available at www.oecd.org/pdf/M00031000/M00031130.pdf.

Cancer Report (WHO, 2003) expects a steep rise in cancers in part due to poor diets – eating too much fat and not enough fruits and vegetables. There are no incentives for processors to sell only simple foods: for example, value-added fruit juices (lots of water plus a little fruit) make more money.

The health toll of diet-related disease is a very large financial problem for affluent countries. Table 2.5 gives a breakdown of the direct and indirect costs for a number of key diseases related to diet in the United States. These costs are immense, even for a rich society like the United States. Table 2.6 shows how general healthcare costs are rising rapidly in many developed economies. The growth of health expenditure is sometimes higher than the growth of GDP. The UK healthcare system, for instance, costs £68 billion for a population of just under 60 million people, costs that the Treasury expects will rise to between £154 bn ($231 bn) and £184 bn ($276 bn) by 2022-3 in 2002 prices (Wanless, 2002). At constant prices, the healthcare costs are doubling.

The WHO has now stepped up its appeal to both developed and developing country governments to act to prevent the double burden of food-related ill-health problems associated with under- and over-consumption coinciding in the same countries. In effect, the WHO and the FAO are now in agreement that the productionist era in food policy has come to an end. Mere quantity is an inadequate policy goal. Quality, distribution and externalised social costs also have to be central to the policy framework (WHO/FAO 2003).

The enticing possibility is that realisation of the size of health and other external costs could change the politics of food. Concern about rising health costs could explain why many Finance Ministries are so concerned about diet-related ill-health. The insurance industry is also worried, one factor behind President George W. Bush's launch of a high-profile US initiative against rampant obesity.

6   Possible sources of change

The costs of diet-related ill-health and the fiscal burden of healthcare may seem unlikely triggers for a re-think about the political economy of food and about the attractions of the industrial and intensive approach to the food supply. But fiscal pressure, driven in part by rising numbers of post-retirement elderly, is already proving a strong motivation for states to re-think pension systems and promises of old-age retirement, made in the great era of affluence of the late twentieth century when stock markets were booming and there seemed no end to the consumerist bargain. Framing the food supply chain to help reduce healthcare costs will become increasingly pressing as those costs rise in affluent societies, and as degenerative diet-related ill-health grows in societies without sufficient GDP to afford expensive healthcare and health insurance systems.

Another potential source of change is public pressure, the preparedness of consumers to act, not just think, like citizens with long-term commitments beyond the checkout counter/point of sale. The appeal to consumers to act differently and to see beyond cheapness can come from various sources. It ranges from individual survival ('your or your family's health') to ecological sustainability ('the planet'). To take one example, the rapid rise in meat consumption that accompanies rising disposable income has implications for land use and grain production to feed the demand for meat. Meat production is an industry already under some consumer scrutiny for factory farming, associations with burger culture (cheap products, high fat, poor ecological impact), and for public health problems (for example, prophylactic use of antibiotics weakening their viability for real human health need).

Public pressure can be highly effective. If food power is concentrating, even large corporations are vulnerable and exposed to sudden changes in public sympathy. When European food safety procedures were found wanting in the 1990s, arguments from consumer campaigners for more ecological systems of food production found popular resonance and moved from the fringe to centre-stage in public policy (Lang, 1996). Politicians intervened in the supply chain because consumers realised that they had little control at the point of sale. The consumerist bargain (cornucopia without consequences) looked momentarily shaky. In the EU, this culminated in the crisis over BSE (mad cow disease) which forced the President and Council onto the defensive (Santer, 1997; Lobstein et al., 2001). Other crises, for example over contaminated feed in Belgium and a wave of food safety scandals in the UK, for instance, highlighted the vulnerability of the industrial food system. The policy question was raised that prices might be cheap, but at what social, health and environmental cost? The implications of this question are still being struggled over within the supply chain, with companies investing hugely in traceability systems while consumer and health analysts argue that the externalised costs are not just microbiological. Indeed, these represent a small fraction of the total burden (Pretty et al., 2003).

Environmental pressures such as climate change and global water shortages could also pose direct and real threats to affluent countries. Water becomes highly sensitive not just for direct human consumption but for use in intensive irrigation and cropping systems (UNEP, 2002; Barlow and Clarke, 2002). The implications of climate change are still unclear but some academic prognoses suggest that cash crops such as tea and coffee – central to the development agenda, let alone the taste buds of affluent consumers – could fall by significant amounts; a one degree rise in temperature can lead to 10% yield reductions in tropical crops (UNEP, 2001). The impact on the economies of countries like Uganda or Kenya, already vulnerable to mono-commodity production downturns, could be serious.

In conclusion, although this chapter has argued that industrialisation and concentration have developed in a mutual cycle of development, it has also argued that some fragility is discernible in the fabric of efficiency that has been woven throughout the food supply chain. It would be foolish (and historically myopic) to pronounce an end to the industrialised system. Indicators suggest continued rural depopulation, capital investment, application of technology, intensification – all the features of industrialisation summarised earlier in this chapter. And yet, the crises in rich countries suggest the need to give more attention to the potential impact of currently marginal policy issues such as public health, ecological strains and consumer reaction. It would be unwise for developing countries to dismiss these concerns as the luxuries of the affluent.

Chapter 3
Food and Poverty: Insights from the 'North'

Elizabeth Dowler

The role that food and nutrition play in the material definitions of poverty are contrasted with the social construction of malnutrition and poverty, drawing largely on British experience. The consequences for poor health and premature death are briefly examined; in particular, the connection is made to the world-wide growth in obesity, and in cardio-vascular disease, cancers and diabetes. The lived experience of those defined as poor in the North, and the implications of contemporary policy initiatives and responses by state, private and voluntary sectors, are explored. The challenges of the dominant policy framework remain consumer and individual choice, rather than public health and citizenship, which militates against the realisation of true food security.

1 Introduction

It may seem inappropriate to discuss food and poverty in the 'North' in the context of international food policy. How can the extent and depth of poverty, hunger and nutritional inadequacy in rich, industrialised countries be in any way compared to the experience of those in the 'South'? State welfare provision and/or employment and other anti-poverty strategies have been in place for at least a century, alongside public provision of minimal levels of safe water, reasonable housing, and the means of obtaining a livelihood (education, training, employment).

Yet there are good reasons to review evidence on the experience and causes of 'food poverty' in rich countries and to examine contemporary policy responses. Food consumption data contribute to a materialist analysis of poverty throughout the world. Even in Britain, however, the welfare regime, constructed to address 'want', in practice condemns benefit recipients to nutritional intakes and food patterns which contribute significantly to ill-health and premature mortality. Furthermore, the consequences for food purchase and patterns of consumption induced by living on a very low income and/or in circumstances of social and environmental deprivation, many of which are exacerbated by developments in food retailing, have often been ignored in policy responses. There are avoidable lessons for the South, both in implementing welfare regimes and in responding to the spread of a globalised food system.

By way of introduction, it is worth recalling that food and nutrition play a critical role in health and in avoidance of morbidity and premature mortality throughout the life-cycle, and in both North and South (Davey Smith and Brunner, 1997; James et al., 1997; FAO/WHO, 2003). The link between malnutrition and infection is well recognised and researched in literature and practice. During the last three decades or so, research has shown in addition the importance of poor nutritional intake and food patterns in contributing to non-communicable diseases: cardiovascular disease, some cancers, obesity, osteoporosis, dental disease and non-insulin dependent diabetes (Shetty and McPherson, 1997). The most recent report from a joint Food and

Agriculture/World Health Organization Expert Consultation (FAO/WHO, 2003), drawing on the best available scientific evidence on the relationship between diet, physical activity and chronic disease, produces a series of focused – though contested[1] – recommendations for regional strategies and national goals.

Significantly, the FAO/WHO Report concerns the whole world, not just the North. The prevalence of non-communicable diseases is increasing globally, and they now contribute significantly to premature mortality in the South; in five out of six WHO regions chronic diseases dominate the mortality statistics (WHO 2002;[2] FAO/WHO, 2003). The measurable shifts in the health and nutritional status of populations in many parts of the world are attributed to the rapid changes in diets and lifestyles which industrialisation, urbanisation and market globalisation have brought (FAO/WHO, 2003). Delegates to the ninth Asian congress on nutrition in New Delhi (in March 2003) showed that changes in diet, coupled with an increasingly inactive lifestyle in all age groups, have led to rising obesity across Asia, which is contributing to the growth in heart disease and diabetes. For instance, 30% of Indian adolescents from the higher economic groups, 14% of Sri Lankan urban schoolchildren, and 20% of Malaysian adults are overweight (Mudur, 2003).

Indeed, the impact of food and nutrition is not confined to 'adult' experiences: life-course analysis has shown how critical the avoidance of 'insult' is at all stages of life (Wadsworth, 1999; Power et al., 1996). Poor maternal nutritional status probably plays a critical role in increasing the likelihood of degenerative disease in subsequent adulthood, since under-nutrition experienced in the womb can track through to negative health outcomes as an adult, especially if small or thin babies grow poorly in the first year of life and subsequently become obese (Barker and Leon, 1997; Wadsworth, 1999). Social and biological factors in the adult's life interact with very early nutritional experience to increase susceptibility to ill-health.

Finally, the role of food and nutrition as a component of, and contribution to, inequalities in health, is increasingly recognised in academic research and policy response, although the nature and causal relationships are still debated. There are significant public health costs in ignoring their role: WHO estimates the 'costs' of poor nutrition, obesity and low physical activity for Europe, calculated in Disability Adjusted Life Years (DALYs), as 9.7% of total DALYs lost (compared to 9% because of smoking) (WHO, 2000). A Treasury review of the costs of long-term health trends in Britain estimated that the NHS would be spending £30 billion less per year by 2022 if the population ate better, was less obese, smoked less and took more physical activity (Wanless, 2002).

2   The social construction of malnutrition

It goes without saying, but is often forgotten, that the foetal environment, maternal conditions and adult risk factors associated with food and nutrition are strongly socially

---

1. The food industry has objected to the inclusion of sugar and salt as factors in causing obesity and high blood pressure, and in the US has lobbied to reduce American grants to the UN WHO. *The Guardian*, 24 April 2003, editorial.
2. Only in sub-Saharan Africa do infectious diseases, particularly HIV/AIDS, malaria and TB, outweigh cardiovascular diseases, cancers and diabetes. On a global basis, 79% of deaths are attributable to non-communicable diseases (FAO/WHO, 2003: 3).

determined: a mother's health and nutrition during pregnancy depend on her previous health and experience, which in turn are strongly influenced by her family and social circumstances (Graham, 2001). In the UK, Europe and elsewhere in the North, there has been an explosion of research on, and policy attention to, inequalities in health and the link to both material and psychosocial circumstances (see Illsley and Svensson,1990; Gepkens and Gunning-Schepers, 1996; Kunst et al., 1998; Marmot and Wilkinson,1999; Leon and Walt, 2001, from a large literature).[3]

Furthermore, the production, distribution and quality of food are affected by, and contribute to, processes of globalisation and delocalisation (Tansey and Worsley, 1995), which have left many producers and consumers in both North and South poorer and with less control over their food systems. In the South particularly, producers raise crops or animals/fish which they have not grown before, in mono-cropping systems heavily dependent on agro-chemicals which they have to buy, and for buyers in new kinds of food processing or storage systems which they do not own. Migration to the rapidly growing urban sector, where they are increasingly dependent on purchased food, is often the consequence. In other words 'traditional societies are not in the process of "catching up" with the [North] but are caught up in a global system which provides food choice and variety for industrialized societies at the expense of economically marginal peoples' (Beardsworth and Keil, 1997: 41).

In the North, too, those who are poor, unskilled and increasingly destitute are also marginalised in terms of the dominant food culture and choice in their own societies. The environmental consequences of the modern food system, and fall-out from the food safety crisis (of BSE/vCJD, and biotechnological manipulation), have generated consumer anxieties and action, and questions about regulation, control and accountability. These issues are covered in more depth elsewhere (Lang, 1999; Lang et al., 2001; McMichael, 2001); critical issues are the lack of power and control over food for those who are poor, whether producers or consumers. In many ways, the poor of the North and the South have more in common with each other than with the rich in either country.

3   Poverty and food poverty

Social construction matters too, when food data are used to define poverty. Poverty defined in materialist terms of income sufficiency is often used to trigger access to social welfare payments, and 'food' often plays an important, if largely hidden, role. Its use as a component of minimum cost-of-living calculations is accepted because, not only does food represent a continuous basic need, but the lure of nutritional science is to foster the myth that a physiological minimum need can be defined, and translated into a dietary pattern and budgetary cost, which then represents an objective contribution to a poverty line.

The problems with these assumptions are discussed in detail elsewhere (Dowler and Leather, 2000; Veit-Wilson, 1994; Dowler, 2002). In purely input-output terms, requirements are not universal objectively established minima but probability statements of the likelihood of avoiding deficiency or (less often) achieving health.

---

3. See also web/email networks of researchers, such as the Health Equity Network www.ukhen.org, and International Health Equity Network.

More seriously, food standards are in fact socially constructed for a given place and circumstance (Dallison, 1996). As such, they may be unrealistic in their assumption of food usage patterns (Dowler and Leather, 2000). Such definitions and their cut-offs are usually set by professional panels, chosen for their scientific expertise rather than their experience of life lived in multiple deprivation and on the lowest incomes. They can often be based on incorrect assumptions about the price of food in relation to other essentials, and to its physical availability; in other words, problems of access are ignored.

In the UK, for instance, many who live in areas of multiple deprivation face difficulties getting to decent shops offering a reasonable range of foods which contribute to a healthy diet, at affordable prices (for example, Dowler et al., 2001a; Clarke et al., 2002). Food may in fact be cheaper and better stocked (especially fresh produce), but also less accessible, in the major retailers' superstores, than in many of the smaller supermarkets or corner stores, whose operating margins are such that they cannot compete on price (Piachaud and Webb, 1996; Consumers' Association, 1997). In many areas, shops have struggled to survive in the face of competition from the large retailers, whose superstores court the car-owning, and monied, customer (see Blair, 2003; Dowler et al., 2001b for details of one area example). Poverty and deprivation in general have contributed synergistically to food poverty.

Despite World Bank promotion of the 'voices of the poor' (World Bank, 2000), few agencies or governments use consensual budget standards, drawn up by a range of individuals from the society in question with relevant life experience (Middleton, 2000). Nonetheless, there are new approaches being implemented to measuring poverty and exclusion in Europe, which involve asking respondents in large-scale sample surveys to define essential needs (Mack and Lansley, 1985; Callan et al., 1993; Gordon et al., 2000; Gordon and Townsend, 2002).

Each time this method has been used, people have ranked normative expectations of food consumption patterns quite highly in their list of items whose lack delineates households as poor. These indicators are based on foods and meals rather than nutrients; they include, for instance, being able to provide three meals a day for children or two for adults, having fresh fruit most days, or a main meat, fish or vegetarian dish every other day. There is also usually an indicator of ability to feed visitors, or provide celebratory food.

Such an approach does not imply that people must use or consume these commodities in particular ways, nor how often, simply that people should be able to do so; they should have the resources (money, time) and access to express normative choices if they wish. In their choice of food deprivation indices and their ranking, people go beyond basic physiological needs to include social and cultural elements, and often health outcomes as well. In the general public's mind, food is more than a bundle of nutrients; it represents an expression of who a person is, where they belong and what they are worth, and is a focus for social exchange.[4]

There are some parallels in method with the household food security indicators regularly used in national surveys and to contribute to estimates of poverty in the US

---

4. This parallels consistent findings in the South that, even on the lowest incomes, people put some premium on variety and status in food: no-one willingly consumes a 'least-cost-diet' – not because they do not know how to construct it, but because even the poorest value culture and diversity (see Berhman, 1988, for an early discussion), and, where possible, hospitality.

(Radimer et al., 1990; Andrews et al., 2000) and elsewhere. These surveys also focus on perceptions and experiences of household members (such as going without food, or types of food, regularly being hungry, and running out of money for food). In the UK, some surveys now also ask about distance to food shops and quality of local provision, range and price of goods available, and, for households with school-age children, about the experience and quality of school meal provision.[5]

Thus, food and nutritional concerns in poverty definition and measurement have moved some way from costing a minimal diet for subsistence, to an acknowledgement of the realities of managing on low incomes and in physical areas of multiple deprivation. The term 'food poverty', which has begun to gain some currency in the UK, can be seen as a useful synonym for 'food insecurity', in that the resonance with recent research and thinking about wider dimensions of poverty than mere physical efficiency and its measurement by minimal cost of living, draws in elements of social and cultural participation. The term has been variously defined, but usually refers to the inability to acquire or consume an adequate quality or quantity of food in socially acceptable ways, or the uncertainty that one will be able to do so (Riches, 1997, 2002; Dowler et al., 2001a).

Whichever methodology is used to define and measure food poverty or insecurity in the North, the general results have been similar: those living on low wages or state benefits, or in areas of deprivation, have lower nutrient intakes and worse dietary patterns than those not living in such circumstances. Meals are missed, and people rely on snacks, sometimes with cigarettes to dull hunger (Dowler et al., 2001a; Whelan et al., 2002). The range and variety of foodstuffs is greatly reduced, so the food base is considerably less diverse. Where budgetary costings are employed, it is clear that many such households could not afford to purchase sufficient appropriate food to meet healthy dietary guidelines or nutrient requirements laid down by government committees of experts (for example, Parker et al., 1998). They have insufficient money, however well they budget, shop and prepare food.

Actual food expenditure, measured in household expenditure surveys and small-scale studies, demonstrates the relationship with income. For instance, in the UK Family Expenditure Survey, households in the lowest income decile spend the highest proportion on food of any group (23% of their income goes on food, as against those in the top 10% who spend 14% on food).[6] Nonetheless, in common with survey findings elsewhere, those in the lowest income category spend much less than richer households in absolute terms (in 1999/2000, for instance, about £25.20 a week as against £106.00 spent by the highest income decile. Households with incomes below £96 a week spent about £1 a week on fruit, while households with incomes above £940 a week spent about £4.40 a week on fruit alone – which is about a sixth of what the poorest households spent on all foods (Office of National Statistics, 2001)).

Small-scale studies suggest expenditure is even lower when other demands – such as rent, debt repayments or utility bills – are pressing: food is the flexible budget item

---

5. The Food Standards Agency has commissioned a national survey of nutrition and diet in low-income households which will include investigation of food security and food access.

6. Although, as in all expenditure surveys, the proportion of income spent on food has fallen in all deciles over the last three decades, as average incomes have increased, and the income distribution has widened. For those in the lowest decile, expenditure on rent and utilities has increased disproportionately, as these costs have increased.

(Dobson et al., 1994; Dowler and Calvert, 1995; Dowler, 2002). Indeed, this is a critical and common finding: food is cut back at the expense of other more immediate demands coming from agencies which can threaten, fine or imprison; the personal costs of poor diets remain hidden, while the potential cost to the household and the state from long-term ill-health or premature mortality has only recently been valued (Wanless, 2002).

4   State, private and voluntary sector responses

There is no shortage of evidence to show what kind of diet is most consistent with health. However, there is considerably more controversy about how to achieve dietary change at the population level. Food culture and advertising are recognised as critical influences on food choice but are seen as too difficult to tackle through intervention.[7] Instead, the inability of those living in poverty to purchase sufficient or appropriate food has often been attributed to personal, domestic failures to buy and cook the right foods, or a propensity to spend too much money on cigarettes and crisps. Public health improvements are then usually regarded as 'prevention strategies', i.e. that people could implement change if they had a mind to.

Knowledge about food, nutrition and health can indeed play a part in determining the kind of food people eat, as can cooking skills. These dimensions of personal agency have long been seen as open to influence by the state and are re-emerging on the research and intervention agendas (Dibsdall et al., 2003; Steptoe et al., 2003).[8] For instance, the UK Department of Health website, in discussing barriers to eating sufficient fruit and vegetables, highlights 'attitude and awareness' along with access and availability. A nation-wide programme to promote consumption of 'five-a-day' fruit and vegetables, with an initial tranche of funding from the National Lottery, is largely focused on development of local-level initiatives, many of which address these individualist elements. Recent analysis suggests that strategies to promote healthy eating and dietary change are among the most cost-effective methods of preventing cardiovascular disease (Brunner et al., 2001) or cancer (Gundgaard et al., 2003).

However, there are dangers in assuming that the failure to live on state benefits or low wages can be taken to signify inefficiency or incompetence (Dowler and Dobson, 1997), rather than a recognition that levels have been set unrealistically low. Public policy readily becomes the familiar 'teaching the poor how to budget and cook' (Travers, 1995). Food plays a significant part in marginalising and blaming those who are poor for their own circumstances.

Some who have lived most of their lives in difficult social and economic circumstances do not actively express the desire for the type of diet which conforms to contemporary healthy eating advice,[9] and some do not express a desire for better shops or cheaper food either (for example, Dibsdall et al., 2003). People have learned to

---

7. Sustain, a public interest non-governmental agency in the UK, published a report calling for the state to prevent food advertising during TV programmes aimed at young children (Sustain, 2001). A backbench MP has taken up the challenge, but has to date not been supported by the Department of Culture, Media and Sport. http://news.bbc.co.uk/1/hi/uk_politics/3004857.stm.

8. The UK Food Standards Agency has commissioned research into cooking skills and their improvement. see website: http://www.food.gov.uk/science/research/NutritionResearch/

9. Such as eating low-fat or wholegrain commodities and products, with at least five portions of fruit and vegetables daily and regular oily fish.

accommodate their practice and expectations to the continual realities of life which they do not expect to change. Parents with young children, especially lone parents, are likely to refer to cost, and their own meagre cash available for food, when discussing shopping habits; they pay little active attention to 'healthy eating', preferring to choose what they know their children will eat so as not to waste food (Dowler and Calvert, 1995; Whelan et al., 2002). Those who live on low incomes do not experiment or try new foods. They often prefer not to shop in large superstores except the cheapest, to avoid embarrassment and temptation (Dowler and Dobson, 1997). The picture is a complex one, with practice and motivation varying according to age and social, demographic and geographic circumstances (Dowler et al., 2001b; Whelan et al., 2002). It is not only those claiming means-tested state benefits who face problems; those earning at or, in reality below, the minimum wage also have difficulty feeding themselves and their families well (Morris et al., 2000; Abrams, 2002; Toynbee, 2003). They, too, have insufficient money, and may lack time for shopping and food preparation as well. Shift workers, for instance, may have limited or no access to decent food for health at work; many rely on snatched snacks and/or take-away food, both of which are likely to be high in fat and salt. This is not to suggest a necessarily wilful disregard for future consequences; rather that, for those who lack money and power, choosing and enjoying a diet conducive to health is difficult when their main focus is survival, both of the household unit and in terms of daily living.

Similar analysis applies to other aspects of the food-health nexus. Recent figures show £1.4 billion was spent on crisps in the UK (BBC, 2003); crisps, snacks, confectionery and fizzy drinks are favourite targets for promotion, particularly to children[10] (Tansey and Worsley, 1995). But again there is a social dimension. For those who live on tight budgets, there is continual anxiety over whether or not their children can or will exhibit the sophistication required to resist the persuasiveness of advertisements, and the need to ensure that their children are not victimised because they do not eat the latest 'fashionable' food. Food can be a marker for social exclusion for children as well as adults. The structural factors which contribute to these cultural contexts have largely been bypassed in policy response.[11]

There has been an acknowledgement of the importance of food availability and affordability in UK policy documents relating to inequalities in health and to some extent in poverty and exclusion (for example, Acheson, 1998; Social Exclusion Unit 1998; Department of Health, 1999a, 1999b, 2000). The complex processes which link inequalities in diet and health outcomes with the decline in public and private services in deprived neighbourhoods (Speak and Graham, 2000), and with developments in the retail sector towards edge-of-city food-superstore building are being explored in multi-disciplinary research (Wrigley et al., 2002). Distribution of free fruit in primary schools, development of five-a-day initiatives in areas of deprivation (and promotion of local food in public procurement) are new, challenging policy initiatives. But they are only a start towards addressing the more fundamental structural issues in food poverty.

---

10. See recent campaigns by Walkers' Crisps (books for schools; walkers.corpex.com/cr15p5/index.htm), and Cadbury's (for sports equipment; see http://getactive.cadbury.co.uk/).

11. The poorest are also the most likely to smoke; cigarettes are highly addictive and hard to give up for those with stressed lives and low self-esteem or sense of control (Marsh and McKay, 1994).

All too often community-based initiatives, such as food co-operatives or cooking clubs, are what happens in practice, and are seen as the main solution. While food co-operatives, like other local food projects, provide considerable social benefits for those involved, they are small-scale in comparison to the decline in local shops and the viability of neighbourhood retailing. They cannot address longer-term changes needed in economic structures or food access, and in practice they can arguably divert attention from the realities of life lived on a low income, faced on a daily basis by diverse households.

In some instances, local food projects have empowered some members of hitherto excluded communities to speak for themselves over issues of retail siting and management, food provision of all kinds in schools, and usage of locally produced food for public procurement. However, local food projects are often used as something of a 'quick fix' to address exclusion, poor food access or skills, or hungry and disaffected schoolchildren. The rhetoric of dignity and self-help is easily employed to cover up a lack of fundamental change and to locate both the 'problem' and the 'solutions' as belonging to those labelled – and living – as 'poor'. Planners and funders in fact need to harness the energy, vision and skill development within local food projects, and to develop the capacity to build on and listen to the experience of local people engaged in them (Dowler and Caraher, 2002).

5 Conclusions

The dominant policy framework for food remains one of consumer and individual choice, rather than public health and citizenship. There is an argument for considering food as a basic utility product which, like water, should be seen as part of a public health service. In contemporary Britain and other countries in the North, people have to pay for water and its delivery, but there are usually cross-subsidies and, on the whole, withdrawal of service for non-payment is avoided where possible. Clean water, waste sewerage treatment, housing and other elements of public health may be provided by the private sector, but the state plays a role in quality and economic regulation, and does not expect community-level provision to step in where the private sector fails.[12]

Why is food treated so differently? No agency has statutory responsibility for measuring and monitoring food access (economic and physical) or food security on a regular basis, except in the United States. Much investment has been made in Europe at national and regional level in monitoring and maintaining food safety, yet, like water, food has also to be seen as a necessary condition of public health for all, rather than only for those who can afford it (Dowler and Caraher, 2002).

In the late twentieth/early twenty-first century, food has been reconfigured as part of a consumerist commodity culture, with the responsibility shifted from the state to the individual, whose rights as a citizen are ignored in relation to food. Indeed, one major state response to food poverty is to address it entirely as an individual need: to provide food which is essentially 'surplus', to be obtained by begging, from food banks or distributed via charitable outlets (Hawkes and Webster, 2000; Riches, 2002). Ironically, this solution is provided by the very sector – the major retailers – which has often

---

12. See Nicol and Slaymaker (2003), which addresses how Demand-Responsive Approaches can address poverty reduction, sustainability and livelihoods issues in securing access to clean water in the South.

contributed to the problem through its development policies and employment practices. This challenges the very notion of 'security', of social appropriateness and dignity, and ignores the elements of the human right to food.

Chapter 4
The Nutrition Transition in the Developing World

Barry M. Popkin

This chapter explores shifts in nutrition transition from the period termed the receding famine pattern to one dominated by nutrition-related non-communicable diseases (NR-NCDs). It examines the speed of these changes, summarises dietary and physical activity changes, and provides some sense of the health effects and economic costs. The focus is on the lower- and middle-income countries of Asia, Africa, the Middle East and Latin America. The chapter shows that changes are occurring at great speed and at earlier stages of countries' economic and social development. The burden of disease from NR-NCDs is shifting towards the poor and the costs are also becoming greater than those for under-nutrition. Policy options are identified.

1 Introduction

Two historic processes of change occur simultaneously with or precede the 'nutrition transition'. One is the demographic transition – the shift from a pattern of high fertility and mortality to one of low fertility and mortality (typical of modern industrialised countries). The second is the epidemiological transition, first described by Omran (1971): the shift from a pattern of high prevalence of infectious disease, associated with malnutrition, periodic famine and poor environmental sanitation, to one of high prevalence of chronic and degenerative disease, associated with urban-industrial lifestyles (see also Olshansky and Ault, 1986).

The nutrition transition is closely related to the other two. Large shifts have occurred in diet and in physical activity patterns, particularly in the last one or two decades of the twentieth century. Modern societies seem to be converging on a diet high in saturated fats, sugar and refined foods and low in fibre – often termed the 'Western diet' – and on lifestyles characterised by lower levels of activity. These changes are reflected in nutritional outcomes, such as changes in average stature, body composition and morbidity.

The nutrition transition is described in more detail in Figure 4.1. In Stage 1, famine begins to recede as income rises. In Stage 2, changes in diet and activity pattern lead to the emergence of new disease problems and increased disability. In Stage 3, behavioural change begins to reverse the negative tendencies and make possible a process of 'successful ageing' (see Manton and Soldo, 1985; Crimmins et al., 1989). The changes are all driven by a range of factors, including urbanisation, economic growth, technical change and culture. For convenience, the patterns can be thought of as historical developments: however, 'earlier' patterns are not restricted to the periods in which they first arose, but continue to characterise certain geographic and socio-economic sub-populations.

Figure 4.1: Stages of the nutrition transition

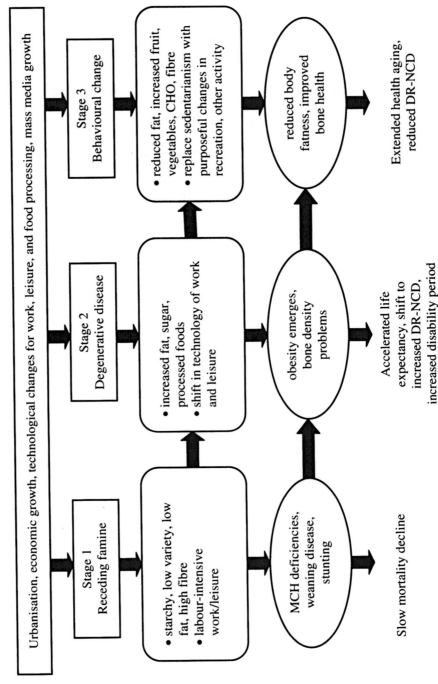

Source: Popkin (2002a).

2   Dynamics of the food system and related changes

2.1   Dietary shifts: more fat, more added caloric sweeteners, more animal source foods

The diets of the developing world are shifting rapidly, particularly with respect to fat, caloric sweeteners and animal source foods (Popkin, 2002b; Popkin and Du, forthcoming).

Edible oil

In the popular mind, the Westernisation of the global diet continues to be associated with increased consumption of animal fats. Yet the nutrition transition in developing countries typically begins with major increases in the domestic production and imports of oilseeds and vegetable oils, rather than meat and milk. Between 1991 and 1996/7, global production of vegetable fats and oils rose from 60 to 71 million metric tons (USDA, 1997). In contrast, the production of visible animal fats (butter and tallow) has remained steady at approximately 12 million metric tons. Principal vegetable oils include soybean, sunflower, rapeseed, palm and groundnut oil. With the exception of groundnut oil, global availability of each has approximately tripled between 1961 and 1990.

Fat intake increases with income, but there have also been dramatic changes in the aggregate income-fat relationship. These are displayed for the period 1962-90 in Figure 4.2. Most significantly, even poor nations had access to a relatively high-fat diet by 1990, when a diet deriving 20% of energy (kcal) from fat was associated with countries having a GNP of only $750 per capita. In 1962, the same energy diet (20% from fat) was associated with countries having a GNP of $1475 (both GNP values in 1993 dollars).

Figure 4.2: Relationship between the % of energy from fat and GNP per capita, 1962 and 1990

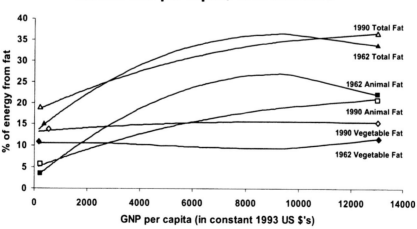

Source: Nonparametric regressions run with food balance data from FAO, UN and GNP data from the World Bank for 132 countries; Guo et al., 2000.

This dramatic change arose principally from a major increase in the consumption of vegetable fats. In 1990, these accounted for a greater proportion of dietary energy than animal fats for countries in the lowest 75% of countries (all of which have incomes below $5800 per capita) of the per capita income distribution. The change in edible vegetable fat prices, supply, and consumption is unique because it affected rich and poor countries equally, but the net impact is relatively much greater on low-income countries.

Caloric sweetener

Sugar is the world's predominant sweetener.[1] For this chapter, however, we use the term caloric sweetener instead of added sugar, as there is such a range of non-sugar products used today. High fructose corn syrup is a prime example as it is the sweetener used in all US soft drinks.[2]

The overall trends show a large increase in caloric sweetener consumed (see Table 4.1). In 2000, 306 kcals were consumed per person per day, about a third more than in 1962; caloric sweeteners also accounted for a larger share of both total energy and total carbohydrates consumed.

Unsurprisingly, Table 4.1 shows that all measures of caloric sweetener increase significantly as GNP per capita of the country and urbanisation increase. However, the interaction between income growth and urbanisation is important. Figure 4.3 shows the relationship between the proportion of energy from different food sources and GNP, for two different levels of urbanisation (see Drewnoswski and Popkin, 1997 for a description of the analysis). In the less urbanised case (Panel A), the share of sweeteners increases sharply with income, from about 5% to about 15%. In the more urbanised case, the share is much higher at lower income (over 15%), and hardly increases with income. The analysis confirms previous observations, that people living in urban areas consume diets distinct from those of their rural counterparts (Popkin and Bisgrove, 1988; Solomons and Gross, 1995).

Animal source foods

The revolution in animal source foods (ASF) refers to the increase in demand and production of meat, fish, and milk in low-income developing countries. IFPRI's Christopher Delgado has studied this issue extensively in a number of seminal reports and papers (summarised in Delgado, forthcoming; Delgado et al., 1999). Most of the world's growth in production and consumption of these foods comes from the developing countries. Thus, developing countries will produce 63% of meat and 50% of milk in 2020. It is a global food activity, transforming the grain markets for animal feed.

---

1. It is not clear exactly when sugar became the world's principal sweetener – most likely in the 17th or 18th century, as the New World began producing large quantities of sugar at reduced prices (Galloway, 2000; Mintz, 1977).
2. Under the name sweeteners, the FAO includes products used for sweetening that are either derived from sugar crops, cereals, fruits, milk or produced by insects. This category includes a wide variety of monosaccharides (glucose and fructose) and disaccharides (sucrose and saccharose), which exist either in a crystallised state as sugar or in thick liquid form as syrups. Included in sweeteners are maple sugar and syrups, caramel, golden syrup, artificial and natural honey, maltose, glucose, dextrose, glucose (also known as high-fructose corn syrup), other types of fructose, sugar confectionery and lactose. In the last several decades, increasingly larger quantities of cereals (primarily maize) have been used to produce sweeteners derived from starch.

It also leads to resource degradation, rapid increases in feed grain imports, rapid concentration of production and consumption and social change.

Table 4.1: World trends in caloric sweetener intake for GNP and urbanisation quintiles

	Quintile 1	Quintile 2	Quintile 3	Quintile 4	Quintile 5	Total
A. Quintiles of GNP (using 1962 GNP levels for each country)						
Caloric sweetener (kcal/capita/day)						
1962	90	131	257	287	402	232
2000	155	203	362	397	418	306
% caloric sweetener of total energy						
1962	4.5	6.2	11.9	12.0	13.5	9.5
2000	6.4	8.3	13.4	13.7	12.7	10.9
% caloric sweetener of total carbohydrates						
1962	6.2	8.5	16.8	17.7	24.4	14.6
2000	9.0	12.1	20.6	22.4	24.6	17.7
GNP						
1962	216	478	983	2817	12234	3282
2000	435	839	2836	5915	28142	7198
% urban						
1962	10.0	21.6	37.3	46.7	66.2	36.1
2000	27.7	41.3	58.7	70.0	78.0	54.9
B. Quintiles of % urban (using 1962 values for each country)						
Caloric sweetener (kcal/capita/day)						
1962	79	131	236	335	389	232
2000	151	201	339	403	441	306
% caloric sweetener of total energy						
1962	3.8	6.3	11.0	13.2	13.8	9.5
2000	6.5	8.1	12.3	13.7	13.9	10.9
% caloric sweetener of total carbohydrates						
1962	5.4	8.5	15.4	20.3	24.1	14.6
2000	6.0	12.1	19.2	22.7	25.7	17.7
GNP						
1962	287	734	1294	4696	9606	3282
2000	653	1798	8798	11739	20568	7198
% urban						
1962	7.1	20.4	33.9	47.6	73.0	36.4
2000	27.0	42.3	57.6	64.9	84.0	54.9

Source: Popkin and Nielsen (forthcoming); FAO, FAOSTAT data set for food balance data.

Figure 4.3: Relationship between the proportion of energy from each food source and GNP per capita and urbanisation

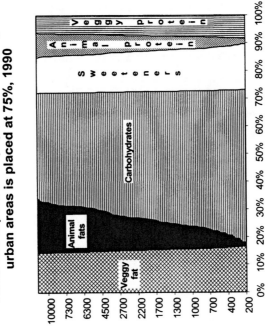

Panel A: Proportion of population residing in urban areas is placed at 25%, 1990

Panel B: Proportion of population residing in urban areas is placed at 75%, 1990

Sources: Drewnowski and Popkin (1997); food balance data from the FAO; GNP data from the World Bank; regression work by UNC-CH.

Summary of food changes: the China example

Data from China are useful for summarising these changes for a typical fast growing economy (Table 4.2). The shift in the Chinese diet follows a classic Westernisation pattern (for more detail on these Chinese changes, see Du et al., 2002; Popkin et al., 1993).

Table 4.2: Shift in consumption in Chinese diet (mean intake grams/per capita/per day)

Food	Urban		Rural		Low income		Mid income		High income		Total	
	89	97	89	97	89	97	89	97	89	97	89	97
Total grains	556	489	742	581	811	615	642	556	595	510	684	557
Coarse	46	25	175	54	226	68	98	43	78	30	135	46
Refined	510	465	567	527	585	546	544	513	517	479	549	511
Fresh veg.	309	311	409	357	436	356	360	357	335	325	377	345
Fresh fruit	14.5	36	14	17	5.5	8	13	18	26	38	15	21.7
Meat and meat products	73.9	97	44	58	36	40	58	64	67	96	53	67.8
Poultry and game	10.6	16	4.1	12	4.1	7	6.6	10	7.7	20	6.1	12.7
Eggs and egg products	15.8	32	8.5	20	6	14	11	22	16	32	11	22.7
Fish and seafood	27.5	31	23	27	12	16	29	26	33	40	25	27.9
Milk and milk products	3.7	4	0.2	0.9	0.8	0.1	0.2	1.4	3.5	3.6	1.3	1.7
Plant oil	17.2	40	14	36	13	32	16	37	16	42	15	37.1

Source: China Health and Nutrition Study, 1989-97, for adults age 20 to 45.

First, we find that intake of cereals decreased considerably during the past two decades in both urban and rural areas and among all income groups (Table 4.2). During the eight-year period from 1989 to 1997, the total intake of cereals decreased by 127g per capita per day (67g for urban residents and 161g for rural residents). The decrease in the low-income group was the largest, at 196g per capita, compared with their counterparts in mid- and high-income groups (86g and 85g respectively). However, there remains an inverse relationship between income and cereal intake. For example, in 1997, the intake in low-, mid- and high-income groups was 615g, 556g and 510g per capita, respectively.

The shift away from coarse grain consumption such as millet, sorghum and corn, is a key component of this change. CHNS data showed a 38g decrease in refined cereals between 1989 and 1997, but an even larger decrease in coarse cereal consumption of 89g.

Second, consumption of animal products increased, more so for the rich than the poor, and for the urban than the rural. As shown in Table 4.2, urban residents' intake of animal foods per capita, per day in 1997 was higher than for rural residents (178.2g for urban vs 116.7g for rural) and also showed a larger increase (46.7g vs 36.8g) from 1989 to 1997. The amount and growth of intake of animal foods were positively associated with income levels. The intake level and the increase in the high-income group from 1989 to 1997 were almost three times those in the low-income group.

Third, and partly as a result of this change, data from the CHNS also show a shift in the diet away from carbohydrates to fat (Table 4.3). Energy from carbohydrates fell for all residents, and by over 20% for urban residents. Energy from fat increased sharply, from 19.3% in 1989 to 27.3% in 1997. Other data show that over 60% of urban residents consumed more than 30% of energy from fat in 1997.

Table 4.3: Shifts in energy sources in Chinese diet for adults aged 20 to 45 (%)

	% energy from fat				% energy from carbohydrates			
	89	91	93	97	89	91	93	97
Urban	21.4	29.7	32.0	32.8	65.8	58.0	55.0	53.3
Rural	18.2	22.5	22.7	25.4	70.0	65.6	65.2	62.1
Low-income	16.0	19.3	19.7	23.0	72.9	69.2	68.6	64.4
Mid-income	20.3	25.2	25.5	27.1	67.5	62.6	62.2	60.3
High-income	21.5	30.0	31.5	31.6	65.4	57.5	55.4	54.8
Total	**19.3**	**24.8**	**25.5**	**27.3**	**68.7**	**63.2**	**62.1**	**59.8**

Source: China Health and Nutrition Survey, 1989-1997.

Finally, when we specifically examine the combined effect of these various shifts in the structure of rural and urban Chinese diets, we find an upward shift in the energy density of the foods consumed (Popkin and Du, forthcoming). The kcal of energy intake from foods and alcohol per 100 grams of food in both urban and rural Chinese adult diets increased by 13% between 1989 and 1997. These are really very rapid shifts.

2.2 Critical related reductions in physical activity

There are several linked changes in physical activity occurring jointly. One is a shift away from the high energy expenditure activities such as farming, mining and forestry towards the service sector. Elsewhere we have shown this large effect (Popkin, 1999). Reduced energy expenditures in the same occupation are a second change. Other major changes relate to mode of transportation and activity patterns during leisure hours.

China again provides interesting illustrations. Table 4.4 shows that the proportion of urban adults (male and female) working in occupations where they participate in

Table 4.4: Labour force distribution among adults, aged 20 to 45, by level of activity (%)

		Light		Vigorous	
		1989	1997	1989	1997
Urban	Male	32.7	38.2	27.1	22.4
	Female	36.3	54.1	24.8	20.8
Rural	Male	19.0	18.7	52.5	59.9
	Female	19.3	25.5	47.4	60.0

Source: China Health and Nutrition Survey, 1989-1997.

vigorous activity patterns has decreased. In rural areas, however, there has been a shift for some towards increased physical activity linked to holding multiple jobs and more intensive effort. For rural women, there is a shift towards a larger proportion engaged in more energy-intensive work, but there are also sections where light effort is increasing. In contrast, for rural men there is a small decrease in the proportion engaged in light work effort.

In China, 14% of households acquired a motorised vehicle between 1989 and 1997. In one study we showed that the odds of being obese were 80% higher (p<0.05) for men and women in households which owned a motorised vehicle compared to those which did not own a vehicle (Bell et al., 2002).

Television ownership has skyrocketed in China, leading to greater inactivity during leisure time (see Du et al., 2002).

2.3 Resultant changes in obesity, diabetes and mortality profile

The interaction of dietary shifts and changes in physical activity has significant consequences for obesity, diabetes and mortality. The burden lies most heavily on the poor.

Obesity
In a series of papers published in a recent issue of *Public Health Nutrition*,[3] the current levels of overweight in countries as diverse as Mexico, Egypt, and South Africa are shown to be equal to or greater than those in the United States. Moreover, the rate of change in obesity in lower- and middle-income countries is shown to be much greater than in higher-income countries (see Popkin, 2002a, for the overview).

Figure 4.4 presents the level of obesity and overweight in several illustrative countries (Brazil and Mexico, Egypt and Morocco, South Africa, Thailand and China).

Figure 4.4: Obesity patterns across the developing world

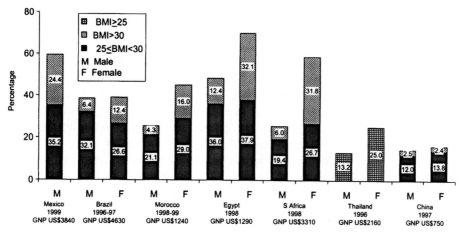

Source: Popkin (2002a).

3. All available as pdf files in the Bellagio papers section of www.nutrans.org

Most interesting is the fact that many of these countries with quite high overweight levels are very low-income. Moreover, it probably surprises many people that the levels of obesity of several countries – all with much lower income levels than the US – are so high.

Figure 4.5 shows how quickly overweight and obesity status has emerged as a major public health problem in some of these countries. Compared with the US and European countries, where the annual increase in the prevalence of overweight and obesity is about 0.25 for each, the rates of change are very high in Asia, North Africa, and Latin America – two to five times greater than in the US.

Figure 4.5: Obesity trends among adults in selected developing countries (annual % increase in prevalence)

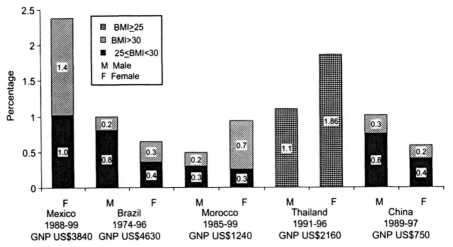

Source: Popkin (2002a).

Diabetes

The rising burden of non-communicable diseases (NCDs) has been the most globally pervasive change among nutrition-related health transitions. There is a growing literature documenting rapid increases in diabetes in many lower-income countries, caused mainly by diet change and inactivity (Levitt et al., 1993; Hodge et al., 1996, 1997, Zimmet, 1991; Zimmet et al., 1997). Diet is, however, the least understood determinant. A clear literature has shown that, in terms of mechanisms and epidemiology, obesity and activity are closely linked to Non-Insulin Dependent Diabetes Mellitus. Several reviews lay out the case for these factors.

The prevalence of this debilitating and health care-intensive disease in a number of regions of the developing world, particularly Latin America, North Africa, and the Middle East, is such that the prevalence is already equal or greater than in the US (King et al., 1998). Furthermore, the prevalence already covers 4% of Chinese adults and 2% of Indian adults. Together there are more new cases each year in these two countries than in the rest of the world combined (ibid.). Interestingly, the age-specific prevalence in the developing regions of the world shows a higher proportion of new cases occurring at younger ages than in the higher-income countries.

Mortality

The most comparable set of mortality patterns by cause, as well as projections of mortality, come from the global Burden of Disease project (Murray and Lopez, 1996). These and other studies show that a remarkable decline in deaths related to infectious and parasitic morbidity has occurred in China and is still occurring in India. At the same time, the rapid increase in NR-NCDs is already leading in China to an increase in mortality caused by heart disease and cancer. The same will occur soon in India.

The burden is shifting towards the poor

In a forthcoming paper, we show that a large number of low- and moderate-income countries already have a greater likelihood that adults residing in lower-income or lower educated households are overweight and obese relative to adults in higher income or education households (Monteiro et al., 2003). This study, based on multi-level analysis of 37 nationally representative data sets, shows that countries with a GNP per capita over about $1700 are likely to have a burden of obesity greater among the poor. It also provides some idea of the set of risk factors causing obesity and other NCDs that are changing rapidly, including poor diets, inactivity, smoking, and drinking.

3   What are the costs?

Malnutrition of various kinds carries significant costs in all countries. Data from India and China illustrate both the general point and the relative importance of under-nutrition compared with 'new' nutrition problems. The data come from a series of studies conducted in 2000-2002, using large national health service cost data obtained from the 1998 National Survey of Health Services for China, and the 1995-96 National Sample Survey for India. A study of the costs of diet-related non-communicable diseases (focusing only on the diet component, DR-NCDs) was undertaken and linked with another study of under-nutrition undertaken by Horton (Popkin et al., 2001a, b; Horton, 1999; Ross and Horton, 1998).

It is true that under-nutrition accounts for significant economic costs in China and India. For China, individual nutritional deficiencies account for between 0.5% and 1.8% of lost GDP, and for India between 0.7% and 1.1%. The overall cost of under-nutrition, also including cognitive costs, is almost certainly higher. The costs of under-nutrition are projected to diminish by 2025 for China (when individual nutritional deficiencies account for 0.2% of lost GDP), but remain important for India (ranging from 0.4% to 0.7% of lost GDP).

However, the costs of DR-NCD are already substantial and will grow rapidly. Taking health care costs alone, these amounted to 1.6% of GDP for China and 0.35% for India.[4] By 2025, the patterns change considerably in each country. Using current

---

4. In 1995, they accounted for 22.6% of costs to the health care system in China. Costs include hospitalisation costs, out-patient costs, and prescription drugs; the large majority of costs were state expenditures. In India, the corresponding share was 13.9%; private expenditures constitute approximately 90% of the costs and the rest are state expenditures.

health and nutrition data combined with government and WHO projections, predictions of future health costs were made. The economic analysis shows that, for China, current costs of DR-NCDs are of similar magnitude to costs of under-nutrition, but that DR-NCDs will dominate by 2025. For India, current costs of under-nutrition are greater, but the two are more likely to become equal by 2025.

4 Why have these changes occurred?

How do we understand the causes of the changes that have occurred?

First, economic theory would clearly predict the changes in diet and activity that we see. Obtaining a more varied and tasteful diet and a less burdensome work pattern is an important choice desired by most individuals. The choices being made are rational. Preferences for dietary sugars and fats are regarded by many as an innate human trait. Sweetness, in particular, serves as the major cue for food energy in infancy and childhood, and preferences for sweet taste are observed in all societies around the globe (Drewnowski, 1987). An argument has been made that preferences for dietary fats are also either innate or learned in infancy or childhood (Drewnowski, 1989). References to the desirable qualities of milk and honey (i.e., fat and sugar), cream, butter and animal fats are found throughout recorded history.

Second, an important factor is the interaction between income and consumption preferences. As we have shown in several studies, not only is income increasing, but the structure of consumption is shifting, and additional higher-fat foods are being purchased with additional income (Popkin and Du, forthcoming; Guo et al., 2000). The China example illustrates the point: for the same extra dollar of income, an average Chinese person is purchasing higher calorie food today than s/he would have done for the same extra yuan a decade ago.

A third element is lower food prices. Delgado (forthcoming) documents the large long-term reduction in the real costs of basic commodities in the developing world over the past several decades. He has shown that inflation-adjusted prices of livestock and feed commodities fell sharply from the early 1970s to the early 1990s, stabilised in the mid-1990s in most cases, and fell again thereafter (Delgado et al., 2001). Others have shown how important cost constraints might be (Guo et al, 1999; Darmon et al, 2002).

Fourth, we might point to the centralisation of the mass media and the generation of major pushes to promote selected dietary patterns directly and indirectly via these media. There is as yet little in the way of rigorous analysis to link shifts in mass media coverage to the consumption or work patterns in the developing world, but there is an emerging literature on increased television ownership and viewing (for example, Du et al., 2002; Tudor-Locke et al., 2003). There is a profound cultural side not only to the globalisation of mass media, but also to the related penetration of Western-style fast food outlets into the developing world. There is some evidence that these changes affect the entire culture of food production and consumption (Jin, 2000; Watson, 1997).

Fifth, an added push has come from technological factors that affect work and leisure, productivity and effort. Most of the changes affecting home production, from piped water to electricity to microwave ovens and lower-cost gas and butane ovens, reduce domestic effort. Similarly, the onset of mass transportation, the availability of cheap motor scooters and cycles and buses reduce energy expenditure in transportation. Similar profound changes affect all types of work. The computer revolution, the availability of small gas-powered systems for ploughing and many others affect the work of farmers and other workers. Importantly, the reduction in the cost of producing and distributing food, and of work-related technology, is affected by urbanisation. More dense residential development cuts the costs for marketing, distribution, and even production in many cases.

Finally, there are other changes in household purchasing, preparation, and eating behaviour that matter greatly. These include location of the purchase, consumption of food, and the processing of the foods purchased, *inter alia*. Elsewhere we have discussed the rapid shifts in sources of calories away from at-home preparation and consumption to away-from-home purchase and consumption (e.g., Nielsen et al., 2002; Bisgrove and Popkin, 1996; McGuire and Popkin, 1989). There are few systematic studies of location of preparation and consumption in the developing world; however, it is clear that many important changes are occurring in both the level of processed food consumed at home and the proportion of meals consumed away from home. As the food system changes and as incomes rise, these changes are expected to intensify. Reardon and Berdegué's work on supermarkets in Latin America represents one example of a major shift in the marketing of food in the developing world (Reardon and Berdegué, 2002).

5 Policy options

This chapter provides a strong case for public investment to find ways to improve the dietary and activity pattern and body composition patterns in developing countries in a way that will prevent the shift towards high levels of NR-NCDs. Health has been seen as a major component of international development for some time; however, most of the focus in the developing world has been on infectious diseases and under-nutrition (World Bank, 1993). For example, the World Bank's 1993 *World Development Report* on Investing in Health focused its entire assessment in the diet and nutrition area on under-nutrition. This chapter highlights the important economic and nutritional burden facing just two of the many countries confronting this transition. It shows that for many countries more than a quarter to as many as two-thirds of adults are overweight and obese and face a lifetime associated with enormous health care costs and unstudied related social costs and reductions in productivity.

From the individual perspective, having a tastier higher-fat and sweetened diet is desirable. Similarly, a reduction in stressful activity in market and home production is desired. The critical issue is finding effective social investments and regulations that will enhance the components of lifestyle that will reduce these NR-NCDs and provide for a healthier population. Solutions in the food system and physical environment are critical factors to consider. In particular, it is important to focus on changes that affect the poor, as they are the ones least prepared to incur the costs of these NR-NCDs and most likely now or in the future to face the greatest burden from these problems.

Issues to be addressed from the food sector include learning how to increase the intake levels of fruit and vegetables and higher fibre products, and to reduce the intake of caloric sweeteners and fat. We should note that there is great controversy about the need to reduce total fat intake or just the intake of selected types of fats (transfatty acids, erucic acid, saturated fats) (Bray and Popkin, 1998; Willett, 1998). Clearly all agree that the removal of carcinogenic or artherogenic edible oils is important, but the role of total fat is not as clear. Similarly there is some debate about the role of caloric sweeteners. For instance, an expert committee of the WHO has recommended a maximum of 10% of energy from caloric sweeteners, a level above that of caloric sweeteners consumed in diets in high-, low-, and moderate-income countries (WHO/FAO, 2002). In contrast, the US Institute of Medicine conducted the same review and concluded that 25% of energy from caloric sweeteners was appropriate (Panel, 2002).

Similar shifts in the physical environment to enhance physical activity exist. There is a growing body of knowledge that points to the role of a spread of environmental factors ranging from connectivity of streets to availability of walking options and street safety to the organisation and layout of buildings and communities. Higher density of, and proximity to, opportunities for physical activity, such as recreation facilities (for example, private and public facilities, parks, recreation centres, green spaces, shopping centres) and transportation options (for example, sidewalks, cycle paths, public transportation, high road connectivity, and lower automobile transportation density), will increase physical activity levels and decrease overweight prevalence. Conversely, constraints to physical activity, such as crime and air pollution, will decrease physical activity and increase overweight prevalence.

For each of the desired changes in the food supply and the physical environment, there are clearly myriad options, some easy to implement and many quite complex. A few countries are already beginning to take some steps forward to address these issues (Coitinho et al., 2002; Zhai et al., 2002). There have also been some limited successes in the higher-income world (Puska et al., 2002).

Chapter 5
Redirecting the Diet Transition: What Can Food Policy Do?

Lawrence Haddad

The diets of consumers in the developing world – rich and poor, rural and urban – are changing. More calories, saturated fats, added sugars and added salts are being consumed, resulting in 'over-nutrition'. Combined with lower physical activity levels these changes are causing increased levels of chronic diseases such as heart disease and diabetes. However, the shifts are taking place in the presence of persistent under-nutrition problems, creating a co-existence of under- and over-nutrition. This chapter identifies the drivers of these changes, and asks what food policy (including policies directed to production, marketing, retailing and consumption) can do to re-direct the changes towards better health. The policy trade-offs inherent in the co-existence of under- and over-nutrition are highlighted.

1 Introduction

Where good data on food consumption are available they show that the availability and intake of foods that are risk factors for chronic diseases – such as cardiovascular disease, diabetes, and some forms of cancer – are increasing rapidly in both urban and rural areas and across all income groups in developing countries. Increases in overweight and obesity rates in the developing world show similar patterns (see Popkin 1998, 2001; Guo et al., 2000a). The co-existence of a double burden[1] of under-nutrition and 'over-nutrition'[2] adds to human suffering and economic costs (see Popkin et al., 2001 for estimates of these costs for some Asian countries). It also complicates the design of food policy.

What can food policy do to redirect the transition in diets towards healthier outcomes? This chapter reviews the drivers of changes in diet and then reviews the potential of both demand- and supply-side food policy options to influence the drivers. The chapter ends by highlighting the difficult challenges posed to food policy design by the co-existence, linkages and trade-offs between under- and over-nutrition.

---

1. See WHO website (www.who.int/nut/db_bmi.htm) for data on the population co-existence of underweight and overweight and see Garrett and Ruel (2003) for the co-existence in the same household.
2. In a scientific sense the term 'over-nutrition' lacks consensus. In this chapter we use the term as useful shorthand for excess consumption of added sugar, processed meats, red meats, starch from refined grains and potatoes, dairy products, trans isomers of fatty acids (found in partially hydrogenated vegetable oils found in some margarines and shortening), saturated fat, cholesterol, and overall calories – no matter the source – which leads to overweight and obesity. The term over-nutrition is problematic in that it focuses on excess consumption of some diet components, but what is displaced from the diet by these unhealthy foods matters as well. In particular, the consumption of fruits and vegetables, nuts and pulses, poultry and fish, healthy oils and fats, and whole grains are thought to be health-promoting and increased intakes should be encouraged (see WHO/FAO, 2002; Willett and Stampfer 2002; McCullough, 2002).

2   Drivers of diet and nutrition trends

The drivers of consumption trends include (a) income growth, (b) changes in relative prices caused by technological, institutional and policy change and (c) the socio-economic and activity changes associated with urbanisation.

2.1 Income growth

We know that as income grows, consumers want to diversify out of cereals and other starchy staples. Data from USDA (Regmi, 2001) on how food expenditure responds to increases in income (food expenditure-income elasticities) across a number of developing countries show that the poorest countries have the highest elasticities. Fish, then dairy and then meats have the highest values followed by fruit and vegetables, oils and fats and lastly cereals. Elasticities may increase in the short term; for example, data from China (Guo et al., 2000b) show that the income elasticities for pork and oil increased between 1989 and 1993, more so at the lowest income levels, especially for edible oil.

2.2 Relative prices

Basic economics tells us that if the relative price of a foodstuff increases, demand for it will decrease. How have the relative prices of different foodstuffs changed over time?[3] In the United States, the relative prices of dairy products, fats and oils, eggs, meat, poultry and fish, and sugar and sweets have dropped dramatically over the period 1982-97, as has the price of non-alcoholic beverages (dominated by carbonated sweetened soft drinks) (Putnam and Allshouse, 1999). Future projections of the internationally traded prices for non-staple non-fruit and non-vegetable goods, whenever available, indicate a further decline in their prices relative to cereals (Delgado et al., 1999).[4]

More analyses need to be undertaken from a health perspective of past trends in producer and retail food prices. For example, we do not have consumer food price trends by fat content or, even better, by type of fat content. Such trends would help identify the main sources of any decline or increase in the price of fat or added sugar – obviously important for policy formulation. In addition, there need to be more studies linking price trends to health outcomes. There are many linking under-nutrition outcomes to price changes (for example Pitt and Rosenzweig, 1986), but few linking rates of chronic disease or levels of obesity to relative price changes, controlling for a range of other factors. One of the few such studies to do so, using US data, suggests that 40% of the growth in weight of the US population between 1976 and 1994 was due to

---

3. One price that we do not examine here is the wage rate, which has risen for occupations that tend to be less physically demanding. This, of course, is the other side of the coin, but one which, for now, we ignore with respect to what food policy can do.

4. Preliminary simple regression analysis of FAOSTAT's producer price series (no retail prices were available) for Nigeria, South Africa, India and China did not demonstrate any significant systematic differences in relative price increases by food category, with the exception of China where oils low in saturated fats (soybean, sunflower, rapeseed, and sesame seed) posted significantly higher price increases over the 1976-95 period compared to palm oil which showed one of the lowest price increases over that period.

technology-based reductions in food prices (see Lakdawalla and Philipson, 2002; Philipson and Posner, 1999).

Technology may be one important source of change in the relative prices of foods that pose a chronic health risk; institutional change is another. Examples of the latter include (a) trade policy governance and (b) changing food distribution mechanisms. An illustration of the first is the entry of China into the World Trade Organization, expected by many (for example, Fang and Beghin, 2000) to lead to a 20% decline in the prices paid by consumers in China for soybean oil and related products. More research is needed from a health perspective on how trade liberalisation will affect the prices of different foods that represent different health risks.

An illustration of institutional policy changes, fuelled in part by technology changes, is the rapid transformation of food retailing in Latin America. Reardon and Berdegué (2002) report that the percentage of food distributed by supermarkets in retail outlets in the region grew from 10-20% in 1990 to 50-60% in 2000, driven by liberalisation of financial flows and developments in inventory management technology. These changes are also happening in Asia and Africa (Reardon et al., 2003). Do these supermarkets provide poorer consumers with increased access to more unhealthy processed foods (for example, those with high levels of trans fatty acids)? Do they also provide increased access to fresh fruit and vegetable products and other healthy diet components? What happens to the choice sets of those who do not use supermarkets? These issues have not been investigated yet. More research is needed to identify the trade-offs between healthy foods and healthy profits.[5]

2.3 Urbanisation

Urbanisation is proceeding rapidly in the developing world. Urbanisation is marked by a reduction in physical activity for the majority of the labour force. The density of residence of urban populations also lowers the per person cost of mass-media advertising, where the spending power of food manufacturers and processors certainly outweighs that of public health authorities. The urban environment is also marked by a greater physical distance between places of work and of residence, and by smaller household sizes. In this environment, where time is scarcer, at least for those gainfully employed, and where the fixed costs of food preparation are higher in smaller families, more food tends to be purchased outside the home, even for poor households.

Good data from the developing world are hard to obtain but foods purchased outside the home tend to be more processed and prepared. If so, they will tend to be higher in salt and fat and will often be fried, sometimes using oil that has been refried – a particularly unhealthy diet component because of the high concentration of trans fat. These foods are often purchased from street vendors, so-called 'street foods'. Street foods are a significant source of food (and income generation) for many urban dwellers, both in terms of energy intake and food expenditure. In some settings, this may be particularly true for poorer urban dwellers compared to the more wealthy group. A recent Accra-wide study (Maxwell et al., 2000) finds that households in the poorest

---

5. Reardon and Berdegué (2002) note that profit margins are highest on fresh fruit and vegetables, but are also high on dairy and processed foods.

expenditure quintile obtain on average 31% of their total calories away from home, compared to 22% for the top quintile (see Figure 5.1).

Figure 5.1: Calories from food away from home (% of total), Accra 1997

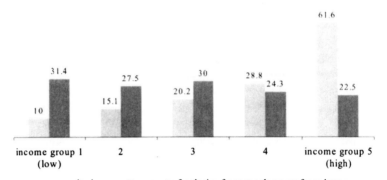

per capita income ■ percent of calories from meals away from home

Source: Maxwell et al. (2000).

Tinker, in her study of street foods in seven countries of Asia and Africa, shows expenditures on street foods ranging from 16% in Manikgani (Bangladesh) to 50% in Ile-Ife (Nigeria), and higher street foods expenditures among the poorest quartiles in both Bangladesh and the Philippines (Iloilo) (Tinker, 1997). Very little information is available on the contribution of street foods to the daily nutrient intake of consumers. In the Philippines, commercially prepared foods were found to contribute 25% of the energy intake of urban working women and 45% of their fat intake (Bisgrove and Popkin. 1996). In the US, data from the Department of Agriculture (Lin et al., 2000) show that the saturated fat content of foods consumed at home has dropped steadily over the 1980s and 1990s, whereas the fat content in fast food restaurants and in schools has remained high (see Figure 5.2).

Figure 5.2: % of calories from saturated fats by location of consumption, US

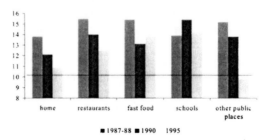

■ 1987-88 ■ 1990 1995

Source: Lin et al. (2000).

Location clearly matters, but does it matter when price and income are controlled for? That it does is clearly shown by a modelling exercise for China, where food consumption shifts due to rural-to-urban migration were modelled, controlling for prices and income levels (Huang and Bouis, 1996). The results are presented in Figure 5.3. Interestingly, in this case, urbanisation seems to have led to a large increase, all things being equal, in the consumption of fruit, a moderate increase in the consumption of meat, fish, milk and eggs, and a moderate decline in the consumption of all other foods. Clearly, one cannot generalise too much about the urban experience before more studies of this type are undertaken.

Figure 5.3: % change in consumption caused by rural-to-urban shift, controlling for income and prices, China, 1991

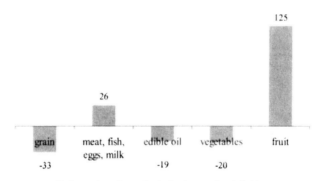

% change due only to urbanization-large and capital cities

Source: Huang and Bouis (1996).

3   What can food policy do?

3.1 The rationale for public action

Table 5.1 summarises the rationale for public action to influence the diet transition towards a healthier outcome. Perhaps the most obvious rationale is information asymmetry between producers and consumers about what is healthy and what is not. There may also be negative externality effects if health care resources are directed away from infants to middle-aged individuals, and in terms of the intergenerational transmission of obesity from mother to baby (see Parsons et al, 2002). There will also be a case for public intervention if private sector incentives result in poorer consumers being priced out of access to healthier food options, especially basic processed foods.

Table 5.1: The case for public policy intervention
to improve diet quality

Rationale for public action	Example of broad areas in which public intervention may be justified
Underprovision of 'public goods'	If generation of affordable healthy food is not available to poorer consumers
Externalities not captured	Negative externality if obesity of mothers is risk factor for child obesity. Health care costs diverted from prevention
Information asymmetries	Case for providing healthy alternatives. Case for labelling; nutrition education
Capital market failure	Investing in anti-low birth weight interventions
Universal access and equity concerns	Obesity is linked to more marginal groups in US, UK
Health insurance market failure	Prevention and treatment of chronic diseases

3.2 Food policy options

Options emanate from the supply side and the demand side, although success will obviously be enhanced via the effective interaction of both. Table 5.2 summarises the food policy options available to moderate dietary fat intake, based on US experience (see Sims, 1998; Ralston, 2000). Although focused only on dietary fat and only on US policy instruments, the table highlights several points. First, there are many stages in the food system where policy can act – both on the supply side and on the demand side. Second, many of the instruments may have small effects – either because behaviour is hard to change in the desired direction or because there are off-setting effects (for example, moving to lower-calorie foods, but consuming additional portions: Sims, 1998). This is a rather sobering conclusion and one that should be kept in mind during the process of policy formulation throughout the developing world. Third, several instruments have ambiguous effects on fat intake – either because they have not been evaluated (for example, harmonisation of fat descriptors between regulatory agencies) or because their direct effects may be overwhelmed by their indirect effects (for example, restrictions on beef imports may result in a reaction from domestic beef producers and a search for new outlets for beef products). The table represents a menu of options that need to be evaluated if their impacts are to be maximised in the desired direction.

Table 5.2: Food policy instruments for influencing dietary fat

Stage of the food system	Types of policy instrument	Examples used in the dietary fat issue	Effectiveness in controlling fat intake
Food production	Commodity price subsidies/ supports	Feed grain subsidies for feedlot animals Dairy price supports	Negative Negative
	Import/export quotas	Export incentives for US vegetable oil Restrictions on beef imports	Uncertain Uncertain
Food processing	Meat grading standards	Beef grading (changes from choice to select)	Positive
	'Standards of identity'	'Standards of identity' changed for low-fat milk and yoghurt	Positive
	Food labelling	Food label descriptors (e.g. 'low fat', etc.) changed for fluid milk, ice cream	Quite positive
Food distribution and marketing	Marketing orders for dairy	Changes in milk marketing orders	Negative
	Food labelling	Use of '% lean' claims on ground beef	Slightly negative
		Restaurant labelling of menu items with 'low fat' claims	Slightly positive
	Food advertising	Harmonisation between the FTC and FDA on ads using fat 'discriptors'	Uncertain
Food consumption	Food labelling	Fat descriptor information on food label	Positive
	Dietary information	Dietary guidelines Food Guide Pyramid	Positive Quite positive
	Commodity promotion boards	Promotion of cheese, ice cream, milk, beef, pork	Negative

Source: Adapted from Sims (1998).

4 Supply-side interventions

(i) *More public investment in technology to deliver high-productivity, low-cost vegetables and fruits and low-fat livestock products to poorer consumers.* The bulk of agricultural technology development in high-value commodities such as livestock and fruits and vegetables tends to be undertaken by the private sector for larger farms. The high cost of cold chain systems reduces access by small farmers. Increasing the productivity of fruits and vegetables and lower-fat livestock products and reducing the transactions costs of delivering them to growing markets are an important area in which agricultural research and development can have a larger health impact.

(ii) *Eliminate price incentives on growing high-fat foods and relax quantity restrictions on growing healthier foods.* The commodity composition of these kinds of price and quantity instruments reflects the economic, social and political importance of the various crops and growers' associations and the small and large industries that rely on them. Whenever the welfare of small sub-groups is weighed against the broader interest, the politics of hurting a small but powerful group will usually outweigh the smaller negative impacts on a much vaster set of individuals (Nestle, 2002). When small welfare losses result, over time, in a large cumulative disease burden, the economics of such trade-offs needs to be revisited.

(ii) *Evaluate food trade policy from a health perspective.* GATT and the World Trade Organization use a number of agreements to navigate health issues, including the Sanitary and Phytosanitary (SPS) Agreement and the Trade Related Intellectual Property Rights (TRIPs) Agreement. Can these Agreements be used to regulate the health content of food imports? Past experience suggests 'yes', if scientific risk assessments show the danger (Millstone and van Zwanenberg in this volume). Beyond obvious health-related trade instruments, can the health community influence the trade community in much the same way as the labour and environment communities have done? Do we know whether the commodity-protection profiles of different countries are pro- or anti-health? If we did, would the health community be able to influence trade policy? If it could (which must, at this point in time, be considered improbable), are there non-health downsides for poor farmers and consumers from an altered pattern of trade? These issues have not been explored to date, and this is surely an area for future research as the percentage of food consumed from trade increases.

(iv) *Impose tougher standards on the fat content of food away from home and in schools.* In the US, for example, the menus in many public schools fail to meet US Department of Agriculture dietary guidelines (Brownell, 2002a, b).

(v) *Reduce malnutrition in utero.* The so-called 'Barker Hypothesis' posits that maternal dietary imbalances at critical periods of development in the womb can trigger an adaptive redistribution of foetal resources (including growth retardation). Such adaptations affect foetal structure and metabolism in ways that predispose the individual to later cardiovascular and endocrine diseases (Barker, 1998). The correlation between low birth weight or early childhood stunting and later cardiovascular disease and diabetes may arise from the fact that nutritional deprivation in utero, or in early childhood, 'programmes' a newborn for a life of scarcity. The problems arise when the child's system is later confronted by a higher-fat, higher-sugar diet, in combination with lowered activity patterns. If this hypothesis is borne out (and evidence is accumulating both for and against) it will serve to remind us that one food policy option for attenuating the impacts of the diet transition is to reduce intra-uterine growth retardation. For example, based on a balanced review of the evidence as of 2000, Popkin et al. (2001) conclude that in China approximately one-third of diabetes can be traced back to low birth weight and stunting in infancy, with this percentage declining in 2020, on the assumption that low birth weight and stunting will decline. There are a number of interventions to address low birth weight at term, ranging from the immediate (for example, improving the food intake quantity and quality of adolescent girls and expectant mothers and improving the quality of pre-natal care) to the underlying (for example, improving women's status relative to men's in terms of resource allocation decisions).

5   Demand-side interventions

(i)   *Increase the relative price of unhealthy choices.* This is an option that those familiar with anti-smoking campaigns might find appealing. It often underlies discussions of what food policy can do to increase the healthiness of the diet transition (for example, Guo et al., 1999). However, it is difficult in practice to identify a food for which an increase in price will not reduce access to healthy components of a diet – components that in a developing country context may be in short supply. Examples in Figures 5.4 and 5.5 illustrate this for US data on meat and edible oil consumption. As Figure 5.4 shows, an increase in the price of meat does have a negative impact on fat and cholesterol intake, but it also has a negative impact on a wide range of diet components that are crucial to diets, especially those of infants and women, such as iron and calcium, which are not found in high densities in non-animal source foods (Huang, 1996). For the same demand system estimates, Figure 5.5 shows that an increase in edible oil prices does decrease fat consumption and increase the consumption of nearly every other diet component because of a substitution towards other foods. This is more in line with the kind of results we might be seeking. However, in a developing country context, edible oil is often used to increase the energy density of infant diets.

Figure 5.4: Responsiveness of nutrients (%) to a 1% increase in price of meat, US price elasticities

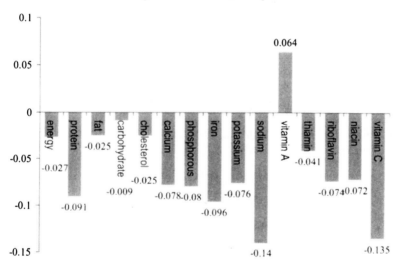

Source: Huang (1996).

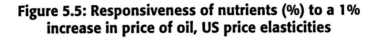

Figure 5.5: Responsiveness of nutrients (%) to a 1% increase in price of oil, US price elasticities

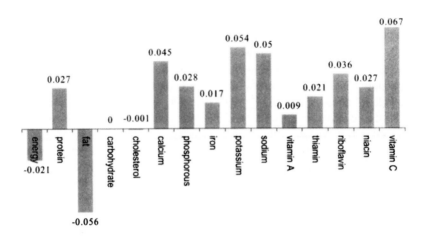

Source: ibid.

(ii) *Clearer information about product contents.* Food labelling can help in reducing information asymmetries, but it can often be confusing, it is obviously of limited value in areas where literacy is weak, and it may be better at discouraging certain types of behaviours perceived as risky than encouraging healthy behaviour (for example, Verbeke and Ward, 2001 on BSE in Belgian beef).

(iii) *Better awareness about consequences of poor diet.* A number of initiatives have been employed in developing countries to raise awareness of the causes and consequences of poor diet. These include a mass media campaign to reduce overweight in Brazil; dietary guidelines for nutritional well-being in China; and school-based training for improving diet and activity levels in Singapore (Doak, 2002). Evaluations of the effectiveness and cost-effectiveness of these attempts to change behaviour are badly needed.

5.1 Policy trade-offs accentuated in a developing country context

Policy formulation on diet change in the developing world must build on the evidence accumulated in the industrialised world. However, the developing country context is very different and policy-makers must remember that:

- Food consumption deficits are still widespread. When looking for foods to discourage the consumption of, remember that many groups require the *other* nutrients contained in the food (for example, the micronutrients in livestock).
- Certain groups of individuals, for example infants, will need to consume even foods that might otherwise be discouraged, for example, edible oils.
- The capacity to influence preferences via the public sector is likely to be lower than in the industrialised world. Whether the imbalance between public and

private sector power to communicate nutrition messages is growing in the developing world is an open question, but with multinationals backing much of the nutrition messaging, one would not be surprised to see the public sector caught on the back foot (Hawkes, 2002).

- On the supply side, anything done to discourage the consumption of a locally produced food considered harmful to health above some cut-off will harm the income-generating ability of many smallholder farmers. They may not have the political strength of industrialised country farmers, but the economic impact on the rural economy of an attempt to alter consumption could be large.
- Many developing countries are desperate to increase foreign direct investment, not to discourage it. Attempts to discourage foreign supplies of foods that are designated 'less healthy' will have employment and livelihood consequences that need to inform any decision taken.

5.2 The uniqueness of food

Finally, it is important to note that food represents a class of commodities that is difficult to influence in a predictable manner. In particular, the temptation to apply the model that was so successful in curbing tobacco consumption (World Bank, 1999) to food should be resisted. Comparisons may be more valid in some countries with powerful judicial systems for those who can take advantage of them (for example, the US and the recent lawsuits taken out against fast-food retailers). But even in the industrialised countries there are some important differences between the two situations – i.e. poor diets are not the same as a smoking habit. First, there is a difficulty in identifying the 'offending product'. Second, with tobacco, there are no obvious consumption trade-offs with positive outcomes as outlined above. Third, there are fewer obvious private externalities (there is no such thing as 'secondary eating'). Finally, there is a broader constituency for food farmers than for tobacco farmers.

Because of these and other differences, the 'triggers' for strong public action are not yet in place (Kersh and Morone, 2002). Table 5.3 is adapted from Kersh and Morone (2002) and it lists the 'triggers' for public action in health and assesses their strength in the US as applied to the obesity problem there. The authors conclude that only the first three of seven triggers have been tripped: social disapproval, evidence from medical science and the evidence of self-help groups. Such constructs help us to remember that evidence is only one ingredient in the formulation and implementation of public health policy.

Table 5.3: 'Triggers' for successful government regulation of private behaviour when a 'political window' opens

Trigger	Comments	Power of obesity triggers in US
Social disapproval	Recognition by society as a 'bad thing'	There is a popular disapproval of obesity
Medical science	Role is to challenge myths	There is strong evidence linking diet to obesity and obesity to chronic disease
Self-help	For example, Alcoholics Anonymous	Overeaters Anonymous, Weight Watchers
Demonise the user	Fearing the drug culture	Obesity does not play on fears. No evidence of trigger yet
Demonise the provider	For example, Big Tobacco	No 'Big Chocolate' yet. 'Fast Food Nation' gaining consciousness. No evidence of trigger yet
Mass movement	Protests, rallies	No evidence of anti-obesity campaigns (possibly the opposite, re: accepting body image). No trigger yet
Interest-group action	Lawyers and lobbyists	Yet to be achieved. No trigger yet

Source: Adapted from Kersh and Morone (2002).

6   Information and analysis gaps

Research in the area of the diet and nutrition transition in developing countries is in its infancy. Most of the work has been spent documenting it and analysing its causes, and much of it has had to make do with crude food data (national supply, not household-level availability or individual intake). Very little research has focused on policy analysis. The following areas deserve much more attention from the research community.

- There is a need to use *existing* nationally representative household survey data systematically to chart trends in the availability of 'bad' food components. These datasets are available for a large number of countries, but are solely used to estimate poverty rates.
- The location of consumption and the health content of that consumption need to be better connected, with more data collected on the characteristics of the points of sale, whether they are street-food vendors or supermarkets.
- Food price elasticities need to be generated that are disaggregated enough to be policy-relevant (for example, 'meat' is not useful, but 'high saturated fat beef products' might be).
- The trade-offs in terms of the consumption changes of different diet components of different population subgroups resulting from the change in the price of a single community need to be spelled out, as do the implications for smallholder income generation.

- There need to be more evaluations of non-price interventions to change diets, both in terms of quality and quantity.
- There has to be more research on the investments and institutional innovations that smallholder farmers need to link up with growing domestic and international markets for healthy foods.
- More research needs to be done that links trade policy with health outcomes, perhaps via the linkage of computable general equilibrium models (CGEs) and micromodels of individual welfare outcomes (for example, Cogneau and Robilliard, 2000).
- Research on the policy process and the role of information will be useful to help us to understand why the public health response to chronic disease has varied in terms of effectiveness.
- More research needs to be done on identifying institutional mechanisms for win-win public-private partnerships (for example Buse and Walt, 2000) to reduce the amount of unhealthy fat and added sugar entering into the developing country food supply.
- Too much of the evidence cited in this chapter has come from one country, China. A similarly concerted effort needs to be undertaken in other large countries for which there are indications that the diet transition is accelerating – for example, India, Brazil, Indonesia, South Africa and Nigeria.

7 Conclusion

The diet transition in the developing world seems to be accelerating. It seems to be a transition towards an increased burden of chronic disease. It is increasing human costs in terms of mortality and the disease burdens. It is increasing economic costs in terms of lower productivity. It is driven by changing preferences fuelled by growing incomes, changing relative prices, urbanisation, changing food choice options fuelled by changes in food technology, and changes in the food distribution systems; and by a legacy of low birth weights from the previous generation. Is there a case for public investment in efforts to influence the transition towards increasingly healthy outcomes? The existence of information asymmetries and negative externalities suggests that this is so.

What can food policy do? We have identified a number of options from the food supply and food demand sides. These options have had mixed success in the industrialised countries. The policy trade-offs in the developing world are even more complicated. For example, efforts to overcome over-nutrition might well undermine efforts to overcome under-nutrition. The public health anti-smoking policy model offers some insights, but it should not be leaned on too heavily; food is not tobacco. There are plenty of areas in which additional technical research is needed to assess competing risks and to help develop policy options, and we have outlined some. But there is also a very great need for research to engage actors in the policy process underlying the diet transition. In a debate where so much is at stake – market shares, profits, livelihoods, and life itself – there is a potentially powerful role for the generators of balanced evidence to bring different actors to the table. This may help to improve the decision-making processes underlying the attempts of food policy to redirect the diet transition towards healthier outcomes.

Chapter 6
Value-chain Governance, Public Regulation and Entry Barriers in the Global Fresh Fruit and Vegetable Chain into the EU

Peter Gibbon

Supermarkets' increased sourcing of fresh produce from developing countries has been generally accompanied by a decline in the proportion of this produce accounted for by smaller-scale producers. This follows from supermarkets' growing use of 'buyer power' to demand more services and lower prices from suppliers. This chapter reviews regulatory interventions by public authorities in the EU, South Africa and France that have been aimed, at least indirectly, at restraining 'buyer power' to the benfit of smaller-scale producers. Although now politically unfashionable, two of these interventions can be regarded as having had a measure of success.

1   Introduction

A key element of the new food policy discourse concerns the exponential growth of large supermarkets sourcing on a global basis, the corresponding opening up of more profitable opportunities in fresh produce for developing country producers, and the nature of the new supply market entry barriers that are introduced at the same time. In relation to this issue a growing body of research is concluding that, far from benefiting from the new openings, developing country small-scale producers are experiencing marginalisation and exclusion. This is of concern since many of the latter are poor, and fresh produce has traditionally offered them higher returns than other crops.

If this is so, what can be done to mitigate the consequences? As in the case of the literature concerning the exclusion of smallholder producers from non-food export crops, most efforts to address this question consider public support to outgrower schemes and contract farming as a way forward. While broadly agreeing that answers need to be sought in this direction, this chapter takes a somewhat different tack. It seeks to examine the extent to which public *regulatory* interventions can lead, or have led, to a mitigation of supermarket 'buyer power' (or the power of other lead firms), in ways that lead to smaller-scale producers remaining a part of global fresh produce chains.

The chapter is divided into three main sections. Section 2 rehearses the arguments concerning the whys and wherefores of smallholder exclusion. Section 3 examines three types of public regulation that have had, amongst their aims, mitigation of buyer power and hence maintenance of entry barriers at a level that ensures continued participation by smaller-scale producers. Section 4 concludes with a short review of the effectiveness and political viability of these types of regulation.

2   Kenyan fresh vegetables and UK supermarkets

Dolan and Humphrey's (2001) paper on Kenyan fresh fruit and vegetables (FFV) has become the central reference point for discussion of the relation between the rise of 'buyer-driven value chains' in the developed world and the exclusion of smaller-scale developing producers from key areas of new export growth. Global-value or commodity chains (hereafter GVCs) are sector-based structures of international trade, arising from the twin phenomena of dispersal of production (through outsourcing) and market integration (through trade liberalisation). 'Buyer-driven' chains link large retailers and branded marketers, mostly based in the North, to decentralised networks of producers in low-cost Southern countries. According to the founder of global commodity chain analysis (Gereffi, 1994), buyer-led chains are actively 'driven' in the sense that large retailers and branded marketers use them not merely to source products, but increasingly also to reshape their own portfolios of functional activities and to achieve higher levels of flexibility. Functional activities that supermarkets in the Anglo-Saxon countries have typically sought to externalise include analysis of sales data to forecast demand, procurement of a 'category' of products rather than a single item, inventory management, quality assurance and new product development.

The forging of such chains creates opportunities for at least some actors in the South, over and above participation in international trade as such. Those actors who can move into roles embracing some of the functions that lead firms seek to offload, and/or otherwise provide these firms with greater flexibility, can attain significant levels of upgrading. In practice, though, relatively few producers in the South (and particularly in sub-Saharan Africa) have these capacities. Therefore, the more demanding the functional attributes that lead firms seek from suppliers, the more these suppliers will experience economic differentiation.

Dolan and Humphrey document the growing dominance of large supermarket chains within UK food retailing, and the increasing interest of these chains in selling FFV (to a point where supermarkets in aggregate controlled 76% of all UK FFV sales by 1997). This interest reflects the relatively high demand elasticity of these products in relation to food products generally. Against this background, large UK supermarkets became interested in sourcing a very wide range of FFV on a year-round basis; in assuring consistency in supply, taste and appearance; and in encouraging the emergence of new products and forms for presenting/packaging them. At the same time, because of the 'due diligence' requirements of the UK Food Safety Act (1990), on the one hand, and rising consumer concern with environmental and labour issues, on the other, they have also become interested in assuring full traceability.

During the 1990s, as their interest in FFV crystallised, UK supermarkets shifted to reliance on a relatively small number of specialised importers, rather than on traditional wholesale markets. Importers were expected to engage in active global procurement, as well as to organise the provision of a series of new services that supermarkets required. At the same time, supermarkets themselves established a role in direct monitoring of growers and exporters.

Turning to the leading African supply source for higher-value fresh vegetables into the UK market, Kenya, Dolan and Humphrey go on to link this story to that of the restructuring of the country's horticultural export sector. Prior to the 1980s the latter was characterised mainly by smallholder producers cultivating chillies, okras, etc. for the diasporic Asian market in the UK. Producers sold on a spot basis to family-owned Asian export companies, which in turn sold into UK wholesale markets. This picture began to change in the 1980s with the entry of a group of better financed exporters, interested in selling European vegetables through UK retailers' dedicated importers. This business took off with growing smallholder participation. Jaffee (pers. comm., 2003) states that smallholders' share of total FFV exports was as high as 50-55% around 1993. Dolan and Humphrey give a figure of under 20% for 1999, although this refers only to exports bound for UK supermarkets. However, while this may exaggerate the extent of declining smallholder participation, nobody disputes the latter's status as a trend.

Dolan and Humphrey explain this transition in terms of UK supermarkets' triggering of rising entry barriers for exporters. Supermarkets' demands implied that exporters had to invest heavily in post-harvest cool chain facilities, guarantee high and consistent volumes, respond very quickly to orders and assure traceability. To do so profitably implied optimising economies of scale, both in fixed investments and in monitoring quality. This implied a shift towards vertical integration, which was also favoured to better assure quick response. In the process, smallholders were replaced by estates (and estate labour), and small exporters by large companies – in some cases very large.[1]

Dolan and Humphrey's findings have been broadly confirmed by subsequent, more detailed, studies of UK-destined horticulture in Kenya (Jensen, 2000; Jaffee, forthcoming) and Tanzania (Jensen, 2002). Jaffee (forthcoming) argues that supermarket buyer power influenced smallholder participation more indirectly than Dolan and Humphrey suggest, however. The major reduction in smallholders' role in the industry followed from new product development, in the sense of the growing dominance of runner beans and snow/snap peas in Kenyan exports. Runner beans require artificial lighting for cultivation in Kenya and thus could be grown only by farmers with electricity. Meanwhile, the introduction of snow/snap peas entailed an extended learning process for exporters, which they decided to keep in-house until the technicalities of these crops were mastered. Outsourcing of these crops has subsequently increased and in 2002 smallholders accounted for around 27% of all Kenyan fresh vegetable exports (not just those bound for UK supermarkets). There may therefore be a shift back to smallholders, mainly for risk management purposes, i.e., to hedge against both localised weather conditions and the spread of plant disease.

---

1. Latest estimates (Jaffee, forthcoming) suggest that six companies control 90% of all exports by value. Kenya's largest exporter of fresh vegetables and cut flowers is Homegrown, with 6,000 local employees and its own nightly DC8 flight to the UK. In 2002 the company, which had operated its own importing arm in the UK, took over two British companies to form Flamingo Holdings Ltd. One of the companies was Flower Plus, a flower importer/bouquet supplier that had recently become Marks & Spencer's lead cut-flower supplier. The other was Flamingo UK, an importer, packer and distributor. Subsequently, Flamingo Holdings acquired Zwetsloots, a UK flower supplier specialising in imports from the Netherlands and Spain. In 2003, Flamingo Holdings became the UK distributor for the large Zimbabwean fresh produce exporter, Hortico, and expanded in Kenya itself by taking over the Commonwealth Development Corporation's stake in Sulmac, formerly the country's leading carnation exporter. After the absorption of Zwetsloots, Flamingo Holdings' 2002 sales were around GB£ 155 million. To raise funds for the acquisitions, Homegrown borrowed from venture capital funds, including Modern Africa Fund Managers.

While the more recent studies note that the processes described here are less marked in FFV value-chains originating in Kenya but destined for elsewhere in the EU, they do predict a gradual convergence of outcomes. For example, mainland EU retailers are increasingly likely to make demands on their suppliers for 'due diligence', as a result of recent EU Minimum Residue Level (MRL) regulations for pesticides, as well as the imminent introduction of a Community-wide requirement for 'farm-to-table' traceability of all food and food ingredients.

3   Supermarket power and public regulation

Very recently, upgraded entry requirements and subsequent economic differentiation have been identified also in Latin American countries, where the market share of supermarkets in food retail has expanded rapidly to reach between 50 and 60% in 2000 (Reardon and Berdegué, 2002). A parallel study has gone on to predict similar outcomes in southern Africa, as a result of the growth of supermarkets in this region too (Weatherspoon and Reardon, 2003). The authors imply a global convergence.

There are instances, however, at least with respect to FFV chains into the European Union, where public regulation has been undertaken in forms aimed partly or wholly at restraining or modifying this outcome. This section examines three regulative experiences of this kind. The first concerns external trade regulation by the EU. The second concerns export market regulation in a producing country exporting to the EU. The third concerns domestic market regulation in the EU, other than in the UK.

3.1 Trade regulation at EU level: the banana regime

Of all FFVs, bananas have the largest share of total trade, accounting for over one-third of all FFV exports. The EU is the largest market for them. Historically, banana production for export has been of two types. Plantations and large estates have been the source of virtually all bananas emanating from Costa Rica, Guatemala, Panama and Honduras and have also played an important role in Ecuador. Smallholder production has been the source of virtually all bananas emanating from the Windward Islands (Dominica, Grenada, St Lucia and St Vincent and the Grenadines) and has also played an important role elsewhere in the Caribbean and – to a lesser degree – in Africa.

Prior to the introduction of the EU single market, most member countries had implemented some form of Lomé Convention-related preference for ACP bananas. However, the only really significant preferences were those granted by the UK to the Windwards, Jamaica, Belize, Surinam, Côte d'Ivoire and Cameroon, and by France to the last two of these plus its own overseas territories. In 1993, with the single market, the EU inaugurated a common Banana Regime. Even though the primary objective of the regime was to protect the market of banana producers in the EU itself (Greece) and in Spanish and French overseas territories, it extended similar protection to the smallholder production systems of the Caribbean, which otherwise would have been out-competed by plantation ones. Smallholder systems would have been eliminated not only on grounds of unit production costs – which in the case of the Windwards were almost double those in the Central America – but also because the huge dollar-zone exporters like Chiquita, Del Monte Fresh and Dole could offer the many add-on services that supermarkets were demanding (year-round supply, call-off delivery, full traceability, etc.).

The regime extended a diluted form of UK and French preferences to all member countries, while also guaranteeing access to all countries for non-ACP bananas. Duty-free quotas of around 850,000 tonnes each were given to EU/EU overseas territory producers and to the ACP countries, while a tariff-based quota of 2 million tonnes was reserved for all further imports from whatever source. A differential tariff, at a penal level for non-EU and non-ACP producers, was applied once these quotas had been reached. The regime also included a highly contentious import-licensing system which in effect gave importers traditionally associated only with the EU and ACP crops control over a share of dollar-zone imports as well (McCorriston, 2000).

This set-up proved unable to withstand repeated GATT and WTO challenges from the US and some dollar-zone producers, orchestrated by the leading plantation-based exporter from this region, Chiquita. As a result, modifications to the regime in favour of dollar-zone bananas occurred in 1994, 1998 and 2001 and the EU has had to promise that all quota restrictions within the regime will be abolished completely by 2006. The objections from dollar-zone producers followed from the fact that – on the basis of penalising their exports in markets like Germany which they had previously dominated – the regime led to an increase in ACP market share in the EU of 15% between 1993 and 1996 (WTO, 1997).

Yet, while indeed having this effect, the regime failed to protect smallholder production systems, especially after the EU was forced to scrap individual country import quotas. At the same time as they were challenging the regime through the WTO, the major dollar-zone exporters established plantations in the ACP, particularly in Côte d'Ivoire and Cameroon. In the context of stagnation in consumer demand and falling prices, smallholder production systems became less, rather than more, competitive. Exports from the Windwards fell considerably and the number of smallholder producers fell from 25,000 in 1993 to 11,000 in 1997.

3.2 Regulation of citrus exports by exporting countries

Most of the major citrus-exporting countries present in the EU market have been characterised by production systems in which there were both large and small growers. In Spain, which remains the EU's single most important source of citrus, smaller-scale growers formed producer associations, one of whose functions was to conduct exports, while larger growers exported on their own account. In other major export sources like Israel, Morocco and South Africa, there were single-channel export systems based on *de facto* mandatory membership of producer associations.

Producer associations and apex single-channel export bodies typically worked on the principle of rewarding volume rather than quality, with the same unit prices being paid to all growers.[2] Prioritisation of quantity reflected one of the main arguments for their existence, namely, that commanding massive volumes protected their members by

---

2. Theoretically, single-channel export bodies could have rewarded quality too, via premiums to specific growers (or co-operatives). Systems of this kind have been applied to traditional tropical export crops, although they are costly to implement and prone to rent-seeking. Their historical absence in the case of citrus was linked to the lack of a clear public quality and grading convention for this fruit, unlike the case of most tropical export crops.

establishing heightened bargaining power vis-à-vis other players in the chain – including supermarkets. There is some qualitative evidence to support the idea that they did so. For example, prior to 1997 when the South African Outspan/Capespan export monopoly was scrapped, UK supermarkets were unable to impose any significant service demands on South African exporters. Most notably, they were unable to impose their desired product mix (Mather and Greenberg, 2003). The other main argument for the single-channel system was the creation of economies of scale in the provision of services and credit to growers themselves, and recovery of credit at source. On this basis, the single-channel system had a strong inclusionary dynamic – albeit one limited in South Africa by apartheid discourses and laws. It was only in the last years of Outspan/Capespan's monopoly that active attention was given to promoting exports by black growers.

In any event, the 1990s witnessed a pattern of 'competitive liberalisation' amongst citrus exporters. First Morocco and then Israel abolished its single marketing channel. The arguments used were similar in both cases, namely, that by rewarding producers only according to volume, incentives for innovation with regard to product development and quality were restricted and international market share was threatened. In addition, resources were being wasted on inefficient producers who survived only on the basis of cross-subsidisation. South African citrus remained under a single marketing channel system until 1997 when, in the context of similar arguments, Outspan/Capespan lost its monopoly and growers became free to leave the co-operatives that sold through it.

In Morocco and Israel a handful of large private concerns, usually formed by mergers between the largest and most resourceful growers, have come to dominate the sector (GEDA in Morocco, Mehadrin in Israel). Large private concerns have emerged also in South Africa (Colours and Katope), although as yet these are not on the same scale. In all three countries, commercialised continuations of the former single export channel (Moroccan Fruit Board, Agrexo/Carmel and Capespan) still play important roles, but – to a greater or lesser extent – have lost out in the UK supermarket trade to the private companies. As a result they are exporting increasingly into less remunerative EU, Central and Eastern European and Middle Eastern markets.

It is possible to provide a very rough evaluation of whether or not the more inclusive single marketing channel system 'worked' for South Africa prior to liberalisation, independently of the assumptions about the general properties of such systems described above, by examining market share and unit price trends in the most 'buyer-driven' of major South African end markets (the UK) during the period 1991-8. The effects of liberalisation can be traced by continuing the story up to 2002 (Table 6.1).[3]

Prior to liberalisation, South Africa's market share of UK citrus imports (Category 805) was rising, although its relative unit prices were in slight decline. The latter trend, although not particularly pronounced, lent some support to the pro-liberalisation argument concerning the effects of single-channel marketing channels. Yet, what is more striking is that liberalisation seems to be associated with a sharp acceleration of

---

3. The evaluation is necessarily rough as the internal composition of South African citrus exports between higher- (easy peeler) and lower-value (Valencia) citrus may have changed from year to year.

both tendencies. Market share increases faster than in earlier periods,[4] but South Africa's unit prices drop in nominal terms (prior to liberalisation they had been increasing) and the relative unit prices commanded by South Africa's exports suffer a sharp deterioration. This occurs against the background of a stable level of total UK imports[5] and without major increases in supply from elsewhere. This seems to suggest that loss of bargaining power vis-à-vis supermarket customers has counteracted any improvements in unit prices that might otherwise have followed from improvements in quality and service provision. Certainly, there is anecdotal evidence that since 1998 UK supermarkets have explicitly used the decline of the Rand to drive down prices in GB£ terms, in a way that did not occur in earlier periods (Mather, pers. comm., 2003).

Table 6.1: Market share and unit price (€/kg) for Category 805 imports from South Africa to the UK, 1991-2002

	Market share by volume (%)	Average unit price (all imports)	Unit price SA imports	SA unit price/average unit prices (%)
1991-4	12.5	0.46	0.44	95.7
1995-8	14.1	0.58	0.54	93.1
1999-2002	18.7	0.63	0.53	84.1

Source: Eurostat Comext data base.

3.3 Regulation of domestic FFV markets in Southern Europe

Since Dolan and Humphrey's contribution, supermarkets' share of all UK FFV sales is generally reckoned to have risen to 80%. None of this is sourced through wholesale markets. Rather, it comes direct from the big branded marketers who dominate the banana trade (but who in some cases have diversified into other crops), and dedicated procurers who are either predominantly domestic in their supply base like Greenvale, Geest and Redbridge, or who are predominantly importers like Thames Fruit, Muñoz-Mehadrin[6] and M&W Mack.

In France there are almost similar levels of concentration in food retail generally to those in the UK. Indeed, the market share of the top five food retailers is actually marginally higher (at 77%, according to mm.eurodata) than in the UK. But, because of the ongoing importance of independent FFV retailers, French supermarkets account for only 37% of sales of this group of products (Cadilhon et al., 2003). Of this share, roughly 60% is sourced direct by supermarkets, while the remaining 40% is sourced through wholesalers. The latter overwhelmingly dominate sales to independent retailers,

---

4. It seems unlikely that any of the post-1994 volume increase is attributable to a re-designation of South African exports previously routed through, for example, Swaziland to avoid sanctions. The UK market share of Swaziland's citrus exports almost doubled (from 0.6% to 1.1%) in the four years following the end of apartheid relative to the preceding four years (Eurostat Comext database).

5. Total Category 805 UK imports averaged 658,000 tonnes in 1991-4, 685,000 in 1995-8 and 682,000 in 1999-2002 (Eurostat Comext database).

6. Formed by a merger of the largest Israeli private citrus exporter (also amongst Israel's longest established growers) and one of the five largest Spanish ones. Thames Fruit is also Spanish in origin.

including those operating in street markets, and to the catering sector. A very considerable proportion of the FFV import trade also goes through wholesalers, who buy at auctions at the ports from importers selling on consignment.

Supermarkets have not been able to exercise much leverage in the FFV chain in France due to a complex of regulatory and cultural conditions. Between 1973 and 1996 three separate laws were passed restricting supermarket expansion in urban areas and thus preserving the role of independent retailers nationally (ibid.). Possibly even more important has been the regulative support provided to the wholesale trade over the last half century. Under a law passed in 1953, a network of 'Marchés d'Intérêt Nationale' (MINs) was created with public participation. The intention of this law was to concentrate wholesalers of *all* fresh produce (including meat, dairy and fish), and not merely FFV, in 16 sites around the country. To enforce this, wholesalers were prevented from operating in areas up to 20 km. radius around these markets (Cadilhon, pers. comm., 2003).

The result has been to reduce substantially retailers' transaction costs for buying through wholesalers. This applies particularly in the Paris region, where the Rungis MIN occupies a dominant role, with annual sales worth around €7 billion. Rungis and a number of other MINs are sufficiently large and diverse to have led several French supermarket chains (for example, Auchan) to set up procurement offices and delivery centres within the markets themselves (Garcia and Poole, 2002). In other words, a system has developed with regulatory support that is competitive with the UK supermarket sourcing model. A similar regulatory situation and set of institutions (MERCASAs) and outcomes prevails in Spain, where 65% of FFV is sold through wholesalers. The position appears to be similar also in Italy, in this case in the absence of a formal network of publicly-owned regional markets. Reportedly, Italian supermarkets source *entirely* through existing wholesale markets, at least in the north of the country (Cadilhon et al., 2003).

The existence of networks of large regional wholesale markets for fresh produce in these countries is intertwined with cultural preferences for regionally-specific cuisines. Markets like Rungis in the largest urban centres offer materials for the full range of regional cuisines (ibid.) This again dramatically reduces the transaction costs that would arise if supermarkets were to source separately from all regions.

Imports comprise a much smaller proportion of traded FFV in Southern Europe than they do in the UK, where in 1998 they represented 45% of vegetables and 88% of fruit by value (Garcia and Poole, 2002). Despite the fact that current MRL regulations and upcoming ones for 'farm-to-table' traceability are common to the whole of the EU, and that actors in wholesale markets in France are in the process of establishing more comprehensive cool chains than previously, it is clear that imports admitted to France come in under less stringent food safety conditions than in the UK. According to Garcia and Poole (2002), only Carrefour amongst French supermarket chains implements the European Retail Consortium's EUREP-Gap process-based food quality assurance guidelines, entailing a full traceability requirement. This is in contrast to the UK, where all the leading operators do so. Carrefour is also the only French supermarket that claims to have a mainly centralised buying function for FFV (ibid.).[7]

---

7 . The extent to which this function is really centralised is open to doubt, however, for the company (which had a turnover in France itself of €34 bn in 2001) employs only 30 FFV buyers 'on a national basis'

Because of their low market share for FFV and the regulatively-underwritten 'break' in the GVC for fruit and vegetables that restricts their direct sourcing, French supermarkets are mostly unable to exercise much direct influence over either importers or developing country growers and exporters. As a result, entry barriers into these chains are much lower than for the UK. Indeed, in the case of citrus from South Africa there is direct evidence that France is supplied by those poorer-resourced growers who still sell their produce into co-operatives (Mather and Greenberg, 2003). Similarly, the chain for green beans into France is still supplied – in part at least – by smallholder systems in Burkina Faso and Senegal (although their market share is also falling).

Intermediation by wholesalers and lower entry barriers in France are generally accompanied by inferior conditions of sale in comparison with those commanded by actors in the restructured chains entering the UK. In other words, export into the French market takes place without prices being agreed in advance and even without the sale being guaranteed.

On the other hand, the picture as regards price levels is much less unfavourable. In the case of citrus, for example, average unit prices for all imports into the French market are higher than in the UK, although the difference is steadily falling (see Table 6.2). The unit prices commanded by South African exports to France fell in the period leading up to liberalisation relative to those for UK-bound exports, but they have subsequently recovered to reach very similar levels despite apparently lower levels of quality and service provision.

Table 6.2: Unit prices (€/kg) for Category 805 imports from South Africa to France, 1991-2002

	Average unit price (all imports)	Unit price SA imports	SA unit price/average unit prices (%)
1991-4	0.55	0.46	83.6
1995-8	0.63	0.46	73.0
1999-2002	0.65	0.52	80.0

Source: Eurostat Comtrade data base.

4   Conclusion

'Buyer-driven' value chains for fresh produce could be considered as promoting greater efficiency (by rewarding economies of scale) and welfare benefits (by keeping consumer prices low). It could be further argued that, if smallholder producers could find other more remunerative alternatives than growing FFVs, their elimination from the value chains would be no bad thing. A recent authoritative survey of UK supermarket food retailing (UK Competition Commission, 2000) and a brief consideration of real alternatives to fresh produce production in, for example, Kenya, throw a different light on these arguments.

(Garcia and Poole, 2002). The decentralised buying structure of two of the other five leading food retailers, Intermarché and Leclerc, is underwritten by their federative ownership status.

The UK Competition Commission states that food retail market concentration is so high that the five leading firms are able to engage in oligopolistic pricing, while at the same time using their power as buyers to extract average discounts of 7-8% on base prices from 100 of the country's leading suppliers. This is before their extraction of additional discounts for promotions, etc. (normally 5-10% of the value of sales). At the same time, in countries like Kenya, there are few alternative remunerative crops and certainly none that are equally remunerative (Jaffee, forthcoming).

Regulation can be, and has been, used in ways that, intentionally or unintentionally, imply restrictions on supermarkets' power to restructure value chains to their own advantage and to small-scale producers' disadvantage. This chapter has briefly examined its use in ways that have sought to force them to buy from high-cost countries (by quota systems), or from powerful export monopolies, or via a dispersed network of domestic wholesalers who are themselves too weak to exercise buying power higher upstream in value chains. In the case of export monopolies and the French system of domestic import market regulation, there seems to be evidence that these can protect all producers from price pressure, as well as from the types of service demand that exclude small-scale producers from the export game. Import quota systems, at least in forms that might have had similar effects, were never in place long enough for a judgment of their effectiveness to be possible.

Unfortunately, at least from the viewpoint of smaller-scale producers, regulation in all the forms mentioned has become difficult to maintain and virtually impossible to (re-)introduce. Import quotas of any kind are in conflict with WTO rules on tariffication, and those favouring less developed countries with small-scale producer-based systems over others without them are additionally in conflict with WTO rules on trade discrimination. Where export marketing monopolies did not fall foul of externally imposed structural adjustment conditionalities, they were phased out voluntarily under the influence of domestic spokespersons for the 'free market'. Meanwhile, the legal framework underpinning the French MIN system is subject to complaint in Brussels under EU competition regulations. In practice, however, even if such complaints are successful, MINs are likely to retain a *de facto* powerful role for French wholesalers for the foreseeable future. In other European countries the potential effectiveness of regulation is likely to remain untested until a major turn of the political circle. Here the short-term challenge is to press supermarkets to source through smallholder-controlled schemes, and to press donor governments to support the latter with provision of low-cost services. At the same time, attention needs to be paid to the issue of returns to smallholders *within* supermarket systems. Jaffee (forthcoming) suggests that, for those smallholders who have retained a place in the Kenyan export system, returns are being compressed. Further research is required in this area, but if this suggestion is confirmed, then the actions mentioned should encompass this issue as well.

Chapter 7
Changing Food Systems in India: Resource-sharing and Marketing Arrangements for Vegetable Production in Andhra Pradesh

Priya Deshingkar, Usha Kulkarni, Laxman Rao and Sreenivas Rao

Transformations in the global food system are causing changes in food production and marketing in India at a slower rate than elsewhere in the developing world but there is is a growing domestic market for horticultural produce, in both traditional and exotic vegetables. Production and marketing arrangements are responding to changing demand driven by urbanisation and diet change. Government-sponsored schemes in horticulture have mixed results, generating more jobs than cereal production but reaching larger rather than smaller farmers and landless households. Beyond direct government interventions, new forms of contractual and sharecropping relationships are emerging between private dealers and farmers. These could be useful in developing a model for ensuring that the horticulture sector can benefit small and marginal farmers.

1 Introduction

This chapter is about the changing nature of food systems in India and the likely impact on small producers in rural areas of growing urban demand, changing consumer preferences, and organised retail as well as export-oriented production. The chapter discusses the opportunities and barriers that new production, processing and marketing arrangements present for small and marginal farmers, using the example of vegetable production in Andhra Pradesh (AP). Evidence drawn from village-level research in two districts shows that conventional production and marketing arrangements have excluded the lower castes and marginal farmers, but innovations in resource sharing have allowed some disadvantaged groups to reap rewards from the horticulture boom. These innovations resulted from changing agreements between private dealers and landowners and have not involved the government directly. However, there is scope through pro-poor policy for the government to improve the record of vegetable production in benefiting lower caste and marginal farmers.

Locating the discussion within the literature on changes in international food chains, the next section provides an overview of the changing vegetable production and marketing systems in India and the policies that have been developed to support this at the macro level. The third section reviews key elements of current horticultural development policy, introduces Agri-Export Zones and raises questions about the disputed role of contract farming. The following section uses field data from AP to illustrate how new resource-sharing arrangements have enabled the poor to benefit directly from horticulture. The concluding section compares governmental and non-governmental interventions and suggests what lessons national and state governments in India can learn in order to develop more effective policy.

2   How far has the vegetable value chain developed in India?

International literature on changing food systems in developing countries documents a shift in the ways that food is produced, marketed and consumed (Gaull and Goldberg, 1993). Drivers of new configurations are changes in consumer taste and preferences, which in turn are linked with increasing urbanisation (both within the country and abroad) and the penetration of large supermarkets and contract farming arrangements.

Such changes were documented for fruit, vegetable and dairy products in Latin America in a recent theme issue of *Development Policy Review*. The Latin American studies record fundamental changes in procurement practices, including sudden (and for producers, highly destabilising) switching of 'sourcing' according to prices prevailing in different countries, consolidation of purchases in distribution centres and sourcing networks, increasing chain co-ordination through contracts with wholesalers and growers, demanding new standards and certification requirements, and extended delays in payments after delivery. There has been a shift away from traditional wholesale markets towards new types of specialised wholesalers serving supermarkets. This is happening especially rapidly in some countries such as Argentina (Ghezan et al., 2002), Chile (Faiguenbaum et al., 2002) and Costa Rica (Alvarado and Charmel, 2002).

In Africa, too, the chain linking producers and exporters with UK supermarkets has transformed the agrifood system. Researchers have noted the downside for small producers: they are increasingly excluded from the value chain as supermarkets rely on fewer larger producers who can meet exacting standards for quality, efficiency, transport and storage (Dolan and Humphrey, 2000).

While the international literature demonstrates a high degree of supermarket penetration, India, despite a doubling of per capita incomes in the last 20 years and a tremendous increase in the urban population, has not witnessed a commensurate shift in the way in which fresh vegetables are produced, traded, consumed or exported.

2.1 Current marketing arrangements

India is the second largest producer of vegetables in the world (after China), accounting for roughly 14% of the world's production. Current production is over 87 million MT and the area under vegetable cultivation is 5.9 million hectares (Department of Agriculture and Co-operation) or 3% of the total area under cultivation. The state of Andhra Pradesh is the second largest producer of fruit, vegetables and flowers in India after Uttar Pradesh. AP produced 8.5 million tonnes of fruit and vegetables in 2002 (Department of Horticulture) and its Government (GoAP) envisages production of over 30 million MT by 2020 (Rao, 2001).

Currently, only a fraction of the total fresh vegetables produced in India is exported, and most of the production is geared to the expanding urban market.[1] The

---

1. Studies have shown that the main obstacles to exporting are quality control problems and difficulty in meeting the recently enhanced phytosanitary standards imposed by importing countries.

important vegetable crops produced in India are cabbage, tomato, *brinjal* (aubergine), onion, cauliflower, pea, potato, *okra* (ladies' finger), and *cucurbits* (cucumber, melon, squash). Recently, exotic vegetables like broccoli, parsley, gherkin, asparagus and baby corn have been gaining importance. Traders purchase from primary producers and there may be four or five traders in a chain that usually ends in the nearest town or city. Most of the sale of vegetables occurs through street vendors, small shops and open-air markets and not through supermarkets. India has about 4,000 regulated markets (*mandis*) for fruits and vegetables, most of which are located in urban and semi-urban areas.

Supermarkets have not taken off in India for a number of reasons. Currently, international and national supermarket chains are not major players because direct investment in India remains problematic for foreign investors, owing to rent-seeking, volatility in government and hostile attitudes towards foreign companies. Restrictive zoning legislation limits the availability of land for retail/commercial purposes, even for Indian supermarket chains. Price-sensitive and bargain-driven Indian consumers prefer to buy from cheaper traditional outlets (Pricewaterhouse Coopers, 2002) and believe that traditional outlets have fresher produce than supermarkets. Most people lack the transport required to travel to centralised outlets and prefer to buy on their doorstep from vendors or walk to a nearby shop. Finally, the rise of two-income families in urban areas remains limited.

Currently the largest and fastest growing supermarket chain is FoodWorld, operating mainly in Southern India. Compared to international supermarkets it is very small, having only 80 outlets, but there are plans to expand to 100 outlets by the end of 2003. The largest chain in AP is Trinethra with 42 outlets in Hyderabad. It is expanding into most towns in AP. There may be some direct procurement from farmers and farmers' co-operatives in the future since FoodWorld is planning a number of small outlets with a focus on fresh fruit and vegetables, but the current impact on producers is negligible, except in a limited number of localities. Large business houses like Tata are also planning to enter fresh vegetable marketing.

2.2 Trends in food consumption patterns

Large business houses are keen to expand into vegetables because they expect vegetable consumption among the urban population to increase. Whereas cereals accounted for more than half of all food expenditure in India in the 1970s, this proportion had dropped to just over a third by the 1990s. Data from the National Sample Survey (NSS) have shown that cereal consumption in rural areas declined by 23% between 1959-60 and 1993-4, while real per capita GDP doubled over the same period (Suryanarayana, 2000). Consumption of dairy products, meat, fruit and vegetables has increased in the diets of urban populations (FAO, 1993; Joshi et al., 2002).

Whilst the majority of people in India live in rural areas, the urban consuming class is expected to grow. According to the United Nations Human Settlements Programme, the total number of urban residents will increase from the current level of nearly 300 million to 330 million by 2005, 435 million by 2015 and 566 million by 2025. A large share of the population will move up the affluence and affordability ladder by 2006-7. At present the consumer class[2] comprises 32 million households. This is projected to increase to 75 million households by 2005, accounting for nearly 40% of the population. India's 1.2 million 'very rich' households (earning more than 360,000 Indian Rupees (Rs) per year) will increase to 5.2 million by 2005 (NCAER, 2001).[3] The combination of urbanisation and increased incomes implies an acceleration of the existing dietary shift from cereals and towards higher value products.

2.3 How pro-poor are government plans for a 'golden revolution'?

The national government is also trying to encourage diversification in crop production to match the anticipated shift in demand for vegetables. Great hopes are being pinned on a 'golden revolution' in horticulture and its potential to create employment, increase farmer incomes, feed agro-industrial ventures and generate export revenue.[4] Horticulture contributes nearly 25% to agricultural domestic product, with less than 8% of the cultivated area, and its contribution is expected to increase (Department of Agriculture and Co-operation). Horticultural expansion is to be achieved through incentives to stimulate exports, food processing and replacement of old cultivars with improved high yielding varieties, dissemination of the latest improved technology on production and post-harvest management through demonstration, training and visits, mechanisation, popularisation of on-farm Zero Energy Cool Chambers, and improvements in handling and market intelligence. Allocations to horticulture increased sharply during the eighth Five-Year Plan to Rs 7890 million from only Rs 240 million in the previous Plan. This was almost doubled in the Ninth Plan to Rs 14.5 billion and is likely to increase again to Rs 20 billion during the Tenth Plan (Department of Agriculture and Co-operation).

A major challenge facing the government will be to ensure that the poor somehow benefit from this 'golden revolution'. The main concerns are for smallholder farmers and landless labourers. It is widely recognised that a major constraint to smallholder farms realising the benefits of their greater efficiency in producing labour-intensive horticultural products is the lack of access to organisations for marketing and input provision. India's experience with co-operatives in the dairy sector has shown that landless labourers, women and small farmers can benefit from new economic opportunities. India currently has 70,000 village milk co-operatives and some 9 million members, 60% of them landless, small, or marginal farmers. The scheme has generated an additional income of $90 for each family involved and the milk co-operative business has created an estimated 250,000 off-farm jobs, most of them in rural areas (World Bank, 1997).

Given these positive experiences in the dairy sector, what is the potential for co-operatives in horticulture? In horticulture, experiences have been mixed. The Kerala Horticulture Development Programme, jointly funded by the State government and the European Union, increased the incomes of 60% of the participating farmers by 20%, but it is not clear whether the beneficiaries included small and marginal farmers (Nair,

---

2. It is not clear how this has been defined.
3. In May 2003, £1= Rs 75.
4. Analysts have noted these virtues of horticulture and especially export horticulture across the world (Dolan and Humphrey, 2000; Jaffee and Morton, 1995).

1999). In contrast, the National Dairy Development Board's Fruit and Vegetable Project, Safal, established in 1986, retails mostly in Delhi and a few other domestic markets but has not succeeded as well as Mother Dairy (a private dairy company), because consumers prefer to buy cheaper vegetables from street stalls. An important difference between milk and vegetables is that consumers appreciate the superior quality of pasteurised milk in polythene packs, whereas vegetable quality does not vary to such an extent.

The employment-generating potential of horticulture is not treated as a direct objective, but may be the major benefit. Since at least 40% of the rural population depends on agricultural labour, more attention needs to be given to this aspect. Employment generation through vegetable production varies greatly from place to place and depends on a variety of factors (Singh and Haque, c.1997). In general, however, vegetable production creates more jobs than traditional crops, as indicated by Table 7.1.

Table 7.1: Per acre (labour days) labour absorption in different crops[a]

State	Tomato	Brinjal	Chilli	Paddy
Karnataka	234	-	124	111
Bihar	50	-	57	49
Uttar Pradesh	105	91	-	45
Rajasthan	52	34	39	31
West Bengal	115	80	-	47

Note: a) Data were collected during 1996-7.
Source: Singh and Haque (c. 1997).

3   The 'Golden Revolution' in Andhra Pradesh

The GoAP's vision for state development, Vision 2020, echoes national plans and strategies for horticulture (GoAP, 1999). The government aims to establish a rapidly expanding food processing industry and attract foreign investment. It anticipates that, by 2020, AP will have a thriving horticulture sector and will be the country's leading supplier of fruits and vegetables to both domestic and international markets. Horticulture is expected to account for 10-15% of the state's GDP and contribute convincingly to higher per capita agricultural incomes.

The strategy for achieving this growth in horticulture is through private sector investment in infrastructure and food processing. The Vision also looks to a strengthening of the fresh produce value chain through farmer co-operatives and the provision of institutional support. This assumes that farmer co-operatives will ensure that their members get better prices for their produce, invest in specific, sharable infrastructure, and form nodal points for advisory work by government R&D departments. Institutional support is to be offered by setting up special boards to facilitate the provision of credit, extension, marketing and infrastructure. Geographically, the initial focus of the AP horticulture strategy is in areas where horticulture is already well established, namely, the canal-irrigated coastal districts, areas around Hyderabad and districts in the dry area of Rayalseema.

Horticulture development in AP is also supported by the establishment of Agricultural Export Zones (AEZs). Over the past two years, 28 AEZs have been identified for specific commodities. Companies locating within AEZs are offered incentives to enter contract farming arrangements with producers, with a view to improving standards and cutting wastage related to variety, farming techniques, handling, packaging, storage and processing. The AEZ for fresh vegetables and mango pulp is in Chittoor District of AP where one of the case studies reported here is located. Companies benefit by accessing an assured supply of low-cost, high quality produce, and farmers will have an assured market and technical and financial support. Companies, farmers and the government are to enter into a tripartite contract.

3.1 Contract farming

Contract farming is being encouraged to facilitate the food processing industry and increase the adoption of horticulture among farmers, but it is, perhaps, the most controversial element of Vision 2020. The key question here is how contract farming can benefit poor people. At present there are sharply divided views on its impacts. The AP Coalition in Defence of Diversity, a prominent network of voluntary development organisations, has strongly opposed contract farming, arguing that it will exclude the poor and harm them in the longer term. This is based largely on their assessment of the first phase of the Large-Scale Advanced Farm Project (LSAFP), popularly known as the 'Kuppam Project'. The project was implemented on 200 acres with land procured from 162 farmer households. Boundaries were erased and land shaping carried out with heavy machinery. Heavy capital investment and the use of machinery alongside the transformation of farmers into labourers created resentment. Concerns were raised about the undemocratic operation of farmers' co-operatives established under the project, in particular the lack of transparency in their dealings with farmers regarding financial and contracting matters.

An assessment of the same project by Rao et al. (n.d.), while conceding that the first phase was indeed flawed on several counts, highlighted the potential for vegetable farming to create jobs. According to this evaluation, employment increased from 490 to 964 labour days per farm with drip irrigation systems. Rao and his colleagues stress how lessons learnt by government from this first phase contributed to the design of the second phase which covered 1686 acres belonging to 679 farmers. In the second phase groups of 5-7 farmers shared one drip irrigation system covering 20-25 acres. The performance of this arrangement was viewed much more positively by the GoAP and it is now being scaled up to 10,000 acres in the third phase. A 50% subsidy for tubewells and drip irrigation is to be provided by Swarnjayanti Gram Swarozgar Yojana through the District Rural Development Agency. This amounts to Rs 20,000 per acre.

The study by Rao et al. does, however, show that more than half of the farmers who benefited from the second phase had average landholdings of nearly 7 acres. In addition, the ratio of irrigated to total operated land was high for all categories of farmers, even before the project. Early assessments of the third phase in the same study showed that poorer farmers were unable to enter horticultural production because of high levels of indebtedness and a lack of access to irrigation.

4   Case-study evidence from Andhra Pradesh

In this section we contrast the impacts of vegetable production on small producers in Medak District in the north of the state with those located in the southern part of the state in Chittoor District. Medak District lies in the semi-arid region of Telangana very near the state capital, Hyderabad. The study village, Gummadidala, lies within the industrial belt in the south of the district and is only 40 km from Hyderabad. Chittoor District lies in the semi-arid region of Rayalseema with an average rainfall below 1000mm per annum and is roughly 120 km from Bangalore. The study village Voolapadu is in the dry part of the district, and has suffered from drought conditions for the last four years. It is well connected by road to the cities of Bangalore and Chennai. Both villages are irrigated by tubewell.

Primary data were collected by quantitative and qualitative methods. Seasonal survey data from the Rabi (dry) and Kharif (monsoon) growing seasons show that the main vegetables grown were tomato, potato and cabbage in the Kharif season, and tomato, brinjal, onion, cucumber, chillies, radish and corriander in the Rabi season. Tomato was by far the most important vegetable grown across all villages. Some of the vegetables, such as coriander and radish, were not captured in the quantitative survey. In Gummadidala, just over 23 acres were under vegetable production, whilst in Voolapadu the figure was almost 15 acres. In both cases this constituted around 10% of the total cultivated land.

An overwhelming majority of vegetable growers belonged to the medium[5] land-holding categories. As Table 7.2 illustrates, 70% of vegetable growers belonged to the category of medium or large farmers, compared to only 18% of all farmers. The participation of smaller growers was higher, however, in Voolapadu: here, a third of vegetable growers farmed on small or marginal farms. The data by caste[6] are also revealing. Table 7.3 shows that, in the sample villages, no ST or SC households grew vegetables. However, this is not a particularly alarming figure, given the low proportion of ST and SC households in the village (1% and 13% respectively). What is significant and important about the caste figures is that, amongst vegetable producers, in Gummadidala OC households far outweigh BC castes whilst in Voolapadu the opposite is true. The next section will demonstrate how this difference can be attributed to opportunities for lower caste groups in new, innovative resource-sharing and marketing arrangements in Voolapadu.

---

5. Marginal (0- 2.5 acres of dry land); small (2.5-5 acres); medium (5-25 acres); large (>25 acres)
6. Caste in India is based on a traditional Hindu hierarchical system that ascribes occupation to people in different groups. From bottom to top of the hierarchy, there are four broad caste categories: Scheduled Caste (SC – so-called untouchables), Backward Castes (BC) and other Castes (OC), plus the Scheduled Tribes (ST) which are outside the traditional hierarchy but are generally placed below SCs. BCs were mainly artisans and farm labourers in traditional agrarian society. Economic, political and social power is concentrated in the hands of OCs. In Andhra Pradesh the BC are numerically the strongest, followed by the OC, SC and then ST.

Table 7.2: Vegetable growing households by land category

| Village | Land category | | | | | Total |
	Landless	Marginal	Small	Medium	Large	
Gummadidala	0	1	1	13	0	15
	0%	7%	7%	86%	0%	100%
Voolapadu	0	4	3	5	1	13
	0%	31%	23%	38%	8%	100%

Table 7.3: Vegetable growing households by caste

| Village | Caste category | | | | Total |
	ST	SC	BC	OC	
Gummadidala	0	0	4	11	15
Voolapadu	0	0	9	4	13
Total	0	0	13	15	28
% of vegetable growing households	0	0	46	54	100
% of all households	1	13	60	26	100

4.1 Typical peri-urban vegetable cultivation in Gummadidala

In Gummadidala land is concentrated in the hands of the Reddy (OC) and a few other upper caste farmers. The pattern here is typical of many peri-urban areas which are well connected to urban locations by road. Large and medium farmers grow vegetables mainly on irrigated plots near the roadside. They themselves transport the vegetables to Monda market in Hyderabad by public or private transport. There they sell the vegetables, through a commission agent, to a trader. Vegetable production has been greatly aided by a farmers' co-operative established 12 years ago that supplies inputs of a reliable quality, at a reasonable price and at a time that suits farmers' requirements.

In sharp contrast is the situation of lower caste farmers. Amongst the few that have some land and access to communal tubewells installed by the government, hardly any are growing vegetables. There are several reasons for this, chief among them the total dependence on moneylenders for credit and private traders for inputs. Interest rates are high, usually because farmers have little/no collateral or are already indebted. Whilst, in theory, co-operative membership is open to all, in practice lower castes are excluded. They are therefore limited to growing irrigated crops which are low-risk. These are either crops that they consume themselves or crops which have a guaranteed price set by the government.

4.2 Advanced market and institutional environment, Voolapadu

Changing production arrangements amongst medium and large farmers
In Chittoor District, as the profit margin on the traditional main crop of paddy has decreased and water availability has declined, large farmers have diversified into other crops, including fruit and vegetables. While a few farmers have gone into exotic

vegetables, others have started growing high-value vegetables such as potato and coriander. The choice of vegetables has been determined by private agents who are in search of outgrowers for particular crops. There are two kinds of arrangements.

First, in the case of potato and coriander, agents from Bangalore or Chennai come to the village and offer credit and purchase guarantees to medium and large farmers with irrigated land. Although the agents reduce some of the transaction costs, the arrangement is still risky. For coriander, the price is not guaranteed and profits may vary between Rs 6000 and Rs 60,000 per acre. Coriander is already grown for sale in Bangalore and, whilst there is great demand during the winter months for festivals and marriages, competition is fierce and drives prices down. Potatoes, where earnings can reach Rs 70,000 per acre, are less risky but more difficult to enter. The agents may provide seed and technical support, but not always, and they therefore tend to choose farmers who are already well integrated into input markets and extension services.

Second, in the case of exotic crops, the outsiders provide seed as well as technical support and advice on how to grow the crop. The crops grown are exotic varieties of chilli and aubergines. Neither has a local market and they are intended exclusively for the Bangalore market.

Pro-poor innovations in resource-sharing and marketing
The really significant difference between Medak and Chittoor, with important implications for policy, is the innovations by farmers in resource-sharing and marketing. These pro-poor innovations fall broadly into three types.

(i) Labour-water exchange In this arrangement, marginal farmers obtain irrigation water from neighbouring farmers with tubewells. If water is available, it is used to grow vegetables all year round.[7] They pay for the water with their own labour and never with cash. The exchange usually occurs between members of the same caste mainly because habitations are by caste. Since both parties belong to the same caste, there is mutual trust and transparency in the arrangement and this form of mutual help through social networks is undoubtedly an asset that has helped these poor farmers in gaining access to the horticultural boom.

(ii) Share-cropping Sharecropping is not a new arrangement but it is discussed here because it has enabled poor SC and BC farmers to grow tomatoes. A majority of SC and a few BC households in the village sharecrop tank-irrigated land owned by the Reddy (OCs). Sharecroppers provide labour and landlords supply inputs, with produce shared on an equal basis. This practice is found mainly on tank-irrigated lands perceived as risky by the owner because of deteriorating water availability. They are not expected to yield very high quantities. For labourers, though, this is an important source of livelihood.

(iii) Group leasing of land by marginal farmers A new initiative has emerged over the last 2-3 years where small and marginal farmers lease out their plots of dryland to

---

7. The selling of tubewell water by farmers has been documented by a few studies in India, for example an International Water Management Institute study in Gujarat found that water was being sold at the rate of Rs 20-25 per hour (http://www.iwmi.cgiar.org/iwmi-tata/PM2003/Highlights/06_Highlight.pdf).

outsiders from Karnataka and Tamil Nadu (catering for the urban markets of Bangalore and Chennai). The outsiders are part of a value chain to these urban centres and the chain is not fixed because there are so many stages involved. Thus the produce may end up with supermarkets, be exported or be sold in open markets. The landowners are SCs and BCs. Outsiders acquire the land on a verbal lease and drill a new tubewell. They then grow irrigated crops such as tomato, brinjal, snake gourd, chillies, carrots and radish. The cultivation uses conventional methods and inputs; for example, drip irrigation has not been used. This is a form of contract farming, but there is no written contract and government is not involved in anyway. The outsider enters into the arrangement on the understanding that it will continue for at least five years so that he can recover his investment in drilling the tubewell.

The landowners are offered wage employment on the consolidated farm. Originally they were concerned about the arrangement because they thought the outsiders would take away their land. However, the arrangement has been positive for both sides. The landowners get regular wage work, acquire new skills and inherit the irrigation system at the end of the lease. More and more marginal farmers, particularly those with land near a main road, are entering into such arrangements. Whilst most of the profits go to the outsider and not to the landowners,[8] risk due to price fluctuations for the produce is borne by the outsider and not by the landowner.

The arrangement has worked because partnerships are not imposed by the government but are entered into voluntarily by groups of friends and relatives who have already established relationships of trust. Although contracts are verbal, there are clearly understood rules, terms and conditions which are based on culturally accepted norms. Groups have some collective weight that they can use to challenge the outsider if necessary, though, because these arrangements are in their infancy, there are not many examples of how conflicts are resolved.

The fact that more and more farmers are keen on adopting labour-water exchange, sharecropping and group-leasing arrangements demonstrates their success. There are a number of reasons why these types of initiatives have worked for the poor. First, the groups and institutions that have evolved function democratically and transparently because they are based on social cohesion, a genuinely shared cause and culturally accepted norms of co-operation and sharing. Second, where purchasing is done directly by the outside agents, farmers no longer have to deal with exploitative commission agents at the *mandi*. Third, people with marginal and even sub-marginal land holdings can get access to opportunities in horticulture. (Table 7.2 shows higher levels of involvement by smaller farmers in Voolapadu than in Gummadidala.) Finally, unlike formal arrangements, informal contract farming arrangements do not involve lengthy procedures and bribes to officials.

5   Conclusion

The analysis of horticulture in AP identifies key differences between traditional peri-urban vegetable-producing areas and those where farmers are moving into new types of production and marketing arrangements. First, whilst the larger farmers in Medak grow

---

8. There is clear evidence of this. One outsider from Bangalore who used to come to the village by bus two years ago now comes in an expensive car.

the traditional vegetables such as tomato, brinjal, cabbage and onion, the larger farmers in Chittoor have ventured into exotic and/or high-value vegetables such as coriander and potatoes. Second, there are more small producers and lower-caste farmers participating in vegetable production in Chittoor than in Medak. Whilst government schemes have benefited mostly larger farmers, lower-caste groups are more predominant amongst smaller landholding groups, so when small farmers gain, benefits generally accrue automatically to lower-caste groups. It may also be the case that incoming private sector producers and traders are more open to establishing partnerships across caste groups than long-established local dealers whose monopoly of the *mandis* is partly based on the social and economic power that they can often, but not always, wield on account of their caste.

These differences reflect the overall institutional and market context: Chittoor is more advanced in horticultural extension and marketing and Medak is more typical of the situation prevailing in most of the state. But there are other processes at work as well. The analysis presented has highlighted the factors, in particular new production and marketing arrangements, that have enabled poorer farmers to cultivate and profit from vegetables, and also those that have prevented similar groups in other locations from benefiting in the same way. These kinds of small-scale and location-specific partnerships between farmers and the private sector have worked well and there are important lessons for other parts of India. The examples given here cannot be treated as a reliable model because the overall institutional and cultural infrastructure and market context will vary from place to place. However, they may inform the design of contract farming arrangements and programmes based on co-operatives and farmers' associations.

By comparing these farmer–private sector partnerships with government initiatives described earlier, the lessons for government policy and action are clear. First, contracts need to protect the interests of small and marginal farmers and should be formulated in terms that they can understand. Second, mainstream arrangements involving banks, officials, government departments and traders frequently exclude lower-caste and poor people and the same problems could hamper horticultural development. Third, horticultural policy needs to include labourers in its vision by moving away from a preoccupation with landed producers. Finally, the village, district and state federations of growers' co-operatives (as in the case of dairy co-operatives) could provide a model, but caution should be exercised in trying to replicate this for the reasons given above.

In conclusion, whilst the shifts in India's food systems have not been commensurate with those in other parts of the developing world, there is an opportunity, in the face of growing urban consumer demand and changing dietary preferences, for state and national governments to establish effective ways of benefiting small producers in horticultural production. This will be achieved only if the current monopoly of commission agents and traders at the *mandis* is broken. Primary growers' co-operatives that are federated into district- and state-level unions hold much promise in safeguarding the interests of the poor in the marketplace.

Chapter 8
Small Producer Participation in Global Food Systems: Policy Opportunities and Constraints

Sheila Page and Rachel Slater

Access to markets is increasingly seen as an essential element in providing a route out of poverty, especially for small producers of food crops in rural areas. However, the nature of those markets is changing and bringing about shifts in both levels and forms of participation by small producers in global food systems. Small producers face new difficulties, for example in meeting high standards, but there are also new initiatives, for example by fair trade companies and co-operatives. This chapter focuses on nine initiatives and asks what small producers must do to achieve effective and sustainable access to markets, and how different private and public organisations can contribute to this.

1   Introduction

The growing differentiation of products and markets offers opportunities for small food producers to grow new crops or enter new markets. For example, Deshingkar et al. (this volume), writing about Andhra Pradesh in India, describe the rapid growth of an industry of small-scale producers supplying exotic vegetables, largely to the national market. There are many other examples. However, small producers face multiple difficulties. Examples include: identifying new markets; acquiring familiarity with standards; dealing with legislation and regulation; and accessing capital (IFAT, 2002; Humphrey et al., 2000; IFAD, 2002; PROMER, 2002).[1]

What, then, might be done? And by whom? The next section unpacks the obstacles or barriers that constrain small producers' market access. The chapter then surveys what small producers must do to achieve effective and sustainable access to markets, and how different private and public organisations can contribute.

2   Unpacking the barriers – obstacles to small producer market access

Page (2003) identifies sixteen necessary conditions for market access (Box 8.1). These can be grouped into four categories: (i) understanding of the market; (ii) organisation of the firm; (iii) communication and transport links; and (iv) an appropriate policy environment.

---

1. For a summary of obstacles identified in these sources, see Page, 2003: 45ff.

Box 8.1: Conditions for market access

(a) Understanding of the market
1. Awareness
2. Knowing buyers, including the perception that others can be different
3. Knowing tastes
4. Knowing and understanding standards

(b) Organisation of the firm
5. Production equipment
6. Investment capital
7. Working capital
8. Labour
9. Appropriate technology
10. Quality and reliability of good or service
11. Appropriate organisation of firm

(c) Communication and transport links
12. Efficient local transport and communications
13. Efficient international transport and communications

(d) An appropriate policy environment
14. Appropriate legal framework, for example land tenure
15. Acceptable tariff system and non-tariff barriers
16. Appropriate additional trading environment, for example, exchange rates

---

2.1 Understanding the market

Producers must become aware of the possibility that there is a new product or market, and that they have at least some of the characteristics necessary to enter that market. They must also be aware of the need to change products, to improve them and adapt, because markets and therefore market access are not static. Here, the barriers to small producers are greater than for larger companies because they cannot benefit from economies of scale of knowledge (Tripp, 2001). A similar barrier for small producers is knowledge of and capacity to meet externally imposed production, health and safety standards (see Box 8.2 and Stevens in this volume). Income-related standards (i.e. those that are imposed as consumers' income rises) pose particular problems for developing countries exporting to developed countries and for producers turning to more affluent or informed consumers in their own country. They impose an additional 'difference' between producer and consumer in tastes (making understanding the market more difficult) and they raise costs (on all production or by requiring different types of production for different markets).

Box 8.2: Horticultural standards

For horticultural production, there is now a Euro-Retailer Working Group which sets standards for food safety and pesticides, and also production and labour standards. For the food market in the UK, standards have been developed by both trade associations and NGOs for the products and the processes of production and for how to monitor these. Although these are not legally binding, they are a significant force because the setters include the major retailers and because following them protects sellers from the risk of being perceived to have fallen below an acceptable standard by inadvertence (Dolan and Humphrey, 2001: 19).

2.2 Organisation of the firm

There must be capacity to produce the product. This means access to technical capacity, labour, equipment, and both investment and working capital, as well as to the necessary inputs. New types of production require at least adaptation of existing technology: the greater the change, the greater the possibility of a significant need for external technological and financial inputs. The purchase of new equipment requires funding and neither the surplus from other production nor the normal amount available for replacing capital in existing production is likely to be adequate for an initial investment. Time-lags between initial production or planting and sale also require funding, especially in agriculture. It may be necessary to move from informal systems, where the funding available or the conditions attached to it may be unpredictable and variable, to formal financial systems.

2.3 Communications and transport

A seller needs efficient links to markets. The dispersed nature of agriculture increases the need for and cost of communications and transport. A new product or market may require new services (different types of transport or refrigerated storage facilities, for example) in new locations. Poor facilities impose a continuing extra cost on production, and the need to establish new ones, a 'barrier to entry' into new production. Poor communications will make all the information needs identified here more difficult and/or more costly to meet; high transactions costs have been cited repeatedly as a particularly serious obstacle in Africa (Bonaglia and Fukasaku, 2002: 84).

2.4 Policy Environment

Finally, sellers can suffer from high policy barriers, whether deliberate (tariffs or other trade restrictions) or unintentional (inefficient administration). Other trading conditions are also important. For example, if a country's policy raises its exchange rate above a market-determined level or if macroeconomic policies (or lack of them) lead to large changes in exchange rates, these raise the costs of trading: both directly (uncompetitive prices) and indirectly (obtaining information on and reacting to changes). In countries where trade is still low or considered a risk, there may also be extensive administrative

Table 8.1: How different initiatives affect the necessary conditions for market access

	Integrated foreign investment (long-term)	Large direct private buyers (probably long-term)	Developing country producers (long-term)	Alternative trade companies (some long-term)	Export promotion agencies (and local govt) (usually long-term)	Import promotion agencies (temporary)	Aid programmes (temporary)	Targeted technical research (temporary)	Agencies promoting alternative trade (temporary)	No. of possible contrib-utors
(a) Understanding of the market										
Awareness	Yes	Yes	Yes	Yes	Possibly	No, awareness is a pre-condition	No, and still no trade in PRSPs	Possibly	Yes	7
Knowing buyers	Yes	Yes	Difficult without external contact	Yes	Difficult because also in selling country	Yes, sometimes	No	No, start from product	Possible	5
Knowing tastes	Yes	Yes	Difficult	Possible, but also want to change tastes	Difficult	Yes	No	Sometimes	Possible	5-6
Knowing & understanding standards	Yes	Yes	Possible	Yes	Possible	Yes	Possible	Yes	Possible	9
(b) Organisation of the firm										
Production equipment	Has information & equipment	Has information	Must find	Sometimes	No	No	No: offer less than govt provides in home country	No	No	4
Investment capital	Yes	No	Must find, now easier	Sometimes	No	No	No (except special schemes, but these are for large companies: IFC, CDC)	No	No	3

				Specialised agencies						
Working capital	Yes	Not normally, but depends on credit terms	Must find, can use those already working off-farm	Yes, training	No	No	No	No	No	3
Labour	Possibly training	Possibly training	Must find	Yes	No	No	No, except general support for education, training	No	No	4
Technology	Yes	Yes	Must find	Yes	Possibly information	No	In agriculture, traditional extension work	Some research initiatives now	Yes	8
Quality & reliability	Yes	Yes	No	Yes	Perhaps	Yes	No	Perhaps	No	6
Organisation of firm	Yes	No	Must do	Yes	No	Possibly advice	No	No	No	4
(c) Communications & transport links										
Local & communication	Can offer substitutes	No	No	No	Govt can	No	Yes	No	No	3
International	Yes, in part	Yes, in part	No	Sometimes	Yes, in part	No	Yes	No	No	3-4
(d) Appropriate policy environment										
Legal: eg land tenure	No	No	No	Some: finance can be used to help lease-holders	Other govt, yes	No	Advice, conditionality	No	Advice	4
Tariffs, NTBs	Advice & lobbying	Advice & lobbying	No	Starting	Political intervention	Advice	Yes	No	No	5+
Other trading conditions	Advice & some bypassing	Advice	No	Advice	Yes	Advice	Advice & conditionality	No	No	6
No. of Contributions	15	10	8	13+	9	7	7+	4+	5	

requirements combined with poor administrative capacity of customs services (cf. IFAT, 2002: 33 for a vivid description of the problems of temporary imports in West Africa).

The importance of some of the problems identified here will depend on the particular circumstances of a country (or even a region or product within it). Some (the cost of equipment, need for working capital) will depend on the nature of the product or service, and there will be a choice: to find ways of meeting the cost or to choose a different activity. Some are obstacles any particular producer will face only once; some will be faced for each new product or new market; but some are 'permanent', for example the higher costs of doing business as a small producer and the difficulties and needs for information created by trading with consumers who are 'different' from the producer. While new agricultural production, for example, has some advantages in terms of low initial costs, it has disadvantages such as high demand for working capital, high transport and communications costs, and vulnerability to trade barriers and changes in standards.

These differences mean that it is not possible to say that some conditions are always 'more important' or priorities. At any point, some will be binding, but it is important that ways of dealing with future barriers are known to be planned. If not, the expected later costs will reduce the expected return from new activities. And it is important to recognise that some of the costs are permanent, and therefore need permanent intervention.

3   Intervention options

For some of the obstacles to markets, particularly the ones to international trade, there may be a permanent role for some external agency, whether public, private, or alternative trader, to provide information and services which cannot be provided at national level. For others, more directly related to production and local infrastructure, there may be a permanent need for something at the national level.

In the longer paper on which this chapter is based, Page (2003) identifies nine different ways by which the barriers to market access can be overcome. These are: (i) direct foreign investment and ownership; (ii) interventions by large direct private buyers; (iii) initiatives by developing country producers; (iv) alternative trade companies; (v) export promotion agencies; (vi) import promotion agencies: (vii) aid programmes; (viii) targeted technical research; and (ix) agencies promoting small production. Table 8.1 indicates how each of the initiatives can support each element of market access.

3.1 Direct foreign investment

As Table 8.1 shows, direct foreign investment can provide all the basic marketing and production functions. Investors also have the experience to meet transport needs and to encourage governments to adapt or remove barriers to trade. In addition, the experience of such companies with other markets leads them to try to alter government policies that add to the cost of trading (unlike a local company, they know that there are alternative ways of administering standards or customs, for example), and their size gives them a significant possibility of successful lobbying, in both host and home countries.

However, foreign companies will choose investment only if the advantages of direct control of production exceed the costs of ownership. This is uncommon and decreasing, particularly in agriculture. In the case of coffee production in Kenya, for example, there has been a partial transition from foreign ownership to reliance on local producers, and remaining owners are sceptical about the future of plantations.

An alternative form, of companies from developing countries investing in developed countries (thus obtaining direct access to external markets and to market information), is emerging in some of the larger developing countries, notably India and Brazil. As the Brazilian examples include fruit juice production, this is another way of rural people gaining access to markets (Page, 1998).

3.2 Large direct private buyers

Traditionally associated with clothing and household textiles sectors, this approach, whereby large companies in developed countries provide regular orders, market information, and advice (often mandatory) on technology and means of production to companies in developing countries, without taking the responsibilities of ownership, was adopted by large buyers of horticultural products in the 1980s and 1990s (see Box 8.3).

Box 8.3: Examples of sub-contracting

Dolan and Humphrey (2001) provide a study of the 'networks of Kenya-based producer-exporters, medium-sized UK importers and large UK retailers' in the horticulture sector. In these cases, the UK companies were marketing their sub-contracted products on the basis that they were differentiated in quality from other supplies, implicitly arguing that there was a need for such a guarantee of quality because other undifferentiated products existed and were less desirable, and that the retailer had the competence and reliability to give this quality. To do this, they had to develop strong control of their suppliers, but most did not have the experience or interest to do this through direct ownership. They therefore looked for (and helped to create) companies and groups that could work with them. Some of these, in turn, purchased from smaller producers.

The emergence of external standards may be weakening one of the conditions for this model (the need for a known company to guarantee quality is premised on the absence of any agreed general standards), but this has not yet altered the model. The local companies need to be strong and reliable enough to make commitments on product quality (and increasingly also on processes of production). This is, therefore, a model that needs some initial conditions in the selling country.

3.3 Initiatives by developing country producers

These initiatives arise in the absence of external private or public sector intervention, and are often very successful. In Guatemala, production and export of snow peas was developed by local producers, led by a foreign entrepreneur (providing the market knowledge) (Wadsworth, 2002). There are other similar cases for non-standard agricultural commodities. Organisation is necessary to bridge the conflict between the need for size in trading and the concern to promote small enterprises (*Agriculture and Industry Survey*, 2000) – see Box 8.4.

Box 8.4: Farmers' organisations for market development

In India, the Kerala Horticulture Development Programme (*Agriculture and Industry Survey*, 2000), established 1993, has provided a combination of finance with technical advice and marketing opportunities. It has explicitly tried to increase co-operation among farmers, making groups a condition for obtaining finance and advice. The finance is important in this case because it is available to leaseholders, so it is offering an easing of land tenure constraints. Shared Interest, a UK-based NGO providing credit for trade, is another example. It focuses explicitly on the problem of working capital, providing finance against orders to fund the period of production and shipping. It does this for both fair trade and commercial orders (it is available to all members of IFAT (Humphrey et al., 2000: 30)), so that it is helping some producer groups to make a transition to commercial trade, where the payment terms are normally less favourable.

Obtaining information both about trading in general ('awareness') and then about specific market requirements has become much easier and cheaper with new communications. Examples include using internet resources for obtaining information about demand (weather information to determine agricultural conditions in other potential supplying countries was an example cited by a producer in Zambia), about policy changes, and for marketing and direct selling of their products – see Bonaglia and Fukasaku (2002) for an example from a leather producer in Ethiopia.

Subcontracting from a local trading company to many individual farmers as well as to co-operatives is found among agricultural producers. Some cases could be classified as either contracts by a foreign buyer or initiatives by a local seller; there were initiatives and responsiveness on both sides (cf. Box 8.5 on Kuapa Kokoo), so the model is more 'network' than 'chain'.

One of the traditional barriers to entry by small traders to international markets has been the difficulty and expense of making cross-border payments. The growing use of credit cards and the simplification or elimination of foreign-exchange controls have made possible obtaining these services, including enforcement of payment, in a standard form and at a lower cost.

Although lack of commercial consultancies has been considered a disadvantage for producers in developing countries (WTO/OECD, 1997: 11), local consultancies on trade are emerging in even the poorest countries, to spread the costs of information and of dealing with administrative requirements among a range of potential small producers and exporters. Private financial services are also developing. In agriculture, producer and exporter organisations that exchange information tend to be more established than in other sectors (cf. Zoomers, 1999: 81, on their role in Bolivia).

3.4 Alternative trading companies

The motivations given for establishing fair trade enterprises are discussed in detail in Page (2003), where it is argued that, at both the micro- and macro-levels, fair trade initiatives are fraught with potential inconsistencies about whether markets and ordinary trade are systematically unfair, whether they can develop relationships of concern between seller and buyer and, given these views, whether fair trade must always be 'alternative' – i.e. can ordinary traders be fair traders? The particular views and motivations for fair trade influence the nature of the alternative patterns suggested and may affect how alternative trade can be linked into the rest of the economy. For example, IFAT Africa holds the position that 'most of the trade generated [through fair trade] should be delivered within the IFAT movement'. The desire is to restrict trade as far as possible to other fair traders (IFAT, 2002: 3). This greatly reduces the potential income of any fair trade enterprise because such companies are still a very small proportion of the market.[2]

Does fair trade deliver benefits to small-scale producers? Some evidence is positive. Cafédirect, founded in 1991 by a combination of NGOs and fair trading companies (www.cafedirect.co.uk), offers a premium on the world coffee price. Because of the sharp decline in coffee prices, this stood at just under 100% for arabica and almost 200% for robusta in November 2002. For tea, added to Cafédirect in 1998, the premium is about 25% (Cafédirect, 2002). A study of an ethical trade initiative in Uganda found an increase in income, but no system for monitoring social impact (Malins and Nelson, 2003). Fair trade cocoa, in Ghana, appears to offer both financial and social benefits (see Box 8.5).

Box 8.5: Kuapa Kokoo and the Day Chocolate Company

Following the restructuring of cocoa in Ghana in 1993, which allowed private companies and co-operatives to participate, a farmers' organisation acquired a buyer's licence. It worked with a Fair Trade organisation, Twin Trading, which was looking for a suitable partner to reproduce its existing activities with fair trade coffee. In 1998, Twin Trading and Kuapa Kokoo established a company in the UK, Day Chocolate, in which they share ownership. This takes some of the cocoa produced by Kuapa Kokoo (and exported through a trading company) and, after subcontracting the processing, sells the chocolate through normal retailers. About 40,000 tonnes of cocoa per annum is now marketed through this arrangement.

Producers receive a guaranteed price (a minimum level and a guaranteed minimum differential above the market price). Ronchi (2002: 24) estimates that this added US$1.6 million to Kuapa Kokoo's revenues in the eight years 1993-2001. Of the extra funds, 25% goes directly to farmers. The rest is spent through a Trust Fund on investment in trading and production companies in Ghana and on community projects, including education, health, water, and mills for alternative income (ibid.: 25).

---

2. Fair trade is currently confined to agricultural or 'handicraft' production, and in services, to finance and tourism. In terms of food, the Fair Trade logo has only been defined for coffee, tea, cocoa, honey, bananas, mangoes, orange juice and sugar.

The impact of fair trade companies is therefore like that of private buyers (Table 8.1), with some additional input into production and organisation, and some additional social impact. Their poverty impact may be increased if there is an additional effect through lobbying on aid. Fair trade companies' reliance on their own reputation as the guarantee that standards are met may be cheaper for small producers (external standards, as discussed above, are costly for small producers), but weakens the market power of the producers; they do not have a certificate and reputations that they can use in other markets.

3.5 Export promotion agencies (and other local government policy)

Export promotion agencies exist in various forms in most developed countries, and were encouraged in developing countries in the 1960s and 1970s. Then, in spite of the excellent performance of some countries which depended heavily on them (for example, Mauritius, with MEDIA), they were criticised as ineffective (for example, Keesing and Singer, 1990).[3]

Not surprisingly, more careful study indicates that the agencies were variable in quality. It is important to define what they can be expected to do. They can act as an information point, not directly on the market conditions and standards in a potential importer, but on the sources of information and assistance that exist. They are more likely, therefore, to be useful as a first stop for a new exporter, than as a continuing resource. They also provide a point of contact for potential importers, with the better ones offering introductions to potential suppliers and at least an implicit guarantee that companies introduced are reliable (see Box 8.6 for a Mexican example).

While Latin American examples suggest that responsive agencies, providing services, work best, Asian examples of government intervention indicate that a more active role is possible. There, and in Mauritius, the interventions were not only through the export promotion agency, but through broad co-operation between private sector leaders and the government. This can exclude small and medium-sized producers (except in a small economy like Mauritius).

Box 8.6: Mexican promotion of non-traditional agricultural products

Mexico has a programme for non-traditional agricultural products which looks for 'higher-value small-farm' products. It thus tries to identify products which are particularly suitable for small farmers, rather than assisting small farmers to operate in sectors dominated by large producers and buyers. It starts from the existing farming structure. The government programme provides both market information and links to potential buyers. It meets the problem of reliability where there are no repeated or large contracts with a guarantee of quality and provenance through a seal of quality. It encourages production also for the home market (Ramírez, 2001).

---

3. The studies suggested that support for production, 'supply-side measures', was better than support for marketing. The argument in this chapter is that the stages of market access are complementary, not competing.

3.6 Import promotion agencies

During the 1960s and 1970s, at the same time as developing countries established export promotion agencies, some donors and international agencies established agencies specifically to promote trade from developing countries: GATT established the International Trade Centre in 1964 (now also related to UNCTAD), and the most important single-donor-funded agency, the CBI in the Netherlands, dates from 1971. These had similar roles to the export promotion agencies, and, like them, were not intended to provide production assistance. They therefore deal with companies which are already established. (They also, of course, do not directly assist companies trying to sell to their home markets.)

The CBI remains the standard by which other programmes are judged by exporters who have used it, and the one with which all companies and countries interested in export promotion are familiar. Its mandate is specifically to deal with what it defines as 'export ready' firms, those which are aware of the possibility, which have reasonable production systems, but which need specific market knowledge and the ability to adapt to it. It provides both basic information, on the official and marketing requirements to sell a particular product or service, and specific seasonal information on fashion or other trends. It is able to help small companies. The general information on its web site (www.cbi.nl) gives extensive background information on markets and on legal requirements such as health and labour standards.

Other individual country agencies have provided various parts of these services (all support services as well as goods). Some take a longer view of their assistance and deal with an industry, rather than an individual firm. The UK agency, DECTA, had some country programmes in Ghana and India which attempted to do this, but was generally a responsive service providing particular services or introductions for firms, not a multi-year programme. Although its information and introduction services were considered useful by exporters and importers surveyed (Page, 1994), these were less useful than the wider services provided by the other agencies. Other examples include agencies in Germany (WTO/OECD, 1997), Denmark (ibid.), and the US (Bonaglia and Fukasaku, 2002: 72).

3.7 Aid programmes

As well as the direct assistance to exports provided by the agencies described above, and by targeted aid initiatives, there has in very recent years been a revival of interest within general aid programmes in providing help for trade. In the 1960s and 1970s, both direct intervention and infrastructure to assist private companies were common among multilateral and bilateral agencies, but then there was a period when both were greatly reduced.

DFID, for example, has two new programmes for African exporters, which are intended to look at many of the stages of market access analysed here. Both look at trade as a means of attaining specified goals: poverty reduction (the Africa Trade and Poverty Programme, ATPP) and environmental benefit (a joint programme with UNCTAD, administered by FIELD). The ATPP programme, for example, is intended to build national capacity to analyse the potential poverty reduction effects from trade and then identify the policies and actions which could maximise these, both national policies and international policies where the country can have an influence through negotiation.

3.8 Targeted technical research

As access to suitable technology is a necessary condition for any marketing, and as agriculture often requires national adaptation of international techniques, the extensive international network of agricultural research can be considered an input into market access. By focusing on what is for many countries their principal source of exports, it can provide a major effect on development. It is, however, only recently that the organisations have looked specifically for export markets in developing new crops, and that they have considered the interaction between new production and policy (for example a workshop in 2002 on Poverty Reduction through Transforming Smallholder Systems from Subsistence to Market Oriented). ICRISAT (Nairobi) is trying to tie its research on new leguminous products to developing capacity in the East African countries to look at trade prospects, in the region and beyond it. It has already been working with a US NGO involved in identifying potential buyers and bringing them to producers (Jones et al., 2002: 6-7). They are also seeking co-operation on meeting standards, for example on aflotoxins. This is a supply-driven approach, but could be used by local producers as the basis of market seeking.

3.9 Agencies promoting small production

Within aid programmes, many donors consider supporting small and medium-sized enterprises an effective way of reducing poverty, and there is some assistance to companies to trade under this heading. For example, IFAD's strategic objectives cite 'strengthening the capacity of the rural poor', 'improving equitable access to productive natural resources and technology', and 'increasing access to financial assets and markets' (IFAD, 2002; PROMER, 2002). It identified a new gap in provision for small rural producers following the cutbacks in government support services through structural adjustment. Its assistance is designed to strengthen agriculture and agricultural organisations. Its advantage over export and import agencies is that it targets not only trade, but also production for the local market: 'the availability of new opportunities on world markets… should not obscure the fact that the principal strength of the rural economy continues to be supply of cash and food crops to domestic and subregional markets'. It includes non-agricultural rural activities and other areas like adult education, as tools for this (Quijandría et al., 2001: 62, 88, 104), and considers provision of financial services an essential part of support.

4   Conclusion

Given the wide range of needs and levels of development of suppliers in developing countries, combinations of assistance may be appropriate. The framework suggested here could provide a tool for identifying which interventions are suitable in particular cases. This could be tested and improved by commissioning detailed country studies which would indicate which types of initiative had worked in which circumstances.

There is also a need to create a network which could bring together existing studies and existing information on the ground of the effects of investment and trade on poverty and of the effects of commercial and public sector initiatives on increasing market access.

Chapter 9
Food and Agricultural Biotechnology Policy: How Much Autonomy Can Developing Countries Exercise?

Erik Millstone and Patrick van Zwanenberg

Some commentators assumed the rules of the World Trade Organization and provisions of the Cartagena Biosafety Protocol could facilitate the establishment of uniform global regulatory procedures and standards covering food and agricultural biotechnology, which could be based on scientific risk assessments. However, the science is often uncertain and equivocal, and assessments of the environmental impact of GM crops should be local rather than global. Consequently the tendency towards convergence is severely attenuated. Analysis of judgements of WTO's Dispute Panel and Appellate Body indicates that developing countries might lawfully be able to exercise considerable autonomy when setting regulatory standards if several conditions are met but, given their limited financial and human resources, they may require multilateral collaboration.

1 Introduction

As their agricultural economies become increasingly integrated into the global trading system, the governments of many developing countries find that they need to establish new, or elaborate existing, food policy-making and control regimes. The experiences of the UK and the EU, especially since March 1996 when the British Government announced the emergence of a novel incurable disease, new variant Creutzfeldt-Jakob Disease, most probably caused by consuming foodstuffs contaminated with the Bovine Spongiform Encephalopathy (or Mad Cow Disease) pathogen, show how severe the adverse consequences can be of failing to provide an adequate and acceptable food policy regime. To try to overcome those challenges many European jurisdictions have been establishing new, and reforming existing, regulatory institutions over the last four years (WHO/Europe and Food Safety Authority of Ireland, 2001). All of these jurisdictions are having difficulties deciding and justifying their policies in relation to the most controversial topic that confronts them, namely, genetically modified (GM) crops and foods. The challenges facing the governments of developing countries, in relation to GM crops and foods, are even more complex, and they often have relatively fewer institutional and scientific resources to draw upon.

One reason why regulatory policy-making on GM crops and food is especially challenging is the extreme difficulty in reliably forecasting the ways in which the technologies will evolve and how they will impact on issues such as food security and the structure of agricultural economies. The upheavals in agri-food biotechnology in the EU and the United States since 1998 illustrate some of these difficulties (Millstone, 2000). Not only the technology, but also the science, is at a very early stage of development. The scientific community's knowledge of how to identify, assess and estimate reliably the risks to public health and environmental biodiversity from the introduction of the products of genetic engineering is rudimentary (Royal Society of Canada, 2001). Despite the efforts of the biotechnology industry and its allies to caricature concerns about the risks posed by GMOs as fundamentally irrational and anti-scientific, the debate within the scientific community about the safety of GM crops and food is almost as fractious as that in the broader society (Levidow and Murphy, 2002; Agriculture and Environment Biotechnology Commission, 2001).

Policy-makers in developing countries are confronted by variants of the challenges faced by their counterparts in industrialised countries. In a first approximation, two categories of developing countries can be identified. One group consists of those countries such as Argentina, China and Cuba that are trying to develop a domestic GM seed and/or crop industry. The second group consists of the majority of developing countries for whom GM crops and food are a matter for agricultural, health and environmental policy-makers and not part of their industrial policy.

For the first group there is some tension between the objective of sponsoring and supporting the development of a GM seed/crop industrial sector and that of protecting public health, environmental biodiversity and food security from the risks that its products and processes might pose. If regulatory policy-makers are excessively risk-averse they could stifle the development of the industry, while a narrow focus on promoting technological innovations and economic growth could compromise public or environmental health.

Governments in all developing countries will also encounter the tensions between their domestic policy objectives and commitments arising from international agreements and rule-based institutions such as the World Trade Organization (WTO) and the Cartagena Protocol on Bio-Safety (CPBS) (Secretariat of the Convention on Biological Diversity, 2000). WTO rules, for example, mean than countries trying to promote their domestic biotechnology industry will have to judge the health and safety implications of home-produced innovations no more favourably than those of imports. When countries set standards for GM seeds and crops, they may also be anxious that the rules of the WTO and CPBS oblige them to make decisions based solely on grounds of public and ecological health, and to adopt the same standards as those of the countries trying to export into their market. The rules of the WTO and CPBS have been widely interpreted as driving a process of regulatory convergence; if a GM crop is deemed safe for cultivation and consumption in the jurisdiction of an exporting country, then, some argue, it should be accepted for import (European Chemical Industry Council, www.cefic.org; UN Economic Commission for Europe, 2003).

Many developing countries that have ratified (or intend to ratify) the Cartagena Protocol on Bio-Safety and that belong to the WTO will confront the challenge of deciding how to protect their environment and citizens from imported GM seeds and crops without violating their obligations under those agreements. This chapter aims to identify those tensions and to explore the conditions under which it may be possible to resolve them.

2   Orthodox assumptions

The WTO and CPBS rules, or at any rate most orthodox interpretations of those rules, presume that science can provide agreed and definitive assessments of risk that can function as benchmarks against which national policies can be formulated and inter-jurisdictional regulatory disputes can be settled. For example, Article 2.2 of the WTO Agreement on the Application of Sanitary and Phytosanitary Measures (SPS) states that: 'Members shall ensure that *any* sanitary or phytosanitary *measure* is applied only to the extent necessary to protect human, animal or plant life or health, *is based on scientific principles and is not maintained without sufficient scientific evidence ...*' (emphasis added). The rules of the WTO stipulate that, other things being equal, all member countries trading in agricultural commodities should either set food safety standards in accordance with those established by the Codex Alimentarius Commission (Codex) or be able to provide a WTO Dispute Panel and Appellate Body with sufficient scientific evidence to justify any tighter standards they may wish to set.

The Cartagena Protocol on Bio-Safety (CPBS) applies to trans-boundary trade in the products of genetic engineering. It is concerned not so much with ensuring that the protection of consumer health is not a disguised restriction on international trade but rather with protecting the biodiversity of the flora and fauna of the environments into which GM seeds and crops may be introduced. The CPBS empowers potential importing countries, especially developing countries, to exclude GM seeds and crops unless and until they have given 'advanced informed agreement' (Article 7). Industrialised countries have given themselves the power to exercise such control, and the CPBS collectively empowers all those developing countries eligible to ratify the Protocol (namely, all those that have ratified the Convention on BioDiversity) to exercise a similar form of control. Although signatory countries to the CPBS are authorised to withhold consent, they can do so only on condition that their decisions are based on a 'scientifically sound' risk assessment (CBSP, Art. 15 para 1), and one that indicates an adverse impact from the GMO in question. As with the SPS Agreement, the CPBS seeks to minimise the extent to which restrictions on international trade are discriminatory or masquerade as environmental protection measures.

3   Why science is necessary but not sufficient

Although the texts of the WTO and CPBS are phrased as if science would settle inter-jurisdictional regulatory disputes, that assumption is seriously undermined by the fact that our scientific understanding of the risks that GM crops and seeds might pose is chronically uncertain, incomplete and contested.

Despite the best efforts of the US Department of Agriculture, the OECD, the European Commission and biotechnology and food industry trade associations, there is no consensus on how much of which kinds of evidence are either necessary or sufficient to indicate that a GM seed, crop or food will be acceptably safe or unacceptably risky (Gaugitsch, 2002; OECD, 2000). Policy-makers have disagreed about which kinds of effects are within the scope of their assessments and therefore which questions the scientists should be expected to answer and which not, and scientists, in turn, have disagreed about which bodies of evidence are relevant and sufficient when conducting their risk assessments. Furthermore, it has become increasingly apparent that not all policy-relevant uncertainties can be readily diminished by further scientific research, because of the complexities of real life ecological and social systems.

In many industrialised countries, the benchmarks by reference to which governments are making decisions are not only contested but changing (OECD, 2000: 3; Levidow and Murphy, 2002). The range and scope of questions that risk assessors and biotechnology companies have been obliged to address have progressively widened. In the early and mid-1990s their deliberations focused on direct and short-term effects of GM seeds and crops, while in the late 1990s and early years of this century, the scope of their discussions extended to include indirect and long-term effects. Consequently the biotechnology companies have found that over time increasing quantities and kinds of data need to be provided, rather than fewer.

One consequence of the fact that science, on its own, is not sufficient to provide unequivocal and uncontested understandings of risk is that individual jurisdictions have far more scope for the legitimate exercise of discretion than is generally recognised.

4   The scope for discretion

Both the WTO and CPBS texts recognise that science is not always definitive and complete; both agreements allow signatories to adopt provisional, precautionary measures if they are not satisfied that the available data are sufficient. However, they both imply that there has to be some evidence of harm before precautionary decisions can be justified (Gupta, 2002).

Article 5.7 of the SPS Agreement permits the adoption of standards '...where the relevant scientific evidence is insufficient...', but only on a provisional basis whilst the member in question obtains additional scientific information. Similarly, the CPBS acknowledges that 'Lack of scientific certainty ... regarding the extent of the potential adverse effects...shall not prevent the Party from taking a decision, as appropriate ...' (Article 10, para 6). Unlike the provisions of the WTO, however, there is no requirement that precautionary decisions must be provisional, and/or that the signatory must seek additional information (Zarrilli, 2000). The exporting country denied market access can, however, request that the signatory review its decision following the production of additional scientific evidence.

Although the recognised scope for exercising precaution permits some discretion, the extent of that discretion, in the event of any dispute, will turn on questions such as 'Which kinds of uncertainties are deemed relevant?' and 'How much uncertainty is deemed sufficient to invoke precautionary measures?'. It will also depend on who is responsible for providing the evidence, who is responsible for interpreting it, and who is required to justify their position.

On this latter issue, the burden of persuasion in each of the Agreements differs slightly. Under the WTO regime, an importing country wishing to set a standard higher than that agreed by Codex, or higher than the standard adopted by the country wishing to export into its market, must produce its own risk assessment in order to justify its policies. Under the provisions of the CPBS, the onus of persuasion is also on the importing country, but it can demand that the exporters conduct and/or finance adequate risk assessments prior to their taking a decision (Article 15).

In one important respect, however, there appears to be much greater scope for autonomy under the CPBS as compared with the SPS Agreement, because the task of assessing the potential impact of GM crops on environmental biodiversity is qualitatively different from that of assessing the risks that might arise, for example, from the introduction of a new GM food ingredient or a new chemical food additive. The former is potentially far more complex and diverse than the latter.

5   Risk assessments of environmental biodiversity: global or local?

The impact on consumer health of using Sodium Nitrite as an anti-bacterial agent, or Saccharin as an artificial sweetener, will almost certainly vary within a national population, but it will be similar across different countries. The impact of GM crops on biodiversity, however, could vary within and between different jurisdictions, as a function of the variety of ecosystems into which they might be introduced. Introducing GM potatoes into the UK may be relatively unproblematic because the UK is not a source of natural biodiversity for potatoes, but introducing a GM potato into Colombia could have a considerable impact, not just on commercial potato crops but also on the natural reservoirs of potato biodiversity. It would therefore be unrealistic to imagine a centralised global body, analogous to Codex, that could assess the environmental risks posed by particular GM varieties that could apply to all, or even many, environments. While the orthodox assumption is that a globally-uniform standard can be set for the health impact of a GM food, no-one pretends that the environmental impact of a GM crop would be uniform across the globe.

The 1990 European Directive on the Environmental Release of the Products of Genetic Engineering tried to treat Europe as if it was just one uniform environment, but that Directive was repealed and replaced.[1] Currently each EU Member State is at liberty to conduct its own domestic risk assessment, and to sub-divide its territory into different environmental types. China has adopted a policy of assessing the risks of the environmental release of GM crops on a province-by-province basis, although some have argued that many Chinese provinces contain rich varieties of environments (Keeley, forthcoming). Since environmental risk assessments must be specific to particular localities and ecosystems, individual countries can, within the rules of the WTO and CBSP, potentially exercise greater discretion over the acceptance or rejection of GM crops than over food ingredients for which Codex provides standards of potentially global application. That much is recognised by the CBSP, the text of which acknowledges that, given diverse environments, the criteria to be taken into account and the data to be generated in a risk assessment cannot be internationally prescribed (Gupta, 2002).

The implications for developing countries when deciding whether or not to permit imports of GM seeds under the CBSP are that they can either demand that studies are conducted in the intended receiving environment, or can require data from studies conducted outside their jurisdiction, but in sufficiently similar environments for their

---

1. Directive 90/220/EEC on the deliberate release into the environment of genetically modified organisms; Directive 2001/18/EC of 12 March 2001 on the deliberate release into the environment of genetically modified organisms and repealing Council Directive 90/220/EEC.

findings to be deemed adequately relevant. Developing countries will also be able to exercise considerable autonomy when specifying the scope of those studies and the criteria by which they are to be interpreted. Unless and until scientific studies deemed adequate by the importing country have been conducted, and unless and until the administration responsible for that environment is satisfied that the proposed introduction of those genetically modified seeds, crops or organisms is acceptably safe, the government of the receiving country can forbid the proposed introduction.

How much discretion governments can exercise is not something that can be determined solely by scrutinising the texts and rules of the WTO and CBSP. The outcomes of any disputes will be settled in any particular case by reference to questions such as 'What counts as a scientific risk assessment?' and 'What counts as sufficient evidence of harm or sufficient evidence of safety?'. We need, therefore, to examine how the rules have been interpreted in practice, and that can most clearly be seen in relation to international disputes, and the judgements of the WTO in those disputes.

6   WTO trade disputes over food safety

Two disputes are particularly relevant in this context. Both have been between the United States on the one hand and the European Union on the other.[2] The first, and better known, dispute has been concerned with beef hormones, the second with a genetically modified hormone, recombinant Bovine Somatotropin or rBST, which, when injected into dairy cows, raises milk yields.

6.1 The beef hormones dispute

The dispute about beef hormones has been long lasting and acrimonious. Several synthetic hormones are permitted for use in beef production in the US but have been banned in Europe since the mid-1980s. The import of US beef into Europe is also banned, unless it can be certified as produced without these hormones. US government regulatory institutions have evaluated the hormones and deem them, and the beef produced with their use, to be acceptably safe, as has the Codex Alimentarius Commission. The US repeatedly complained to the Europeans, but their ban on imports of US beef remained. The US Government eventually responded by taking the EU to a dispute at the WTO.

In 1997, a WTO Dispute Panel found against the Europeans, and the WTO's Appellate Body confirmed most aspects of that Panel's judgement (WTO, 1997). The US Government is exercising its right to impose financial penalties, at the rate of some $160 million a year, on selected European imports, and using the revenue to compensate US beef farmers for their lost sales.

Many commentators, on both sides of the Atlantic, initially interpreted the outcome of that dispute as implying that regulatory standards can and will be harmonised by reference to internationally agreed scientific judgements, and that countries with relatively weak standards could compel countries with higher standards to lower theirs to match the lowest international common denominator, and to accept

---

2. In the beef hormones case Canada was also a party to the dispute – but that has no bearing on this analysis.

their exports. If the details of the case are scrutinised more carefully, a very different picture emerges.

The WTO Dispute Panel and Appellate Body found in favour of the US on the grounds that the EU had failed to conduct a proper and appropriate science-based risk assessment. The WTO did not rule, however, that the use of synthetic beef hormones was risk-free, or that beef produced using synthetic hormones is acceptably safe. Nor did it rule that the EU had no scientific evidence, but merely that the EU had not followed the rules concerning the conduct of, and requirements for, an appropriate science-based risk assessment.

The judgement went against the EU because the scientific evidence of risk that the European Commission provided derived from studies of direct human exposure to hormone products, for example in pharmaceutical formulations, and not from studies of the likely effects on consumers of ingesting beef produced using the hormones. As the Appellate Board stated, the evidence: '... constitute[s] general studies which do indeed show the existence of a general risk of cancer; but they do not focus on and do not address the particular kind of risk here at stake – the carcinogenic or genotoxic potential of the residues of those hormones found in meat derived from cattle to which the hormones had been administered for growth promotion purposes ... Those general studies are, in other words, relevant but do not appear to be sufficiently specific to the case at hand' (Appellate Body Report, para. 200). In other words, the scientific evidence used by the Europeans to justify their measure was too indirect.

The EU's response has not been to lift the ban on US beef but to commission further scientific studies intended to provide more direct and relevant evidence and to plan to conduct revised risk assessments once the results of these studies emerge. Commission officials and members of their expert scientific advisory body are confident that, in the near future, they will have gathered sufficient evidence to enable them to conduct a new risk assessment, and that they will then be able to persuade the WTO to revise its judgements (pers. comm. with E. Millstone, London, May 2001).

Importantly, the EU has chosen to ask a slightly different and broader range of questions about the risks posed by beef hormones than were addressed by the US authorities and Codex, and which may therefore produce a more comprehensive assessment to support its case. That evidence has to be sufficiently specific to the risks in question, but it has, for example, included studies on the possible adverse effects on not just average consumers but especially on vulnerable groups, and in particular on pregnant women and pre-pubescent children, while in the US the assessments of risk have not focused on those specific groups. There appears, however, to be nothing in the WTO statutes or case law that prevents a jurisdiction from refining the scope of its consideration of risks in that kind of way.

At least two other aspects of the beef hormones dispute hold important lessons for policy-makers in developing countries, particularly in relation to agricultural biotechnology. First, both the US Government and the Appellate Body of the WTO confirmed that all signatories have the right to set any level of protection they choose (including a zero risk) in response to any possible risk (Appellate Body Report, para. 186). In other words, just because one country, however powerful, deems a particular risk to public or environmental health to be acceptable, it does not mean that other countries are not at liberty to set and maintain different benchmarks of acceptability, even a requirement that a risk be demonstrably zero. That fact was not sufficient to justify the European ban on US beef, but only because the Europeans had failed to assess the particular risks that beef might cause. The implication is that, if the EU had conducted an assessment of the risks from consuming beef produced using those hormones, it might have been able to reach a science-based conclusion sufficient to sustain the restrictions which it had imposed on imports of North American beef, just as long as some scientific evidence indicated some non-zero risk.

Second, in their judgements on the beef hormones dispute there were important differences as between the Dispute Panel and the Appellate Body. The former argued that risk assessments had to be quantitative, and that governments had to specify in advance of conducting a risk assessment the quantitative benchmarks by reference to which acceptability would be judged. The Appellate Body over-ruled the Dispute Panel on both these points. The WTO rules therefore allow governments, including those of developing countries, to decide for themselves what is and is not acceptable in the light of their own risk assessments. They can set their hurdles as high, or as low, as they like, but they do not need to specify the height of the hurdle before assessing particular risks, even though that might be a practice the US sometimes adopts.

The Dispute Panel and Appellate Body also confirmed that, whatever benchmark is set, it should be applied in a non-discriminatory manner; that is, it must be applied uniformly and consistently to all risks of a particular type, irrespective of whether they arise from domestically produced commodities or imported ones. This stipulation would not be problematic for the Europeans in relation to beef hormones because no European companies are requesting permission to market domestic beef produced using synthetic hormones implants. The requirement that decisions be made in a non-discriminatory fashion, however, may well have ramifications for other similar risk issues that fall within the remit of the SPS Agreement, as well as for decisions made under the CBSP.

The significance of the requirement not to discriminate will, inevitably, depend eventually on how governments, WTO Dispute Panels and the Appellate Body interpret the concept of 'similar' risks, but the case law to settle, or even provide guidance on, that issue has not yet been made. The available evidence does suggest, however, that if a developing country has no plans to encourage the development of a domestic GM crop industry, it can be as strict as it likes in its assessment and evaluation of the impact of GM crops on its biodiversity, without violating the rules of the WTO.

Countries such as China, Cuba, India and Argentina that are trying to gain a share of the global market for GM seeds and crops will be obliged to apply their benchmarks of acceptability in consistent and non-discriminatory ways, but that requirement still leaves them with considerable scope for exercising discretionary judgements. They will not need to adopt the same benchmarks as their competitors, no matter how powerful those competitors might be.

6.2 The rBST dispute

The European Community, as it then was, refused to authorise the introduction of rBST in the mid-1980s, not because the European Commission had conducted a risk assessment and deemed it too risky, but because European dairy farmers were already producing a surplus of milk and dairy products for which no market could be found and because consumers indicated that they did not want their milk produced using rBST.

Following the outcome of the beef hormones dispute, many in the US and Europe expected that the US would initiate an analogous dispute to challenge Europe's ban on rBST. The evidence suggests, however, that the European Commission had learnt lessons, from the beef hormones dispute, about how to sustain a policy in the face of a challenge from the US. In the aftermath of the August 1997 WTO Dispute Panel's judgement on beef hormones, the European Commission arranged for two separate groups of experts to conduct thorough and detailed science-based risk assessments following procedures that were consistent with WTO rules. One group assessed the potential risks to human consumers of ingesting milk and dairy products from cows treated with rBST, while the other group assessed potential risks to the health of the cows.

As with the beef hormones cases, the European Commission extended the scope of the risk assessments beyond that previously adopted by the US Government and Codex. Whilst the latter had confined their focus to possible adverse effects on human consumers, the Commission included the health of cows within its assessment. Furthermore, it asked the experts investigating the human effects to '...assess the possible direct *and indirect* adverse effects on public health caused by the use of BST *under normal conditions*' (emphasis added). The inclusion of the word 'indirect' and the phrase 'under normal conditions' extends the scope of the assessment beyond that required if they were absent, and again there appears to be nothing in WTO statutes or case law that prevents a jurisdiction from refining the scope of its consideration of risks in this kind of way.

The committee concerned with the potential risks to public health did not conclude that the use of rBST was demonstrably hazardous to human consumers, but it did conclude that there were some *prima facie* indications of a possible risk and that many important uncertainties remained unresolved (European Commission, 1999a). The committee on the veterinary side concluded, however, that there was persuasive evidence indicating that rBST treatment of cows can impair their health, in particular by increasing the incidence and severity of mastitis or udder infections (European Commission, 1999b). In the light of these two risk assessments, the EU re-imposed its long-standing moratorium on rBST.

In 1999, when Codex met in Rome with rBST on its agenda, many people expected the US would try to persuade it to set a maximum permissible residue level for rBST, which would have been a vital precursor to initiating a WTO dispute with the Europeans. US representatives at the Codex meeting declined to force the issue; they simply moved 'next business'. The US Government did not challenge the EU's risk assessment, or its ban on rBST. The EU is consequently able to maintain its moratorium without fear or threat of a WTO dispute.

The human health assessment identified some evidence, of a non-conclusive kind, indicating that rBST might exert adverse consequences for consumers; the possibility could not be ruled out, though there was insufficient evidence to rule it in either. If the EU had requested or produced only one risk assessment, and if that had been the one concerned with consumer health, then the EU would, within the rules of the WTO, only have been able to extend the duration of its moratorium temporarily, not permanently, but only if it had also indicated which set of further studies and data it would require before reassessing the risks and the moratorium.

The rules of the WTO would, however, not prevent a country, or multilateral jurisdiction such as the EU, from subsequently accepting the data and studies it had requested, but then temporarily extending the moratorium yet again, while requesting even more data to illuminate some of the remaining uncertainties. The rBST case shows that the amounts of evidence required to exercise that option are rather slight. Governments certainly do not need unproblematic proof of harm before taking precautionary measures.

7   Summary and concluding remarks

The texts and rules of the WTO and CBSP suggest that there will be at least some scope for exercising discretion and that, other things being equal, the scope will be greater in relation to GM crops and seeds under the terms of the CBSP than in relation to GM foods under the SPS Agreement, given that, in the former case, risk assessments will of necessity be local rather than global. Nevertheless, even under the seemingly more demanding requirements of the SPS Agreement, the international disputes over beef hormones and rBST suggest, at least provisionally, that there may be greater scope for exercising autonomy than many have assumed.

Both disputes suggest that it would be unrealistic to assume that scientific risk assessments will provide a basis by reference to which trade-related disputes about risks from GM food can be settled. Different jurisdictions, and not only industrialised countries, can and do legitimately disagree, and nothing in the WTO rules or procedures can compel agreement. Consequently we can expect, not so much convergence of regulatory standards, but rather sustainable diversity. Countries do not have to fall in line with their competitors and accept the importation of GM seeds or crops just because other countries (industrialised or developing) have deemed them acceptable in their own markets and environments, as long as a few conditions are met.

Firstly, jurisdictions will have to comply with the procedural requirements established through case law, such as that of conducting a sufficiently relevant and direct scientific risk assessment. Secondly, jurisdictions must also have some (but not necessarily very much) relevant scientific evidence and/or scientific reasoning to indicate a possible risk. Thirdly, they must evaluate both domestically produced commodities and imports in non-discriminatory ways. These are not especially exacting requirements.

The beef hormones and rBST cases also suggest that different jurisdictions do, and legitimately can, ask slightly different questions of their scientists, and thus conduct and conclude their risk assessments in different ways, and adopt measures that are more restrictive than those indicated by Codex and the exporting country. Furthermore, they may be able to do so and yet not be vulnerable to a WTO dispute, just as long as a scientific risk assessment has been conducted, and as long as it provides a basis for the consequent measures adopted.

As compared with the provisions of the SPS Agreement, the forces tending to compel regulatory convergence on GM crops are, given the CPBS and the local character of environmental impacts, significantly weaker than those driving convergence of most other kinds of food safety standards. Because environments are not homogenous, countries should be able to define the relevant questions, adopt their own decision criteria and decide which data should be generated when considering the environmental release of GM seeds and crops. For example, if countries want to keep GM crops out of their jurisdiction entirely, it may be sufficient for them simply to indicate that before they could be satisfied that a GM variety was acceptably safe they would want to be assured that no adverse effects on soil micro-organisms would occur, effects which have thus far remained largely unexplored. In principle, they could be explored, but it would be prohibitively expensive to do so.

Neither the SPS Agreement nor the CPBS allows signatories to restrict trade solely on the basis of socio-economic considerations; some scientific judgement about possible risks must be part of the rationale (CPBS, Article 26, para. 1). Scientific evidence of risk to health or ecosystem biodiversity is the primary consideration by reference to which importing countries may legitimately adopt differing standards from those of countries trying to export into their market. Yet, the evidence suggests that reconciling their chosen domestic GM crops policies with international obligations may be far less difficult, in principle, for the governments of developing countries than was widely expected in the mid-1990s.

One significant constraint is likely to be a scarcity of expertise and financial resources. The UK established its new Food Standards Agency (which deals with GM food safety but not the environmental impacts of GM crops) in April 2000. In the financial year 2001-2, the Agency's aggregate expenditure was approximately £115 million (equivalent to €161m.) with a London-based staff of 570 people (FSA, 2002). The budget for the European Commission's European Food Safety Authority's first year of operations (i.e. 2003-4) is €40m. and it will employ some 250 people (www.efsa.eu.int/persobudg_en.html). Expenditures of that sort of magnitude are difficult for many developing countries, but there may well be considerable scope for multilateral collaborations amongst several developing countries on a regional basis, to share both costs and skilled personnel (Hilderbrand and Grindle, 1994). The UN Environmental Programme's Global Environment Fund Project on Development of National Biosafety Frameworks aims '…to assist up to 100 countries to develop their National Biosafety Frameworks so that they can comply with the Cartagena Protocol on Biosafety. The project will also promote regional and sub-regional cooperation on biosafety' (see www.unep.ch/biosafety/). The British Commonwealth's Science Council is, for example, collaborating with Trinidad and Tobago to support a project to help develop the capacity of several Caribbean countries to evaluate risk assessments of GM plants and to facilitate risk management decision-making (Commonwealth Science Council, forthcoming). It is too soon to tell how adequate or successful those initiatives might be, but our analysis suggests that investments of this type on the part of developing countries may well be worthwhile.

Chapter 10
Food Trade and Food Policy in Sub-Saharan Africa: Old Myths and New Challenges

Christopher Stevens

Changing agricultural trade patterns and policy have powerful but often misunderstood effects on food security in the medium term – partly because they are indirect and partly because insufficient attention is given to the key changes. Africa, in particular, is being squeezed. Current patterns of importing cereals and exporting other agricultural products depend upon price effects of both OECD protectionism and preferences. In the future changes to both could increase the price of cereal imports and reduce the volume and prices of exports. These shifts are not from the formal Doha negotiations on agriculture but from the re-arrangement of agricultural subsidies in OECD countries, changes in trade preferences, and Africa's limited technical capacity to participate actively in setting standards.

1   Introduction

Patterns of agricultural trade are changing so fast that the effects are likely to be powerful in the medium term. This is especially true for sub-Saharan Africa: change is under way in relation to the agricultural goods that are exported, imported and consumed locally. In brief, Africa is being squeezed.

However, the changes are not necessarily to be found in expected places. Liberalisation of agricultural trade in the Doha Round is unlikely to be significant in either scale or effect. This is true with respect to liberalisation both by major OECD actors and also by African countries. Excessive concern with this *cause célèbre* is getting in the way of addressing the real problems: the erosion of preferences; higher import costs; and standards. Changes in standards, in particular, pose severe challenges to African countries.

To develop this argument, we need to begin by understanding the concept of 'trade policy rents', and how these affect Africa. An important paradox emerges: that Africa's greatest gains from exporting to Europe have been in the products that appear at first glance to be the most heavily protected and to receive the least generous preferences. From this platform, we can then review the 'old' and 'new' trade agendas, and examine the implications for food policy.

By way of introduction, however, it is helpful to recall the pattern of agricultural trade in Africa. The links between trade and food security are complex, of course, because there are so many filters that intermediate the impact on an actual producer or consumer of any trade change (see McCulloch et al., 2001: Figure 4.2).

As far as imports are concerned, the current pattern of sub-Saharan African cereals trade is well known: the region has become increasingly dependent upon imports (see Figure 10.1). Contrary to some popular opinion, this is not primarily a result of food aid, which has formed a relatively small (and declining in the last decade covered) share of the total. At the same time, a significant part of the foreign exchange used to pay for the imports comes from agricultural exports. Hence, any change in either side of the trade equation could affect indirectly the food security of individuals by altering either the total volume of food available in a country or its distribution between different types of food (over which individuals have different entitlements).

Figure 10.1: Sub-Saharan African cereals imports and food aid, 1970–2001°

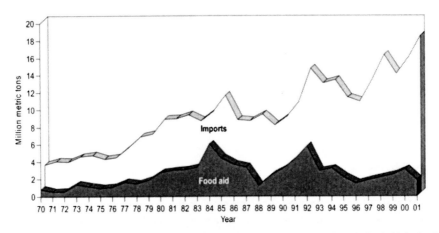

Note: a) It is not clear from the data whether FAO figures for total imports include food aid. It should be clear, since figures for imports should include all imports, but since the figure for food aid comes from WFP and, presumably, is compiled from what donors say they have sent, it is not known if all of what is reported under food aid is also noted under imports. To the extent that food aid is additional, its share of the total is even smaller than the graph suggests.
Source: FAO FAOSTAT Agriculture Data (http://apps.fao.org/page/collections?subset=agriculture).

Africa's agricultural exports fall into three groups in terms of their market characteristics. These are:

- traditional products (such as beverages) that are exported to a relatively undifferentiated, liberal world market;
- other traditional exports (such as beef and sugar) that are exported to markets that are heavily influenced by agricultural protectionism;
- non-traditional products (such as horticulture) that are exported to markets characterised to a greater or lesser extent by protectionism.

The reason for differentiating between these groups is that they face very different 'value chains' and price characteristics. The secular decline in the terms of trade for the first category (beverages, etc.) was forecast over half a century ago in the pioneering work of Raúl Prebisch and Hans Singer, forecasts that have been borne out in reality. African exporters are price-takers on a declining world market. Some appear to have 'lost' their comparative advantage to new entrants such as Malaysia (as in the case of West African palm oil production).

The second category would have been expected, on the basis of the Prebisch-Singer analysis, to have suffered a secular decline in their terms of trade, were it not for the fact that OECD governments (and especially the European Union) have stepped in with policies to support the prices received by their own farmers and have passed on some of these 'benefits' to some African exporters. Consequently, the relative returns from exporting these products have been much more attractive than for other traditional commodities (Stevens and Kennan, 2001: Figure 7.8).

The third category (non-traditional exports) shares the same characteristic – but the scale of the price boost is less marked and the structure of the value chain through which the final price is distributed is very different. In broad terms, Africa's gains from the non-traditional exports have been less substantial than those from the protected traditionals, but the gains are less vulnerable to policy change in the EU.

To understand how this has come about, it is necessary to understand the concept of trade policy rents. This helps to explain the paradox that Africa's greatest gains from exporting to Europe have been on the products that appear at first glance to be the most heavily protected and to receive the least generous preferences.

2   The protection–preference nexus

2.1 How rents are created

What are termed 'trade policy rents' arise when a market is distorted but certain suppliers of imports receive preferential access. The purpose of the distortion is to enable domestic producers to sell goods that consumers would otherwise prefer to buy from foreign producers (whether because they are cheaper, of a preferred quality or whatever). One way to do this is to subsidise the domestic producers – but this tends to be politically unpopular because it is visible, and results either in higher taxes or lower government expenditure on other things. Another, less visible and less politically costly way is to rig the domestic market so that consumers have to pay the higher prices at which domestic producers can compete. One of the fundamental mechanisms to achieve this is to impose protectionist trade barriers that, by squeezing imports, restrict supply and maintain prices at higher levels than would otherwise apply. In some cases, these restrictions (and their price effects) are substantial. The principal intention of these distortions is normally to confer the rents on producers in the distorting state, but there is leakage – often through preferences. All of the OECD countries offer some form of preferential market access to certain developing countries.

In general terms, the protection–preference nexus makes sourcing imports from some suppliers more attractive than from others, but who gains what depends upon the power distribution within a value chain. The trade policy rent may:

- accrue to the producers (processors or shippers) in the preferred countries, increasing the profitability of production and allowing them to:
  - o   increase supply relative to that of non-preferred countries; or
  - o   compensate for production, processing, storage or transport inefficiency relative to that of non-preferred countries; or
  - o   invest in the human and physical capital required for upgrading;

- accrue to the buyers in the importing country (if the price they pay to their suppliers does not increase by the full amount of the import tax cut), increasing the profitability of importing from preferred countries relative to non-preferred ones leading to:
  o increased imports from the former;
  o a need/willingness to shift value-adding processes to the producing country.

To see how the balance between these outcomes arises, consider the way in which rents are created. What is important is both the overall scale of the rent and the architecture of the rules that create it.

Rents are most substantial in product markets that face protectionism so severe that it restricts sharply the possibility of importing from non-preferred sources. This is the case, for example, with beef and sugar, for which the EU import tariffs are respectively 12.8% + €303.4/100 kg (beef) and €33.9/100 kg (sugar), equivalent to *ad valorem* tariffs of 94.5% and 116.2% respectively.[1]

In the case of beef, all African, Caribbean and Pacific (ACP) countries are relieved entirely from the 12.8% *ad valorem* element – but this is of no relevance to most since they are unable to comply with regulations on foot and mouth disease (FMD). For the four southern African ACP countries that can comply (Botswana, Namibia, Swaziland and Zimbabwe) there is an extra preference, namely, that the specific duty is reduced to €24.2/100 kg.

For sugar, some ACP countries have country-specific quotas under the EU–ACP Sugar Protocol. They include Congo, Côte d'Ivoire, Madagascar, Malawi, Mauritius, Swaziland and Zimbabwe (plus Tanzania and Uganda that do not have a surplus to export, and Kenya that has only recently resumed its exports). Under the Protocol the price received is related to the EU domestic price.

At the other end of the scale are items for which protection is so modest as to render any preferences of limited commercial value. For example, the tariff paid by non-preferred countries on exports to the EU of shelled almonds is only 3.5%, compared with preferential rates of 0-3.1%.

In the middle are commodity groups like horticulture. EU tariffs are moderately high (for example, 12.8% for aubergines) and so the duty-free access provided to a range of developing countries is significant. The advantage is available to a large number of countries, and does not appear sufficiently large by itself to exclude totally non-preferred suppliers. The preference is insufficient to offset any substantial price uncompetitiveness on the part of producers or transporters or, of course, any other failings in the fiercely rigorous supply chain required to get perishable items from a sub-Saharan African field to a European supermarket shelf within hours (Dolan et al., 1999).

---

1. The tariffs given are for raw cane sugar for refining (Combined Nomenclature (CN) code 17011110) and fresh or chilled boneless beef (CN 02013000). The *ad valorem* tariff equivalents were calculated using average world import unit values 1995-7 for the Harmonised System 6-digit sub-heads into which the CN 8-digit codes fall.

2.2 The distribution of rents can change

Small rents almost certainly accrue to the importer/retailer/consumer end of the value chain. They do not influence purchasing decisions, and are merely a windfall gain. Depending upon domestic market conditions, they are either retained by the importer, wholesaler or retailer or passed on to consumers. The distribution of large rents is influenced by the structure of the trade policy regime.

In the most heavily protected sectors preferences typically take the form of special quotas allowing some third parties to supply the high-priced market without paying the substantial import duties that either exclude other imports or drastically reduce their profitability. Sugar is the extreme example. One EU processor/distributor, Tate and Lyle, is substantially dependent for its supplies on preferential sugar imports and, in turn, is the monopsony buyer of exports to the EU under the Sugar Protocol. As a cane sugar refiner, the company needs access to imports since domestic European sugar production is of beet. And, because of the high EU tariff, the financial viability of its operations depends upon the continuation of supplies from preferred sources. Since each beneficiary of the Sugar Protocol has a fixed quota, Tate and Lyle cannot play one off against another; if it cannot agree a price with Mauritius, it cannot buy more from Zimbabwe.

At the same time, as the owner of the main cane sugar refineries in Europe, Tate and Lyle is the only feasible purchaser of African (and Caribbean/Pacific) exports to the EU. The alternative of exporting already refined sugar to the EU is not considered to be commercially viable on a substantial scale. The only, very partial, alternative would be to sell outside the European harvesting season to EU beet refineries. But the beet and cane industries are in competition for market share.

A completely different power relationship will evolve from the EU's 'Everything but Arms' (EBA) initiative of 2001. Under this, all least developed countries are able to sell unlimited quantities of any product but arms (including sugar) to the EU. Implementation of the EBA has been partially deferred for bananas (until 2006), sugar and rice (until 2009), but in the interim the least developed countries have duty-free access for an increasing quota of sugar and rice that is set at levels comfortably above past flows.

Unlike the Sugar Protocol, therefore, there are (or will be) no quantitative limits on the sugar that least developed African countries are able to export. But neither is there any built-in protection against the sole feasible large-scale importer (Tate and Lyle) playing one supplier off against another and driving down the price received. For this reason, the least developed sugar-exporting countries have so far agreed to what is effectively a market-sharing agreement with the non-least developed ACP Sugar Protocol beneficiaries. The former will voluntarily limit the quantity of their exports and, in return, will receive a price that is linked to the EU level. Whether or not this arrangement will survive full EBA liberalisation of sugar in 2009 remains to be seen!

2.3 Impacts on producers

The comparison between sugar exported under the Sugar Protocol and under EBA illustrates how the effect of the protection–preference nexus on any given group of producers or countries will depend on many features of the regime's architecture.

Another influencing factor is the way in which any tariffs are calculated. Many of the tariffs imposed by OECD countries on 'sensitive' agricultural products are in the form of specific duties. In other words, instead of the tariff being set at 100% it is fixed at, say, €50/kg.

Such specific duties, unlike *ad valorem* ones, increase the post-tax price of a product with a high unit value by a proportionately smaller amount than one with a low unit value. Because of this, importers may be encouraged to purchase top-quality items that attract higher unit values. This is particularly likely if the item is subject to a tariff quota limiting the volume of imports that can be made. As explained, the EU's preferences for southern African beef include specific duties and also apply tariff quotas.[2] One consequence is that imports from Botswana, Namibia and Zimbabwe are only of higher-quality beef.

This has a range of effects – including on the type of producer able to benefit from the protection–preference nexus and on prices in the domestic market. It will always tend to be the case that 'export quality' will be higher than 'average domestic quality'. But when a specific duty combined with a tariff quota encourages exports to be of only the highest-quality items this disparity is widened. It reduces the chances of poorer producers participating in the lucrative trade because they lack the ability to finance quality production (unless the government makes appropriate provision). At the same time, because each animal contains both higher-value and lower-value cuts, an increase in herd take-off to supply the higher-quality cuts to Europe also increases the supply of lower-quality ones to the domestic market. In turn, this will tend to depress domestic market prices to the benefit of consumers (including poor ones) and the detriment of producers (including poor ones).

3   What won't change?

There are severe challenges ahead for this pattern of trade, many with implications (albeit indirect) for food security. But, too often, they fail to be recognised. This is partly because there is excessive 'background noise' from the ever popular re-discussion of hoary old myths. One of these is that the WTO has already opened up agriculture to free trade, or will do so in the context of the Doha Round. This is wrong in both OECD states and in Africa (though for different reasons).

3.1 OECD protectionism

How high?
There has been much analysis of who would win or lose from a substantial liberalisation of Northern agriculture. This is largely irrelevant as a practical policy concern since we are not about to see anything resembling liberal trade in OECD agriculture, despite the much heralded 'reforms' to the Common Agricultural Policy (CAP) and the on-going agricultural trade negotiations in the WTO Doha Round.

What would a more liberal agricultural regime look like? Liberalisation in the textbook sense means reducing the government taxes and subsidies (and amending

---

2. The tariff quotas are: Botswana 18,916 tons, Namibia 13,000 tons, Swaziland 3,363 tons, Zimbabwe 9,100 tons. Swaziland is a relatively modest exporter.

protectionist rules) that stop high-cost domestic producers losing market share to lower-cost imports. It implies that the global location of production will change over time, with lower-cost producers increasing output and higher-cost producers declining.

An absolutely essential part of this process is the removal of OECD barriers to imports from developing countries. Whilst tariff slashing would not in principle prevent OECD governments from subsidising their farmers sufficiently for them to be able to compete with imports, the fiscal cost would be very high, making the cuts improbable. Without the tariff cuts, it will remain feasible for governments to avoid production relocation through the payment of subsidies.

The EU portrays its CAP reforms as an exercise in liberalisation, but they have little in common with the concept just described. EU 'liberalisation' aims to sustain European production but to reshuffle the subsidies and taxes to make them less costly to the European budget and more easily defensible in the WTO. The EU currently provides €43 billion per year of direct support funded at the Union level. In addition, there is the indirect support of tariffs that make imports artificially expensive, as well as national-level assistance to farmers. The Commission proposals of 2002 seek to shift €25 billion of direct, EU-level income support from one type of support to another. This will have very limited effects on the EU's overall agricultural trade since it will neither decrease production nor increase market access. But it will erode African preferences (see next section on what will change).

The 1994 Agreement on Agriculture (AoA) began a process of reinforcing rules and liberalising trade in temperate agricultural goods, but this still has a long way to go. In return for accepting rules that *could* become constraining after further rounds of negotiation, members were allowed to defer major pain by setting import restrictions and subsidies at high initial levels. The OECD countries retain a huge number of agricultural 'tariff peaks', some of which run into thousands percent.[3] The products that most frequently encounter tariff peaks in the Quad[4] are:

- beef: Canada and EU;
- dairy products: EU, Japan, United States;
- vegetables, fresh or dried: EU, Japan, US;
- fresh fruit: EU, Japan, US;
- cereals and products: EU and Japan;
- sugar: Canada, EU, Japan, US;
- prepared fruit and vegetables: Canada, EU, Japan, US;
- wine: Canada, EU, Japan, US;
- spirits: EU, Japan, US;
- tobacco: Japan, US.

Of these, the product groups with the greatest *absolute* importance for sub-Saharan Africa are tobacco and sugar, plus cotton in the US. In *proportional* terms (i.e. sub-Saharan Africa's share in world imports), the most important are fruits such as oranges, avocado and grapes, fresh cut flowers and tea (in Japan). Whilst many of these are

---

3. The operational definition of a tariff peak is over 15%.
4. Canada, EU, Japan and the US.

covered by the Cotonou Agreement, sub-Saharan Africa still faces tariff peaks in other Quad markets.

The effect of Doha

The existence of tariff peaks is important because it means that apparently substantial cuts may still leave in place barriers so high as to keep imports at very low levels. How likely is it that the Doha Round will bring down tariff peaks to levels at which substantial imports become viable? 'Not very likely' seems to be the answer.

What is known in the jargon as the 'negotiating modalities' were due to be agreed by 31 March 2003 (but were not). They were intended to establish the quantitative targets for liberalisation in the Doha Round. This follows the precedent of the Uruguay Round when, for example, the industrialised countries agreed to convert all their market access restrictions into tariffs which they then reduced by 36% over six years. These figures are not mentioned in the AoA and, by implication, neither will any that are produced for the Doha Round. Rather, the modalities established the cuts that the WTO members had to make to their tariff schedules when producing their 'comprehensive draft commitments'. It is then up to their negotiating partners to check whether the schedules accord with the benchmarks. According to the Doha timetable, the draft commitments are to be adopted at the Cancún Ministerial meeting in September 2003, but this deadline must be in some doubt following the failure to meet the end-March target for the modalities.

While the modalities are not the final word in the negotiations, they are certainly the most important 'first steps'. Only if the formula adopted commits the industrialised countries to reduce their import protection to non-constraining levels will it be possible for the Doha Round to result in increased export opportunities for developing countries in Quad markets. Even then, there will be much to negotiate. On past precedent, the formulas will allow members some latitude in liberalising to a greater extent on some items and to a lesser extent on others. It will be important to follow the negotiations closely to urge that the greater reductions are made on items of importance to poor countries.

In the run-up to the March 2003 deadline the WTO Secretariat produced a summary of member state positions, known colloquially as the revised Harbinson draft, H1 (Rev.1) (WTO, 2003). The H1 (Rev.1) approach, which would reduce higher tariffs proportionately more than lower ones, is as follows; the square brackets indicate the figures for industrialised countries and have not been agreed:

(i)   For all agricultural tariffs greater than [90 per cent *ad valorem*] the simple average reduction rate shall be [60] per cent subject to a minimum cut of [45] per cent per tariff line.

(ii) For all agricultural tariffs lower than or equal to [90 per cent *ad valorem*] and greater than [15 per cent *ad valorem*] the simple average reduction rate shall be [50] per cent subject to a minimum cut of [35] per cent per tariff line.

(iii) For all agricultural tariffs lower than or equal to [15 per cent *ad valorem*] the simple average reduction rate shall be [40] per cent subject to a minimum cut of [25] per cent per tariff line (WTO, 2003: para. 8).

The application of this proposal to the Quad's current tariffs would leave many product groups largely immune to imports. Yet the Harbinson proposal failed to win consensus partly because some members felt that it was too drastic (as well as because others felt it did not go far enough) The principal product areas that would retain tariff peaks of over 50% post-H1 (Rev.1) are:

- in the EU: beef, dairy products, bananas, prepared meat, sugar and grape juice;
- in Japan: meat, dairy products, cereals, sugar, coffee/tea essences and silk;
- in the US: peanuts and tobacco.

In addition to these ultra-constrained products, those facing 25-50% tariff peaks (which will reduce, if not suffocate, trade) include:

- EU: meat (other than beef), fruit, vegetables, cereals, fruit juices, food industry residues, and tobacco;
- Japan: cereal preparations, miscellaneous food preparations;
- US: dairy products, sugar, butter substitutes.

3.2 African protection of agriculture

The reason why African agriculture will not be thrown open to the winds of global competition by the Doha Round is that this has either happened already (largely as a result of structural adjustment) or, if it has not, the Harbinson formula will not fundamentally affect the *status quo* for most items. An analysis of the 600-700 agricultural lines (at the HS6-digit level) on which the Southern African Development Community (SADC) countries have bound their tariffs under the Uruguay Round shows that many followed the example of the OECD countries and set them at high levels (see Table 10.1). In the jargon, a 'bound' tariff is one that has been submitted to the WTO and cannot be exceeded; 'applied' tariffs are those actually in force. In all the countries listed in Table 10.1 the maximum bound tariff is 100% or more and, in most cases, this maximum rate applies to almost all (well over 90%) of products. Only in the Southern African Customs Union (SACU) is the ultra-high tariff cited in the table unrepresentative of the entire range, and tariffs in excess of 90% are more typical of the maximum.

Table 10.1: SADC tariff ranges for agriculture (%)

Country	Maximum		Minimum	
	Bound	**Applied**	**Bound**	**Applied**
Malawi	125	30	125	0
Mauritius	122	55	37	0
Mozambique	100	35	100	0
SACU	597	115	0	0
Tanzania	120	30	120	0
Zambia	125	25	45	0
Zimbabwe	150	40[a]	25	0

Notes: a) Excluding tobacco, alcohol, maté and aerated mineral water, which face high rates but are not food items.

An important feature of Table 10.1 is that in most cases applied rates are much lower than the bound ones. In other words, the SADC countries have taken out an 'insurance policy' in the Uruguay Round by setting the bound tariff at a level that leaves a significant comfort zone above the tariffs they are actually applying. In most of the countries only a small minority of product lines attract the maximum applied rate, which is always below the maximum bound rate.

The application of the Harbinson proposal to the current bound tariffs of the SADC countries shows that, for most items, the 'new' bound tariff would still be above the current applied level. In other words, whilst the reform would reduce the comfort zone (and, for this reason alone, should be accompanied by other reforms – see Stevens et al. 2000), it would not, in itself, result in any significant cuts to the tariffs actually applied at present. Except in the cases of SACU and Mauritius, fewer than 1% of agricultural lines would see the bound rate brought below the current applied level and, in the great majority of cases, the products concerned are alcohol and tobacco; the only 'staples' are some categories of fruit, vegetables and maize in Mauritius. For SACU the list is longer, at almost one-eighth of the items, and broader since it includes a range of meats, dairy products and sugar. However, the 'free trade' agreement that the EU and South Africa have already concluded and are in the process of implementing, plus autonomous SACU liberalisation, is likely to be a much more important factor in liberalisation than is Doha.

4   What will change?

4.1 Preference erosion

Africa's preferences on its agricultural exports to the EU are being eroded. The resulting decline in the relative financial attraction of exporting to Europe will be offset by improvements in other markets only if these continue to use import controls that maintain domestic prices at artificially high levels and provide preferential access to African (and not too many other) countries. There is no evidence that this is happening.

The preference erosion can come in several forms. One (already rampant in the area of horticulture) occurs when the preferences are generalised to a larger number of countries. The extension of sugar preferences to all least developed countries under the EBA is an extreme example. The net effect is to reduce preferences in the European market or to increase the bargaining power of importers – or both. In either case, African exporters lose.

Another form of erosion is when EU policy shifts the ways in which European farmers are supported into forms that provide less for import suppliers. This is happening in the cases of beef and rice. Under the EU's *Agenda 2000* changes, market prices for these products are set to fall, but European farmers will receive direct income support to offset this. If European market prices fall, so will those received by ACP exporters. If ACP exports were unrestricted, it might be possible for some countries to offset a part of this by increasing the volume of exports. But where exports are limited by a tariff quota (as they are for beef and rice), they will have no opportunity to offset the decline in their return per tonne exported by increasing the volume of sales.

4.2 Import costs

The combination of OECD agricultural protectionism and preferences has made the pattern of imports shown in Figure 10.1 more viable financially than it otherwise would have been. Direct and indirect subsidies to OECD cereal producers have depressed the cost of imports. This is most visible when a consignment is subject to a direct export subsidy, but the effect of OECD protectionism and domestic subsidies is greater. These depress world prices by increasing OECD supply and by insulating OECD consumers from the adjustments needed to deal with this. Preferences to two out of three categories of African agricultural exports have increased the foreign-exchange inflows available to pay for the imports. Preference erosion will sap the second of these; the Doha Round may affect the first. Africa will be squeezed from both sides.

The conventional wisdom is that, if and when significant liberalisation occurs, the impact of OECD production cuts on world prices will be mitigated by increases in output from those countries whose agricultural sectors are able to respond quickly to higher prices, for example the members of the Cairns Group. Consequently, total world output will not fall by too much and prices will not rise very substantially. But, if this increased output does not occur during the period in which OECD subsidies and trade barriers remain significant, there could be a larger than expected surge in world prices.

Imports from the Cairns Group are unlikely to rise far if the large OECD markets remain closed to them – as would be the case if the Harbinson proposals were adopted. At the same time, it seems possible that a WTO 'compromise' will see sharp cuts in export subsidies by the OECD countries (especially the EU). These are costly for the subsidisers and especially vexatious to the Cairns Group. The specific intent of such a compromise would be to increase prices in non-OECD markets (so that Cairns exporters would not be undercut by the EU). In other words, the aim is to make the imports from Africa (among others) more expensive.

4.3 Standards

Changes to both the level and form of sanitary and phytosanitary (SPS) standards in export markets will also affect African agriculture. This is an under-researched area – indeed, the lack of research capacity is a part of the problem – but three different types of change in standards can be identified. The experience thus far is that when standards become more difficult to apply in one market, the effect tends to be generalised into others. This was neatly illustrated in 2002 when Zimbabwe, faced with a FMD outbreak that closed off exports to the EU, struck a deal to export beef to Libya. But Libya has the same SPS standards as the EU! It is unclear whether any beef was actually exported.

The three forms of change in standards are:

- more rigorous safety requirements in import markets;
- new areas of health concern;
- new forms of monitoring.

In practice, two or three of these features are often combined, but it is useful to separate them analytically because the possibilities for taking any action to deal with them differ. The most intractable category is the first. It is difficult to see how consumers will ever be persuaded to accept food meeting a lower safety standard if it comes from one source than has been decreed for others. Hence, the idea of 'special and differential treatment' for developing countries in this area appears to be a complete non-starter. The fact that the standards that have been imposed may amount to overkill (and may well have been influenced by agribusiness lobbying as a convenient way of keeping out imports) does not alter the situation. If European consumers have been persuaded that products on sale must be 100% free from genetically modified organisms (GMOs), rather than 99.5% free, then this is sufficient to make the import into Zambia of GMO food aid from the United States a risk to Zambia's future horticultural exports to the EU.

The second category of problems is also difficult, but may be more tractable in some cases. It refers to new health regulations in relation to new perceived problems. For example, in the wake of Europe's bovine spongiform encephalopathy (BSE) scandal, the EU is registering all beef-supplying countries according to their characteristics as potential repositories of the prion that causes BSE. If introduced insensitively (either by accident or with deliberate protectionist intent), regulations based on this classification could undermine southern African beef exports.

The third category is the easiest to deal with in principle – but requires a huge increase in the capacity of African countries to participate in international scientific debate. Some ways of achieving a given SPS standard are easier for some countries/types of producer to comply with than are others. This has been demonstrated in relation to horticulture in Dolan et al. (1999): European supermarket concerns with pesticide residues have encouraged them to concentrate their purchasing on larger rather than smaller farms (with clear implications for food security).

Beef provides another example. There are two main ways to ensure that a herd is free from FMD. One is to vaccinate and keep meticulous records of cattle movements. This approach is feasible only for the more commercialised farmers. The other approach – which the EU has adopted for decades in southern Africa – is physical separation. The disease-carrying buffalo are kept apart from cattle by a series of fences. Any farmer within the FMD-free area can meet the required standard, regardless of size of operations. There is concern that, following the FMD outbreaks in Europe, an attempt might be made to move from the latter to the former method of certification. Small producers might then be disadvantaged.

In order to avoid these new forms of SPS standard adversely affecting livelihoods and food security in Africa, the countries concerned have to be able to participate in the scientific discussions that establish the means by which standards are certified. This they are conspicuously unable to do at present. It needs to be a high priority for action.

5   Conclusion

Trade policy is not the only factor affecting food security outcomes. The Malawi famine of 2001/2 is a case in point: the available data suggest that international trade was not a major contributory cause (Stevens et al., 2002). However, trade policy is a significant factor. Preference erosion and rising import costs seem inevitable, and there is little that Africa can do other than to negotiate delays to give more time to adjust. The implications for food policy will vary between countries – and for food security between socio–economic groups. The 'decision-making' flow diagrams in McCulloch et al. (2001: Figures 6.1, 6.2, 6.3) show the questions that need to be asked.

The issues around standards are different. Changes in standards may favour one type of producer unit over others – but the poverty and food security implications of this are unclear. Current research on the relative contribution to poverty reduction of wage labour in packing houses and larger farms, on the one hand, compared with small-scale farming, on the other, needs to be extended to more countries and products (see, for example, McCulloch and Ota, 2002). Until this is known, governments cannot decide whether to attempt to reverse the trend that favours larger units (for example, by spending resources to help small farmers achieve the same standards) or to ride with it. At the same time, the higher standards demanded on the world market (and the higher cost of feeding the populace from imports) both counsel the need for much more support to the agricultural sector as a whole.

Chapter 11
The World Food Economy in the Twenty-first Century: Challenges for International Co-operation

Hartwig de Haen, Kostas Stamoulis, Prakash Shetty and Prabhu Pingali

Fundamental changes in the world food economy pose new challenges for all participants in the food system, particularly in developing countries. This chapter focuses on the implications of these changes for international co-operation in food and agriculture. Concentrating especially on the FAO, it reviews the responses in monitoring, advocacy, resource mobilisation, regulation and technical and policy assistance activities. It is argued that the emerging food policy agenda, while addressing new challenges, must nevertheless keep at its centre the fight against hunger and malnutrition. However, shifts in the location and nature of hunger require that new approaches be developed to address this persistent and unacceptable global problem.

1 The changing world food economy and the fight against hunger

The world food economy is changing, these changes will continue over the next few decades – and they have implications for FAO. How does FAO ensure that new issues do not distract attention from the fundamental objective of reducing undernourishment and poverty? And are there opportunities for FAO to develop innovative ways of thinking about and responding to food insecurity?

The scale of the changes is not in doubt. They are extensively reviewed in the chapters in this volume, and are summarised in Box 11.1. From an agricultural perspective, key features are the increasing commercialisation of farming, the increasing reliance on technical change as the main source of growth, the growing importance of oilseeds and livestock products in global output, and the growing agricultural trade deficits of developing countries (FAO, 2002a). These changes are both driven by and interact with rapid urbanisation and rapid industrialisation of the food industry. The traditional view of agriculture in developing countries has been of small-scale producers serving largely local markets. There is an increasing need to focus on largely urban markets that are served by sophisticated supply chains which source in both developing and developed countries.

We review these issues in more detail shortly. Before doing so, however, it is worth recalling that the framework for considering the issues is provided by the over-arching goal of reducing hunger. The goal was set by the World Food Summit (WFS) in 1996, and confirmed by the World Food Summit five years later (WFS-fyl) meeting in

Box 11.1: Facts and trends in the emerging world food economy

Slowdown in population growth: The growth rate of 1.35% per annum in the second half of the 1990s is expected to decline to 1.1% in 2010-15 and to 0.5% by 2045-50 (UN Habitat, 2001).

Income growth and reductions in poverty:[a] Per caput income growth in developing countries will increase from 2.4% per annum between 2001 and 2005 to 3.5% between 2006 and 2015. The incidence of poverty will be reduced from 23.2 % in 1999 to 13.3 % in 2015.

Average food intake will increase but hunger will remain high: Daily per capita calorific intake in developing countries will increase from an average of 2681 kcal in 1997/9 to 2850 in 2015. Under 'business as usual', undernourishment will decline from 20% in 1992 to 11% in 2015, but reductions in absolute numbers of undernourished people will be modest – from 776 million in 1990/92 to 610 million in 2015, far from meeting the WFS target.

Slower rate of agricultural production growth: Growth of demand for agricultural products, and therefore of production, will slow down as a result of slower population growth and reduced scope for consumption increases in places where food consumption is already high. For developing countries, production growth will decline from an average of 3.9% p.a. in 1989-99 to 2.0% between 1997-9 and 2015 (FAO, 2002a).

Changes in product composition: Between 1997 and 2015, wheat and rice production in developing countries will grow modestly (by 28 and 21% respectively). However, significant increases are expected in coarse grains (45%), vegetable oils and oilseeds (61%), beef and veal (47 %), mutton and lamb (51%), pig meat (41%), poultry meat (88%), milk and dairy production (58%) (FAO, 2002a).

Production growth based mostly on yield growth: Yield improvements will account for about 70% of production growth, land expansion for 20% and increased cropping intensity for the rest. Nevertheless, FAO projections show that the arable area in developing countries will increase by almost 13% (120 million ha) and water withdrawals for irrigation by 14% by 2030. One in five developing countries will face water shortages (FAO 2002a).

Towards larger farm sizes: As the opportunity cost of family labour rises, small family farm operations for subsistence production become increasingly unprofitable. Landless tenant farmers will gradually find their way to the urban industrial sector. Small landowners will likewise find it more profitable to sell or lease their holdings rather than to cultivate them.

Growing agricultural trade deficits: Agricultural trade surpluses in developing countries are shrinking and, by 2030, will have become a deficit of about US$31 billion, with a rapid rise in imports of cereals and livestock products and a decline in surpluses of vegetable oils and sugar.

Urbanisation: Virtually all of the world's anticipated population growth between 2000 and 2030 will be concentrated in urban areas (UN Habitat, 2001). At the present rate of urbanisation, urban population will equal rural population as early as 2007 and will exceed it from that point on.

Diet transitions: The pace of dietary change, both qualitative and quantitative, accelerates as countries become richer and populations become increasingly urbanised, with a shift in diet structure towards a higher energy density diet in developing countries and a dramatic increase in the contribution to food calories from livestock products (meat, milk and eggs), vegetable oils, and, to a lesser extent, sugar. Average developing country per capita meat consumption has increased from 11kg per year in the mid-1970s to around 26 kg in 2003, and oil crop products from 5.3 kg to 9.9 kg. Increases in saturated fat intake from animal sources, a greater role for added sugar in foods, reduced intakes of complex carbohydrates and fibre, and reduced fruit and vegetables intakes are discussed by Popkin (this volume).

Market structures: Supermarkets are emerging and changing patterns of food procurement in urban areas in many parts of the world, especially in Latin America (see Reardon and Berdegué, 2002a).

---

a) These figures are for developing countries as a whole. It should be acknowledged that reductions in the incidence of poverty will be geographically uneven, with the greatest progress being made in East Asia and the least progress in sub-Saharan Africa (FAO, 2002c).

June 2002. The goal is to reduce the number of undernourished people in the world by half, from 800 million people in the base period 1990-92, to 400 million by 2015. The WFS established a plan of action to achieve the goal, and the priorities contained in it were again confirmed at the WFS-fyl meeting. As summarised in FAO's 'Anti-Hunger Programme: Reducing Hunger through Sustainable Agricultural and Rural Development and Wider Access to Food' (FAO, 2002b), there are five key priorities:

(i)   to improve agricultural productivity and enhance livelihoods and food security in poor communities;

(ii) to develop and conserve natural resources;

(iii) to expand rural infrastructure (including capacity for food safety, plant and animal health) and broaden market access;

(iv) to strengthen capacity for knowledge generation and dissemination (research, extension, education and communication);

(v) to ensure access to food for the most needy through safety nets and other direct assistance.

The Anti-Hunger Programme also draws attention to the policy framework needed at both national and international levels, including a better trade environment and the provision of global public goods.

These priorities remain important because the world is not on track to meet the target of halving the number of undernourished people by 2015. Successive reviews by FAO have shown faltering progress. Whilst the number of people in the developing world who are undernourished continues to decline, at current rates, the 2015 target will not be met until many decades later (FAO, 2002c and Figure 11.1). In order to reach the

Figure 11.1: Number of undernourished people in developing countries: observed and predicted levels relative to the World Food Summit target

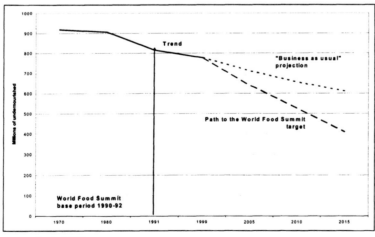

Source: FAO (2002b).

WFS target, faster progress is required (Hussain, 2002). The WFS-fyl meeting concluded that political will was the most important missing ingredient in solving the problem.

2   Emerging issues in the world food economy

There are four kinds of challenges arising from the transformation of the world food economy, relating to (i) agricultural production systems; (ii) patterns of trade in food; (iii) urbanisation and diet transition; and (iv) food markets.

2.1 Challenges emerging from changing agricultural production systems

There are five issues at stake in this area.[1]

First, increases in the opportunity cost of family labour, together with increasing scarcity of natural resources (land, water and biological diversity), will increase the need for technologies which enable sustainable intensification, increases in productivity, resistance to pests, and stress tolerance. New biotechnologies (for example, Genetically Modified Organisms – GMOs) could potentially contribute to fulfilling some production needs, including through applications that respond not only to the needs of resource-poor farmers, but also to the need for improving the nutritional content of crops and livestock products (FAO, 2002d). Thus far, most biotechnology developments have targeted commercial farmers who can afford them. If the poor are to reap this potential as well, public action is needed to create effective demand for research to meet their needs. For this to occur, it is important that the current controversy and uncertainty over the risks and benefits of new technologies be resolved and that acceptable pathways be created through which small farmers can access these technologies. In this context, developing countries, Africa in particular, urgently need technological breakthroughs on various fronts, for which National Agricultural Research Systems, that currently have limited capacity and resources, need to be better equipped.

Second, an increasing commercial orientation of production systems is expected due, *inter alia*, to rapidly rising urban food demand, changing consumption patterns and the increasing integration of domestic and international markets for agricultural products. Some of the resulting changes include: larger operational holdings; reduced reliance on non-traded inputs; and increased specialisation of farming systems. While the speed of these transformations differs substantially across countries, they are all moving in the same direction.

As economies grow, the returns to intensive production systems that require high levels of family labour are generally lower than those from exclusive reliance on purchased inputs. With the expected rise in operational holding size, the ability of the household to supply adequate quantities of non-traded inputs declines. Power, soil fertility maintenance, and crop care are the primary activities for which non-traded inputs are used in subsistence societies. With the increased opportunity costs, family labour will be used less as a source of power and more as a source of knowledge (technical expertise), management and supervision.

---

1. See Pingali (1997) and Pingali and Rosegrant (1995) for more details on these five areas.

Third, rapidly increasing scales of production are being observed particularly in the livestock sector, trying to supply rapidly growing markets for meat, milk and eggs. Both global analyses and country case studies (conducted by FAO in Brazil, India, Thailand and the Philippines) confirm that advanced technology embodied in breeds and feeds appears to be critical to the success stories for poultry around the world, and the same is likely to become true for hogs over time. Much of this technology appears to be transferable, but only at relatively large scales of operation, at least for poultry. Thus there is strong reason to believe that technology itself is a prime driver of the displacement of smallholders from the livestock sector. Small-scale producers obtain lower financial profits per unit of output than large-scale producers, other things being equal. This suggests that, in the absence of deliberate action, small-scale producers will eventually be put out of business by competition from large-scale producers, especially since the better-off producers will scale up.

Fourth, preserving biodiversity will be a formidable challenge. Higher opportunity costs of labour increase farmer reliance on herbicides for weed control for rice and other staple food crops that are currently managed through weeding by hand. Insecticide and fungicide use for high-value crops, such as vegetables and fruit, is substantially higher than for staples, and improper use can increase the incidence of pesticide-related diseases. Although food will, in general, be cheaper, failure to internalise the environmental costs of the expansion and intensification of agriculture will result in the price of food being lower than its social cost, holding back incentives for further research in yield improvements.

Finally, increases in agricultural production and commercialisation are not frictionless processes. The absorption of the rural poor in the industrial and service sectors has significant costs in terms of learning new skills and family dislocations. Also, where property rights are not clearly established, high-value crop production in upland environments could lead to higher risks of soil erosion and land degradation.

So what does this mean for the new food policy? More attention needs to be paid to the development of the overall rural space. Growth in agriculture and in associated non-farm employment can have a broad impact in reducing poverty in rural areas. Two questions follow: How can countries become more competitive in the production of primary agricultural products? And how can the non-agricultural sector add value to primary food products, for instance via reduction in post-harvest losses and via food processing?

2.2 Challenges emerging from changing patterns of trade in food

FAO's projections foresee a continued deepening of the agricultural trade deficit of the developing countries. The net imports of the main commodities in which the developing countries as a group are deficient (mainly cereals and livestock products) will continue their rapid rise. At the same time, the net trade surplus in traditional agricultural exports (for example, tropical beverages, bananas, sugar and vegetable oils and oilseeds) is expected to rise less rapidly or to decline (FAO, 2002a).

Increased developing country imports of cereals and livestock products are due to increased demand combined with the low competitiveness of their domestic agriculture, though the relative weight of these factors varies across countries. Low competitiveness is often the result of insufficient resource mobilisation for the enhanced competitiveness of poor rural communities, the sustainable use of natural resources, the provision of market infrastructure and research.

Growing food imports are also the result of inflows of cheap food from subsidised agriculture in developed countries. Most of the developing countries entered the World Trade Organization without having in place measures of support for their agriculture. They therefore do not have access to special safeguard measures against import surges under the WTO Agreement on Agriculture. This lack of appropriate instruments is certain to be a difficult issue in the final phase of the Doha Round of multilateral trade negotiations. Another issue of concern to poor net food importers is the failure to implement the Marakesh Decision regarding Least Developed Countries (LDCs) and Low-Income Food Deficit Countries (LIFDCs) which had been promised assistance in coping with their rising food import bills and which are now asking for more concrete commitments during the Doha Round.

With regard to agricultural exports, markets for traditional exports are generally saturated, but there is potential for significant gains by developing countries if the processing and marketing of value-added tropical products is moved from consumer to producer countries. However, lack of capacity on the part of the exporters and the presence of tariff escalation in the importing countries both contribute to the loss of potential export revenue. Capacity limitations are particularly felt in markets where access depends on increasingly strict sanitary and phyto-sanitary standards.

In general, the emergence and strengthening of international trade agreements have resulted in a reduction of national control over flows of goods and services between countries. The inclusion of agriculture in the multilateral trade negotiations has led to governments relinquishing more and more control over their domestic policies. The challenge facing the members of the WTO is to manage and further adjust the new rules-based agricultural trading system in a way which is conducive to commonly agreed rules and priorities. In this regard, the Doha development agenda recognises explicitly the food security and rural development needs of developing countries by granting them special and differential treatment.

As agriculture is integrated into the world trading system, there is also an increasing need for regulation. Trade allows the rapid transmission of unsafe foods and animal and plant diseases across borders, so traceability and other regulations have become more important to ensure food safety (FAO, 2002e). The unequal application of standards can be a barrier to successful production and trade; for example, when developing country producers strive to meet developed country standards relating to animal welfare, their products may become uncompetitive.

2.3 Challenges raised by urbanisation and dietary transition

With virtually all of the world's population growth expected between 2000 and 2030 concentrated in urban areas, provisioning the expanding urban markets will be a major challenge for agriculture and food marketing systems in the years to come (UN, 2001). Rapidly rising urban food demand induces an increasingly commercial orientation of production systems, while inefficiencies in the marketing and transport infrastructure will provide incentives for the location of production in peri-urban areas.

The pace of dietary change, both qualitative and quantitative, accelerates as countries become richer and populations become increasingly urbanised. Urbanisation is accompanied by changes in habitual food consumption patterns and dramatic lifestyle changes which include a marked reduction in levels of physical activity. In developing countries which are urbanising, quantitative changes in dietary intake have been accompanied by qualitative changes in the diet. Even when the changes in energy intake have been small there have been large increases in the consumption of animal products, sugars and fats (Horton, 2002; Popkin, 1999).

A number of structural factors also contribute to the differences in urban diets: the organisation of food markets and the opportunity cost of the time of the main food preparers in the household both point to the consumption of a higher share of processed and pre-prepared foods, including street foods (FAO, 1997). There is evidence that smaller and poorer households also rely on street foods for their diets (FAO, 2002f, Ruel et al., 1998). This is, in part, because the purchase of street foods frees up time for income-earning activities. Data from an Accra-wide survey show that households in the lowest income quintile consumed 31.4% of their calorie intake away from home, more than any other income group (Maxwell et al., 1998). The limited evidence available points to the higher fat, sugar and salt content of these pre-prepared foods relative to those prepared at home, which adds to the consequent health burden (ibid.).

The determinants and nature of food security are different in an urban as compared to a rural context (Maxwell, 1999). Compared to their rural counterparts, the urban poor rely almost exclusively on market purchases of food, and depend on wage income or self-employment in the informal sector. Transportation and housing constitute essential (inelastic) components of the expenditure basket of the urban poor. The sheer number of the urban poor makes targeting more difficult. However, concentration and better transport and communications systems facilitate the delivery of social services (such as nutrition education, nutritional programmes and health services) and the operation of safety-nets and other targeted programmes. Food safety issues related to street foods, and hygiene issues related to the transport and small-scale processing of food, are some of the issues which urban food security policy must deal with (FAO, 1997). With respect to agriculture, competition for land for urban dwellings and infrastructure and for urban and peri-urban agriculture will have to be resolved. There is also a need to think about securing food for urban areas through efficient transport and marketing systems.

Finally, there is a need to monitor these transitions. Monitoring of diets, for example, needs to focus not only on undernourishment, but increasingly on obesity, diabetes and other diseases that result from increased proportions of sugar and animal fats in people's diets.

2.4 Challenges resulting from transformation of food markets

Food markets in developing countries are undergoing profound changes that are fuelled by economic development, increase in per caput incomes, changing technology and urbanisation. Higher incomes and increasing numbers of women in the labour force mean greater demand for high-value commodities, processed products and pre-prepared foods (Reardon et al., 2002). Urbanisation increases the scope for economies of scale in food marketing and distribution, while reductions in transactions costs increase the size of the market for distributors and retailers. The result is an impressive increase in the volume of food marketing handled by supermarkets, but also substantial organisational and institutional changes throughout the food marketing chain (Dolan and Humphrey, 2001). Such changes include the setting of private grades and standards for food quality and safety, and the adoption of contracts between buyers and sellers at various points along the food marketing chain.[2] Sub-contracting for products of specified quality and traits is likely to proliferate as a form of interaction between retail food chains and producers. If regions where supermarket retailing is more developed (for example, Latin America) are a precursor of what will follow elsewhere, then supermarkets and large-scale distribution will progressively dominate the food marketing chain in urban areas.

However, concentration of food trade in the hands of a few retailers and large market intermediaries threatens the existence of small traders and small business, central 'spot' food markets and neighbourhood stores. On the production side, these trends may mean the gradual disappearance of those smallholders who are unable to meet the private standards on health and safety set by large retailers and wholesale buyers as well as neighbourhood stores and spot wholesale markets (Dolan and Humphrey, 2001; Reardon and Berdegué, 2002a).

3   Co-ordination, regulation, intervention: what role for international co-operation?

Key roles can be identified for international co-operation in five main areas: (i) advocacy and monitoring; (ii) sustainable intensification of agriculture; (iii) awareness raising and education; (iv) regulation; and (v) capacity-building.

3.1 Reducing global hunger: advocacy and monitoring

Following the World Food Summit Plan of Action, FAO developed the Anti-Hunger Programme (AHP) for the World Food Summit five years later (WFS-fyl) in June 2002 (FAO, 2002b). The AHP is a strategic framework for national and international action to reduce hunger through agricultural and rural development and wider access to food. It proposes public investment of US$24 billion each year to jump-start an accelerated campaign against hunger that could enable the WFS goal to be reached. To promote ownership of the programme by developing country governments, the cost of the agriculture and rural development parts of the programme could be shared equally between the international donor community and the developing countries themselves.

The Heads of State and Government, who gathered at the WFS-fyl, called upon 'all parties (governments, international organizations, civil society organizations and the private sector) to reinforce their efforts so as to act as an international alliance against hunger to achieve the WFS targets no later than 2015'. Together with partners, FAO has subsequently been promoting the realisation of the alliance. Its goal is to mobilise political will, technical expertise, and financial resources, so that the poor and hungry in every country are enabled to achieve food security on a sustainable basis. It would achieve this by facilitating initiatives at local and national levels, with regional and international alliances playing an important role in supporting these initiatives.

---

2. See Reardon and Berdegué (2002b) and Reardon et al. (2002, 2003) for a more comprehensive coverage of the issues related to the proliferation of supermarkets.

Responding to another decision by the WFS-fyl, the FAO Council has established an intergovernmental working group charged to develop, together with stakeholders and in co-operation with relevant treaty bodies, a set of voluntary guidelines to support the progressive realisation of the right to food, in the context of national food security, serviced by an FAO-based secretariat.

FAO has been mandated since its inception to monitor the global situation with regard to hunger and malnutrition in the world. The commitments made in the 1996 World Food Summit (WFS) Plan of Action include support for strengthening information systems for the monitoring of food insecurity and vulnerability at sub-national, national, regional and global levels. As a result, the Food Insecurity and Vulnerability Information Mapping System (FIVIMS) Initiative was launched and an Inter-Agency Working Group was given the responsibility for steering its activities. Over the years FIVIMS has acquired many dimensions, and is now as much concerned with contributing to the monitoring of the Millennium Development Goals, as with conducting multi-disciplinary work at community level to better understand the causes of food insecurity and vulnerability. At national level, inter-agency collaboration and networking need to be reinforced to support the development of methods, techniques and tools for an improved understanding of food insecurity and vulnerability and for assessment and monitoring. The changing food system, and the changing nature of nutrition problems, throw up challenges for the measurement of food insecurity (Hussain, 2002). For example, in the context of the emergence of diet-related non-communicable diseases (NCDs) in the developing world, FIVIMS may need to re-orientate the content of its monitoring systems to focus on both under-nourishment and over-nourishment.

3.2 Increasing agricultural productivity: promoting sustainable intensification

Productivity-based agricultural growth is the cornerstone of FAO's Special Pogramme for Food Security. Intensification, diversification and improving water control are key components.

The need for technologies which correspond to the needs of small farmers, herders and fishers should take into consideration the fact that research and technology development are more and more in the private domain. Biotechnology is a prime example.

Biotechnology holds great promise, but may involve new risks. In most countries, the scientific, political, economic or institutional basis is not yet in place to provide adequate safeguards for biotechnology development and application, and to reap all the potential benefits. Clearly the question is not what is technically possible, but where and how life sciences and biotechnology can contribute to meeting the challenges of sustainable agriculture and development in the twenty-first century, based on a science-based evaluation system that would objectively determine, case by case, the benefits and risks of each individual GMO.

FAO is currently in discussion with private sector companies to share their technologies and information with developing countries free of charge or at minimal cost, particularly when no important market is lost by facilitating such access. The aim is to develop partnerships to set up a public technology bank, which would put key technologies and products at the disposal of poor farmers in the developing world.

As far as water is concerned, significant productivity gains in agriculture over the past half-century have protected the world from devastating food shortages and the threat of mass starvation. Water management, in both rain-fed and irrigated agriculture, was instrumental in achieving those gains. Agricultural policies will need to unlock the potential of water management practices to raise productivity, promote equitable access to water and conserve the resource base. FAO's proposed strategy is to 're-invent' water management in the agriculture sector, based on the modernisation of irrigation infrastructure and institutions, the full participation of water users in the distribution of costs and benefits, and the revival of flagging investment in key areas of the agricultural production chain.

FAO sees broad scope for policy intervention to help to 're-invent' agricultural water management. It recommends a strategic approach to the development of available land and water resources in order to meet the demand for food products and agricultural commodities, and a broader awareness of the productivity gains that can be achieved through wise water use. Individual farmers and households need to be assured 'stable engagement' with land and water resources, meaning land tenure and water use rights that are flexible enough to promote comparative advantage in food staples and cash crops. These rights must be matched by access to rural credit and finance, and the dissemination of technology and good practices in water use.

There also needs to be a re-adjustment in management strategies away from formal irrigation systems and towards pro-poor, affordable technologies, such as small-scale water harvesting. At irrigation scheme level, modernisation programmes will help to extract the full value out of sunk costs and reduce pressure on public funds. Modernisation strategies should transform rigid command-and-control systems into much more flexible service-delivery systems. Agriculture should, and can, shoulder its environmental responsibilities much more effectively by minimising the negative environmental impacts of irrigated production and seeking to restore the productivity of natural ecosystems.

3.3 Towards healthier diets: awareness raising and education

Diet issues are rising rapidly up the agenda. What sorts of advocacy roles might be played by international agencies such as FAO and the World Health Organization (WHO)? There is much to learn in this regard from the experiences of national agencies in the developing world; for example, see Dowler's discussion of food poverty in the UK in this volume and the experiences of school meals programmes (Dowler et al., 2001; Gustafsson, 2002). There are opportunities for nutrition education and health promotion specialists to investigate this area and to devise strategies to promote healthy eating habits and nutritious diets. Shifts in food supply and processing systems within a food chain will have to respond increasingly to consumer demand and become more environmentally, economically and nutritionally viable; thus, more research on supply availability, food chains and consumption is also necessary. There are numerous opportunities for nutrition education and health promotion in these areas which would address both micronutrient malnutrition and the rising trend of nutrition-related non-communicable chronic diseases, including obesity.

3.4 Regulatory roles: the role of Codex Alimentarius

UN agencies such as FAO have the important role of providing technical advice and acting as a neutral forum for discussion and deliberations related to the development of regulatory and other frameworks that are essential in an increasingly globalised world

To help its member countries respond to food safety challenges, FAO is redefining its own approach to food safety and quality issues. In a report to the Organisation's high-level Committee on Agriculture (COAG), it proposes a comprehensive new system that would share the responsibility for providing safe food among all players in the food and agricultural sector, from food producers and processors to retailers and consumer households. This 'food chain approach' would be strengthened by the development of Good Agricultural Practices that would help farmers remove threats to food safety at the source.

The Codex Alimentarius Commission, jointly serviced by FAO and WHO, is charged with the responsibility of developing a food code. Its recommendations are based on the principle of sound scientific analysis and evidence, involving a thorough review of all relevant information. Codex international food standards are developed to protect the health of the consumers and ensure fair practices in the food trade. The Sanitary and Phyto-Sanitary Agreement of the WTO cites Codex standards, guidelines and recommendations as the preferred international measures for facilitating international trade in food. The focus of the Codex is shifting to take account of the changing global food system. At the same time as FAO is exploring relationships with private companies to ensure that biotechnology reaches and benefits small producers, Codex has adopted new food standards, including ground-breaking guidelines for assessing the food safety risks posed by foods that are derived from biotechnology (FAO, 2003).

Risk Analysis – a relatively new paradigm for formal decision-making, encompassing assessment, management and communication of risks – has the ability to take uncertainty into account and to provide advice on the basis of a scientific risk assessment including estimates of uncertainty where natural variability or paucity of data exists. This requires a structured and precautionary approach at all stages of the risk assessment process and in the establishment of recommendations for risk management practices based on the available scientific evidence.

3.5 Capacity-building: enabling better integration of countries in the multilateral trading system

FAO offers direct development assistance and policy and planning advice to governments for improving the efficiency of the production, distribution and consumption of food and agricultural products. Thus the provision of technical assistance and enabling capacity-building is an important task that FAO has undertaken since its inception. However, the priorities with regard to the areas of expertise (in which it makes available assistance and enables capacity-building) in these countries are changing continuously, more so in recent years with the changes in the food economy. For instance, there is increasingly more demand for assistance and capacity-building in areas such as regulation of food safety, plant and animal health and in making food and agricultural policies compatible with the multilateral trade rules established by the relevant WTO Agreements since these impinge directly on international trade in food and agricultural commodities. There is also increasing demand for training to enable developing countries to collect quality information and to be able to analyse this information to address their national policy needs and strategies. This feature of the UN's role in its member states will continue to evolve and change and will make demands on organisations such as FAO to be flexible and adaptable to the changing needs in the food and agriculture sector in the new century.

4   Concluding remarks

UN agencies such as FAO face challenges in this new century which demand mature and balanced approaches in an increasingly resource (both human and financial) constrained environment and in the face of increasing demands from widely divergent directions. The challenges come from the combination of the persistence of old problems (such as extreme poverty and hunger) along with the emergence of new ones, such as the need for food standards, regulation and promotion of healthier diets.

Chapter 12
Responding to Change: WFP and the Global Food Aid System

Edward J. Clay

The WFP has played a key role in international response to the rapidly changing environment and immediate threats to food security. This was achieved by a process of piecemeal, but incomplete adaptation within the severe constraints of the global food aid system with its resource uncertainities and massive donor influences. The rapid shift from a focus on development to a focus on relief and the gradual erosion of the multilateral character of the WFP especially give urgency to clarifying WFP's mandate and providing a clearer basis for determining when food aid is an appropriate international response to food insecurity.

1 How institutions respond to the changes in the global food system

The processes of change within the global food system documented by others in this volume pose a challenge to international institutions with a mandate to promote food security in developing countries. This case study of the United Nations' World Food Programme (WFP) focuses on an institution that has been in the forefront of international response to the rapidly changing environment and immediate threats to food security of poor and vulnerable communities and countries. Two key issues are the rapid shift from a focus on development to a focus on relief, and the gradual erosion of the multilateral character of the WFP.

The underlying assumption is that institutional changes are only partially indicated in formal declared statements of policy. Because the processes of change are never wholly transparent, it is necessary to scrutinise institutional arrangements, budgets and establishments – to look at how resources are being acquired and used. Three broad types of institutional response can be identified (Clay et al., 1998a; Clay and Stokke, 2000; Doornbos, 2000): (i) reformulation or restatement of objectives; (ii) adaptation as an apparently piecemeal process of adjustment; and (iii) reconstruction – the more ambitious reconfiguring of institutions and mandates. In the case of the WFP, the main strategy has been adaptation. Is it now time to take on reformulation and reconstruction?

2 The context: how has the system changed?

Taking a longer view, four features stand out within the global food aid system.[1] Over the past forty years, food aid has become relatively less important in overall aid, and more (or at least no less) dependent on surplus availability and prices in donor countries. There has been a rapid decline in the developmental uses of food aid, and an increase in humanitarian uses. There has also, following a long period of institutional development, been a recent weakening of international management arrangements, especially from a multilateral perspective. Putting these changes together, food aid at present can be characterised as a marginal and uncertain resource, largely used for humanitarian purposes, and increasingly bilateralised.

2.1 A marginal resource

Perhaps contrary to public perceptions influenced by the media coverage of crises and high-profile government and NGO responses, food aid is no longer a major element of aid. Food aid has declined in importance since the early 1970s, from around a quarter of official development assistance (ODA) at that time to under 5% in the 1990s. Amongst donors it is only relatively important, at around 25% of total aid within US foreign assistance. This change is for three reasons:

- Most donors have not allocated increased resources to food aid since the early 1980s. They have budgeted broadly in terms of their commitments to the Food Aid Convention (FAC) and WFP in which there is considerable overlap.
- The US contribution has declined in relative and, during the 1990s, in absolute terms.
- The increase in humanitarian relief has been to a substantial extent funded by reallocations from developmental uses of food aid.

2.2 An uncertain resource

International food aid levels strongly reflect the short-term supply-side influences that determine commodity availability. This is particularly so in the case of the US. These donor supply-side influences are well documented (for example, Benson and Clay,1998), in particular the sensitivity of food aid to prices (negative) and stock levels (positive), and continue to be reconfirmed by more recent econometric analyses (Barrett, 2001; Barrett and Heisey, 2002). In consequence, global food aid flows are procyclical, falling and rising with international cereal market prices. From the viewpoint of aid-recipient countries with chronic food deficits, aid is least available when imports are more expensive, and so balance-of-payments support most valuable. Figure 12.1 illustrates the volatility of food aid.

---

1. Food aid is here understood to include only transactions that qualify as aid under DAC rules on concessionality, provided as humanitarian assistance or for development, and by official aid agencies. In addition, international food aid is restricted to food provided as tied commodity aid from donor sources or financial aid restricted solely to the acquisition of food imported but sourced internationally or locally within the recipient country. There is a grey area of export credits, just as there is with credits for agricultural inputs such as fertiliser or any other goods and services.

Figure 12.1: Global cereals food aid, 1970/1-2001/2

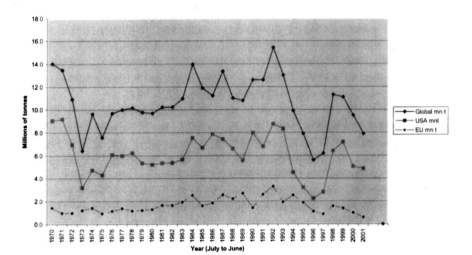

2.3 From development to relief

There has been a gradual shift in the stated objectives of food aid. These began as supporting rehabilitation and mutual defence (the Marshall Plan of 1947 in Europe and the defence treaties in East Asia from 1949). They were then redefined as developmental (Public Law 480 of 1954) (Clay, 1995). They are now a combination of providing immediate humanitarian assistance, alleviating poverty and combating food insecurity. In particular, humanitarian food aid has been growing.

2.4 Weakening multilateralism

Food aid was initially closely linked to US domestic agricultural and trade policy, and continues to be so. The donor basis of support was broadened by agreements including the Food Aid Convention of 1967 and the establishment of WFP in 1962. It became relatively stable through a major restructuring following the 1974 World Food Conference. The global extent of the food aid system also progressively widened as the number of recipient countries expanded to over 100 by the late 1980s. However, a number of changes took place in the mid-1990s, and the US has again become the dominant food aid donor, accounting for 60% of the world total.

3   WFP: from development to relief

Historically, the WFP has an unusual background as 'an autonomous joint subsidiary programme of the United Nations and the Food and Agriculture Organization'.[2] Established in 1962, its original mandate was 'to assist the poor and the hungry, and to

---

2. This account draws heavily on the detailed, informative, if somewhat uncritical, history of WFP up to the late 1990s by John Shaw, a former senior staff member (Shaw, 2001).

be their advocate in word and deed'. It became effectively a separate agency within the UN as a result of changes in its constitution, endorsed by the UN General Assembly in 1991.

The WFP was established primarily as an additional, multilateral food aid window for development purposes, the primacy of development goals being reflected in its mandate. From the internal perspective of senior management, its main focus of attention for most of the first 30 years of its operations was on using food aid in support of economic and social development projects (Shaw, 2001: 67).

The WFP's development portfolio expanded rapidly to achieve what proved to be peak levels in the mid-1980s. Many donors, including the EU member states, the Nordic countries, Australia and Canada, saw WFP as an acceptable, cost-effective channel for their annual food aid commitments. Building upon successful responses to major humanitarian crises, such as those in Bangladesh from 1972 to 1975 and Ethiopia in 1984, large national safety-net programmes were put in place as development projects involving food for work or direct distributions to vulnerable households. The potential for expanding food distribution in response to disaster-related food crises – so-called concertina projects – indicated the safety-net characteristic of these programmes (Shaw and Clay, 1994).

The emerging policy problem was that few projects were able to demonstrate either convincing short-term nutritional or longer-term developmental benefits for the poorest, food-insecure households (Stevens, 1979; Clay and Singer, 1985). Meanwhile, concerns that imported food aid had potentially negative impacts on agricultural development and the agriculturally-related livelihoods of the poor never disappeared (Maxwell, 1991). There was also the problem of 'institutional inertia' (Barrett and Heisey, 2002). As a multilateral agency, the WFP had gradually extended its development portfolio to include over 80 countries by the late 1980s, and had separate country representation outside of UNDP offices. Country programmes had country government stakeholders who were also represented on the governing body.

The position was unstable, however. First, the strengths and weaknesses of WFP's development portfolio had been a subject of continuing controversy since the 1970s (for example, Stevens, 1979; Jackson, 1982). The authoritative joint evaluation sponsored by three important donors, Canada, Netherlands and Norway, in the early 1990s, was highly critical of many facets of performance, and questioning about the lack of evidence on positive impacts (CMI, 1993; Faaland et al., 2000). Second, there were growing and competing pressures on donor resources, in particular, high-profile humanitarian relief operations. And, third, efforts to rationalise internal agricultural policy, within the EU in particular, resulted in the near disappearance of the most important non-FAC source of commodities, surplus dairy products. All these militated against growth on the development side, and in favour of growth on the relief side. This was reflected in resource flows (Table 12.1). In 1989-90, development projects accounted for over half of WFP's activity; by the end of the decade, the share had fallen to less than one-sixth.

Over the same period, the number of countries with development activities reduced by a third. By the early 1990s, the WFP had gradually extended its operations to cover 93 countries, including 83 in which it had regular, multi-year development activities. Resources were geographically concentrated on sub-Saharan Africa, where there were 42 country programmes, especially because of the southern African food crisis. Nevertheless, Latin America and the Caribbean (25 countries) were well represented, as were North Africa and the Middle East (11, mostly middle-income, countries, with relatively lower proportions of undernourished and poor people).

Table 12.1: WFP operational expenditure by category 1989-2002 (US$m.)

Year	Development	Relief	Special operations	Trust funds/bilaterals	Other[b]	Total
1989	499.5	258.1	0	0	0	757.6
1990	498.6	261.2	0	166.2	0	926.0
1991	487.8	586.3	0	252.7	0	1326.7
1992	469.7	868.1	0	234.1	0	1571.9
1993	398.4	865.8	0	217.3	21.6	1503.2
1994	311.5	873.5	0	207.7	20.3	1413.0
1995	340.8	613.9	0	141.6	0.2	1096.7
1996	279.1	737.7	18.5	31.1	11.0	1077.3
1997	332.7	704.3	20.6	15.7	-0.9	1072.4
1998	254.3	915.4	34.1	26.7	6.8	1237.3
1999	246.4	1089.3	34.1	55.4	4.3	1429.6
2000	185.0	920.3	25.9	19.7	7.4	1158.3
2001	231.1	1421.4	32.2	45.8[a]	46.1	1776.4
2002	194.7	1282.8	36.7	38.6[a]	39.4	1592.2

Notes: a) Bilaterals only; b) Operational expenditures such as General fund, Insurance and, from 2001, Trust funds that cannot be apportioned by project/operation.
Source: WFP, *Annual Reports*.

Over the subsequent decade, the WFP has substantially reorientated its activities both towards lower-income countries with higher levels of food insecurity, and also those with humanitarian crises.[3] These include many previously insignificant or new recipients, such as North Korea and East Timor, the Democratic Republic of Congo and conflict-affected West African states. There has also been a substantive involvement in Europe and the Commonwealth of Independent States. Meanwhile, the number of programmes and scale of operations have contracted in the Americas and North Africa. The number of country programmes in the Americas declined from 24 in 1991 to 11 in 2001 and expenditure has also fallen by 39%. This shift of resources shows that gradual adjustment is practicable.

The irony is that the WFP itself has not formally recognised the major change in the nature of its activities. Its latest mission statement, adopted in 1997, reflects its greater autonomy, defining its role as the food aid arm of the UN system, with policies oriented towards 'the objective of eradicating hunger and poverty', leading ultimately to the elimination of the need for food aid (Box 12.1). Key policies and outputs reflect this

---

3. WFP committed itself to providing at least 90% of development assistance in low-income, food-deficit countries and 50% to least developed countries by 1997.

emphasis on poverty eradication and economic and social development (WFP, 1996; WFP, 1999; FAO and others, 2002). The primacy of development goals was being asserted, despite the dominance of relief activities accounting for three-quarters of operational expenditure between 1993 and 1995 (Table 12.1) and the widespread perception, created by media coverage of natural disasters and conflicts, that the WFP was a humanitarian relief agency. This lack of congruence between mandate and what the WFP actually does is an issue for careful consideration.

Box 12.1: WFP purpose and objectives

WFP's *General Regulations and Rules*, adopted in 1997, set out its *purpose* as to:
- use food aid to support economic and social development;
- meet refugee and other emergency and protracted relief food needs;
- promote world food security in accordance with the recommendations of the United Nations and FAO; (food security is defined by the 1992 FAO/WHO International Conference on Nutrition as 'access of all people at all times to the food needed for an active and healthy life').

More specifically the WFP's food aid activities are to:
- support economic and social development, concentrating its efforts and resources on the neediest people and countries;
- assist in the 'continuum from emergency relief to development' by giving priority to supporting disaster prevention, preparedness and mitigation and post-disaster rehabilitation activities;
- assist in meeting refugee and other emergency and protracted relief food needs, using this assistance to the extent possible to serve both relief and development purposes;
- provide services to bilateral donors, United Nations agencies and non-governmental organisations for operations which are consistent with the purposes of WFP and which complement WFP's operations.

---

4   How WFP became primarily a relief agency

The US as major stakeholder was initially opposed to the WFP having a major role in emergencies, then largely understood as responses to natural disasters. There were perceptions that emergency aid was politically sensitive and that the WFP would have difficulty in responding objectively to requests by member states seeking what might be construed as short-term balance-of-payments support. The Sahel drought of 1972/74 was the first major crisis in which the WFP began to play a major role. Then a wider international food security crisis led to significant restructuring of the food aid regime, eventually giving the WFP an enormously enhanced role in humanitarian relief.

The World Food Conference in 1974 established a number of new institutions and modalities, including the World Food Council. Its resolution on emergency stocks led directly to the establishment in 1976 of the International Emergency Food Reserve (IEFR), with a target of 500,000 tonnes as a contingency reserve, with annual replenishment. The IEFR was to be managed by the WFP. However, FAO's Director-

General was to approve individual actions on the recommendation of the Executive Director of WFP. This 'joint key' arrangement was an indication of the perceived sensitivity of an international agency responding to requests from member governments. It reflected, too, the importance that FAO attached to having an operational role in food emergencies in member countries.

In practice, donors were unwilling to meet the target for advance commitments of unrestricted funds. The WFP's capacity to respond on its own initiative and quickly in the first phase of a crisis, or to a rapidly evolving situation, continued to be severely circumscribed. However, the IEFR's flexibility provided a way for donors to co-ordinate and consolidate their responses to major natural disasters, and potentially sensitive humanitarian crises in particular. This was recognised in 1979/80 in the donor response to two coincident crises, the massive and sudden outflow of refugees from Afghanistan to Pakistan and from Cambodia to Thailand. The IEFR target of 500,000 tonnes was met for the first time and WFP emergency commitments jumped by 55% in 1980 to US$192 million. This donor-directed use of the IEFR has been the key factor in the enormous expansion of WFP's role as the multilateral channel for emergency food aid in the 1990s.

The WFP's emergency operations and the IEFR were envisaged as providing short-term relief through commitments of up to 6 months. These modalities of operation were inappropriate for the forward planning and organisation of continued relief to those affected by conflict, without early prospect of repatriation or rehabilitation. Consequently, in 1989, a new sub-category of regular operations was instituted, Protracted Refugee and Displaced Persons Operations (PROs), which could be planned and to which donors could make advance pledges on an annual basis.[4]

The IEFR procedures and donor pledging in commodities were insufficiently flexible to allow the WFP to respond rapidly and directly to a new, unforeseen humanitarian crisis, such as a sudden natural disaster or an unanticipated influx of refugees.[5] The Immediate Response Account (IRA), a purely cash facility, was instituted in 1991 to meet this gap, but, the north Europeans apart, donor support has been disappointing.

The WFP was similarly drawn into the role of logistics co-ordination and monitoring for major country and regional relief operations, such as those in West Africa in 1984/85 and southern Africa in 1992/3. The assessment of overall food aid requirements had previously been undertaken by FAO, focusing on the impacts of natural disasters on production and associated country-level food balances and food import implications. The WFP became increasingly involved with UNHCR in joint assessment of humanitarian relief requirements and refugee crises, and with FAO for natural disasters.

Thus, we can see that the modalities of emergency operations evolved pragmatically in reaction to specific events and agency experiences in increasingly large and complex humanitarian operations. There was no grand design, or inter-agency attempt to rethink the modalities of emergency food aid on a global scale that might be

---

4. PROs were subsequently renamed Protracted Relief and Rehabilitation Operations (PRRO) to make the uses of these resources more flexible.

5. This inflexibility partly explains why NGOs and the Red Cross family have had a relatively more important role than WFP in immediate post-disaster relief and refugee crises.

required by the growing number and scale of humanitarian crises. Instead, there was skilfully piecemeal adaptation, with an implicit change of priority from development to relief.

5   The erosion of multilateralism

A global system for food aid was carefully built up during the period before and after the world food crisis of 1972-4. At the heart of this was the Food Aid Convention, originally agreed in 1967, and eventually an arrangement which guaranteed minimum tonnages of food aid each year. In an extremely tight market in 1995, however, with the highest openly traded price levels for wheat and maize since 1973/4, the resource commitments that underpinned the food aid system proved extremely fragile. The United States and Canada unilaterally announced a reduction in their commitments under the Food Aid Convention. Food aid overall contracted sharply from the high levels of over 15 million tonnes in 1992/3 to under 6 million in 1996: the post-1974 arrangements had partially failed (Benson, 2000).

In the following years, two major donors, the US and the European Union, followed different courses of action, with serious implications for the WFP.

To begin with the US, the 1995 Food Bill seemed to indicate that the US was moving towards reduced internal agricultural support as part of embracing the WTO-promoted liberalisation of agricultural trade. As a result, the future of food aid was unsure, apart from the Title II obligations that were mandated in Congressional legislation and strongly supported by the Food Aid Coalition of private and voluntary organisations, farmers and agribusiness. However, with the cycle of weakening markets and the build-up of stocks in 1997/8, and prior to the Congressional mid-term elections, the Administration acted to increase appropriations. Large commitments of 'crisis' aid were made to Asian countries bilaterally and directed through WFP as emergency aid, reflected in the sharp increase in flows in 1999.

Former Senator George McGovern, who had played a major role in the launching of the WFP 40 years earlier (Shaw, 2001), also proposed a new food for education programme (FFE) – initially supplying surplus food to schools in developing countries.[6] The FFE was embraced by both Congress and the Administration, who expected both US private and voluntary organisations (PVOs) and the WFP to participate in the initiative. The FFE was launched in FY2000, and became a substantial element of US food aid in FY2001 (USAID, 2002). Thus, US food aid bounced back in the years after 1995, and the WFP was a strategic channel for both emergency aid and launching the FFE.

In contrast, those within the European Commission responsible for development and humanitarian aid recognised, after 1995, an opportunity to decouple food aid from international agricultural management, a radical alteration to the regime (European Commission, 1996; European Council, 1996). The Single Market Act that required EU-wide tendering for all but small contracts severely constrained the possibilities for national governments to tie food aid procurements to domestic sources. There was generally less interest in tying EU food aid to internal food sources, as reflected in the

---

6. Literally surplus commodities, that is food temporarily available under Section 416 of the Agricultural Trade Act of 1949 rather than PL480 aid appropriations.

relaxation of the arrangement whereby only 20% of EU food aid could be acquired outside the internal market from developing country sources. So there was little opposition within the Commission, and much support from member government development agencies, for the 1996 Regulation on food security and food aid, that converted the EU food aid budget lines into food security budget lines, allowing a choice between finance or commodities. Food aid diminished as a result.

Meanwhile, ECHO, the EU's own humanitarian office, was intent on raising its profile and was actively extending its support to affected countries directly and indirectly through NGOs. In humanitarian crises, the Commission seemed to regard the WFP as a channel of last resort when its own efforts were frustrated, as in Bosnia (European Court of Auditors, 1998). The share of the now smaller food aid programme available to the WFP fell.

A fuller analysis, beyond the scope of this review, would show how other donors separately reassessed their food aid in the light of what proved to be the 1994-5 grain price spike, and other influences specific to themselves.[7] This trend in policy was not uniform, but inevitably put further budgetary pressures on the WFP.

The aggregate impact of these many interconnecting changes in food aid policy is only slowly becoming clear. Globally food aid shipments have continued to fluctuate strongly (Figure 12.1). Total cereals shipments recovered in 1997/8 and 1998/9 from the 1996/7 level. However, the total is becoming even more sensitive to the increasing share accounted for by volatile US shipments, as other donors' contributions, especially that of the EU, continue to decline.

The implications of donor adjustments are especially serious for the WFP, which has effectively returned to reliance on US resources. By 2001, US contributions had risen to 65% of total resources (Table 12.2), the high level that characterised its initial experimental period in the 1960s (Shaw, 2001). Comparing funding in 2001 with that a decade earlier, overall contributions had risen by 27%, but funding for regular development was 50% lower. US resources were over 140% higher and funding for development had been maintained. European Commission funding was 60% lower, whilst regular support had almost disappeared, falling from over $120 million over the two years 1991-2 to under $2 million in 2001. Support from EU Member States had been somewhat reduced and also mostly accounted for by large reductions in funding for development. Amongst the other major donors, there has been some reduction in support, down 25%, with the contribution to development down 57%.

The cumulative effect of all these piecemeal decisions is that the WFP has, as a multilateral institution, become too reliant on a single funder, with potentially if not already unwanted consequences. Because US aid is so sensitive to short-term supply-side influences, the previously stabilising character of WFP operations may have been lost. The US has historically insisted on separate approval of all WFP development projects. But the geographical distribution and types of activity could be becoming even more closely shaped by American food security policy (for example, food for education) and wider foreign policy priorities (for example, crisis aid to Indonesia in

---

7. For example, Australian and Canadian aid agencies undertook corporate evaluations (AusAid, 1997; CIDA, 1997). These resulted in affirming the priority for emergency relief, confirmed the phasing-down programme that had initially been a response to budgetary pressures and also cut back their regular support to WFP. The Netherlands and the UK effectively phased out food aid, apart from support for relief through both multilateral and NGO channels.

1998/9). The range of resources at WFP's disposal may be too narrow, for emergency relief (Marchione, 2002) and also for development projects in which local purchase or regional or unrestricted international sourcing would be more appropriate and cost-effective (CMI, 1993). Foods that are required, such as white maize, may not be on the US availability list. Health and environmental concerns are being added to those about product suitability for consumers and the disincentive effects of food aid imports. The controversy over the US committing GM maize as emergency aid to southern Africa in 2002 is indicative of this constraint. Whether or not there is any longer more than marginal additionality is debatable. But against that alleged advantage of food aid has to be set the inflexibilities of double tying by source and commodity.

Table 12.2: Contributions to WFP by Food Aid Convention signatories, biennium 1991-2 and 2001 (%)

Donor	1991/2 biennium			2001		
	Total as % of FAC sign.	Development as		Total as % of FAC sign.	Development as	
		% of total	% of donor total		% of total	% of donor total
USA	34.1	20.9	22.3	64.8	41.5	9.1
European Comm.	20.2	11.8	21.3	6.3	0.3	0.7
EU national actions[a]	25.5	25.5	46.7	17.0	28.5	23.7
Other[b]	20.2	34.5	61.9	11.9	29.7	35.5
Total signatories	100.0	100.0	36.3	100.0	100.0	14.2

Notes: a) EU national actions of 15 Member States; b) Includes Argentina, Australia, Canada, Japan, Norway and Switzerland.
Source: WFP, *Annual Reports*.

A difficult issue for other donors is whether they are prepared to complement what the US chooses to make available. For example, as part of the international drought response in 1992/3, the Netherlands funded the overland and internal transport costs of surplus US maize provided under S416 to Zambia. Should other donors have been prepared in 2002 to meet the milling costs to overcome Zambian and other recipient country objections to importing unmilled US GM maize? (IDC, 2003)

6   Adapting to change: successes, failures and unresolved issues

Taking a long-term perspective, the WFP is unquestionably a success story with the UN system, showing that an agency can respond to a changing environment. It grew from a small experimental programme into a separate agency, with a wide presence and the largest budget of any agency apart from the international financial institutions. It has progressively taken on a key position in supplying humanitarian relief, as well as a major role in providing transport and logistics expertise in the delivery of humanitarian aid. Yet there was no grand design. All this resulted from often small incremental changes to modalities and institutional arrangements, and from *ad hoc* crisis measures. However, since the early 1990s, and, it is argued, especially after the pivotal events of

1995, further adaptation has been achieved at the cost of both marginalising the development programme, originally the primary objective of the WFP, and politically costly and operationally inconvenient reliance on a single funder. Meanwhile, the pace of change in the global food system continues apace. These circumstances call for a full rethink of the role of international food aid.

The starting point for a wider rethink should be a country-level reassessment of the role for *food assistance* over the next decade, in the context of wider national strategies for poverty reduction, human development and disaster reduction. In undertaking the assessment, it is necessary to make the clear distinction between *food assistance* – public or NGO interventions that directly distribute food to beneficiaries – and *international food aid* – an aid modality with many uses (FAO, 1996). Currently, the policy context for a reassessment could be as part of the follow-up to a country poverty reduction strategy plan or paper (PRSP). That would be especially useful if the PRSP had spelt out a strategy for social safety nets and risk reduction measures. Where there has been a crisis, then the reassessment could be part of the rehabilitation strategy. The reassessment must explicitly take account of the ways in which the food system is expected to evolve, including internal market liberalisation.

A previous, and deliberately provocative, review of food aid policy issues proposed 'a reconstitution of WFP, to make it the UN's humanitarian and rehabilitation logistics and food support agency, replacing the focus on food aid as a resource with that of ensuring resources and professional capacity appropriate to the objectives defined by humanitarian emergencies and the alleviation of hunger and malnutrition' (ODI, 2000). These are now enormous responsibilities, as reflected in the scale of resources being committed for relief. The distinctive category of development activities would progressively disappear.[8] Of course, the provision of support for relief, rehabilitation and combating extreme chronic food insecurity should also be done in ways that foster and are sensitive to development.

Perhaps without another crisis such as that which led to the 1974 World Food Conference, such a comprehensive rethink is unlikely. These issues were not addressed in the 1996 World Food Summit or the WFS-fyl in 2002 (Shaw and Clay, 1998; FAO and others, 2002). However, it may be that events in 2002 and 2003, including the food crises and the HIV/AIDS pandemic in Africa, and conflicts in Asia and the Middle East, will place such intense pressures on the food aid system that this will generate sufficient impetus to sustain a process of re-examination. Even if the rethink is not a singular process, those involved in each part of the parallel negotiations need to adopt a more consistent perspective on the wider situation.

---

8. Some of what is currently categorised as development would continue, because it meets the criteria for appropriate support to highly food-insecure countries as defined by FAO (2002).

References

Chapter 1

Anderson, I. (2002) *Food and Mouth Disease 2001: Lessons to be Learned Inquiry Report.* London: HM Stationery Office.

Barling, D., Lang, T. and Caraher, M. (2002) 'Joined Up Food Policy? The Trials of Governance, Public Policy and the Food System', *Social Policy and Administration* 36 (6): 556-74.

Berg, A. (1973) *The Nutrition Factor.* Washington, DC: The Brookings Institution.

Berg, A. (1987) 'Nutrition Planning is Alive and Well, Thank You', *Food Policy* 12 (4): 365-75.

Bernstein, H., Crow, B., Mackintosh, M. and Martin, C. (1990) *The Food Question: Profits versus People?* London: Earthscan.

Bickel, G., Nord, M., Price, C., Hamilton, W. and Cook, J. (2000) *Measuring Food Security in the United States: Guide to Measuring Household Food Security.* Washington, DC: United States Department of Agriculture, Food and Nutrition Service, Office of Analysis, Nutrition and Evaluation.

Booth, D. (ed.) (2003) 'Are PRSPs Making a Difference? The African Experience', *Development Policy Review* 21 (2): Theme Issue.

Brown, L. R. and Kane, H. (1994) *Full House: Reassessing the Earth's Population Carrying Capacity.* London: Earthscan and Worldwatch Institute.

Carson, R. (1962) *Silent Spring.* Harmondsworth: Penguin.

Clay, E., Chambers, R., Singer, H., Lipton, M. et al. (1981) *Food Policy Issues in Low-income Countries.* World Bank Staff Working Paper No. 473. Washington, DC: World Bank.

Competition Commission (2001) *A Report on the Supply of Groceries from Multiple Stores in the UK.* Cmd 4842. London; HM Stationery Office.

Conway, G. (1997) *The Doubly Green Revolution: Food for All in the 21ˢᵗ Century.* Harmondsworth: Penguin.

Development Assistance Committee (DAC) (2001) *The DAC Guidelines on Poverty Reduction.* Paris: OECD.

Dolan, C. and Humphrey, J. (2001) 'Governance and Trade in Fresh Vegetables: The Impact of UK Supermarkets on the African Horticultural Industry', *Journal of Development Studies* 37 (2): 147-76.

Dowler, E. (1998) 'Food Poverty and Food Policy', *IDS Bulletin* 29 (1): 58-65.

Dowler, E., Turner, S. and Dobson, B. (2001) *Poverty Bites: Food, Health and Poor Families.* London: Child Poverty Action Group.

Dowler, E. and Jones Finer, C. (eds) (2002) 'Food', *Social Policy and Administration* 36 (6): Special Issue.

Draper, A. and Green, J. (2002) 'Food Safety and Consumers: Constructions of Choice and Risk', *Social Policy and Administration* 36 (6): 610-25.

Drèze, J and Sen, A. (1989) *Hunger and Public Action.* WIDER Studies in Development Economics. Oxford: Clarendon Press.

Eide, B. W. (1996) 'Human Rights Requirements to Social and Economic Development', *Food Policy* 21 (1): 23-39.

Ellis, F. (1993) *Peasant Economics: Farm Households and Agrarian Development.* Wye Studies in Agricultural and Rural Development. Cambridge: Cambridge University Press.

FAO (1996) *Rome Declaration on World Food Security.* Rome: FAO.

FAO (2002a) *Factsheet on Feeding the Cities.* Rome: FAO.

FAO (2002b) *Factsheet on Food Quality and Safety.* Rome: FAO.

Field, J. O. (1987) 'Multi-Sectoral Nutrition Planning: A Post-Mortem', *Food Policy* 12 (1): 15-28.

Gaull, G. E. and Goldberg, R. A. (eds) (1993) *The Emerging Global Food System: Public and Private Sector Issues.* New York: Wiley.

Gereffi, G. and Kaplinsky, R. (eds) (2001) 'The Value of Value Chains: Spreading the Gains from Globalisation', *IDS Bulletin* 32 (3).

Gittinger, J. P., Leslie, J. and Hoisington, C. (eds) (1987) *Food Policy: Integrating Supply, Distribution and Consumption*. EDI Series in Economic Development. Baltimore, MD: Johns Hopkins University Press.

Gordon, D., Adelman, L., Ashworth, K., Bradshaw, J., Levitas, R., Middleton, S., Pantazis, C., Patsios, D., Payne, S., Townsend, P. and Williams, J. (2000) *Poverty and Social Exclusion in Britain*. York: Joseph Rowntree Foundation.

Hewitt de Alcantara, C. (ed.) (1993) *Real Markets: Social and Political Issues of Food Policy Reform*. London: Frank Cass.

Hindle, R. E. (1990) 'The World Bank Approach to Food Security Analysis', *IDS Bulletin* 21 (3): 62-6.

Huddleston, B. (1990) 'FAO's Overall Approach and Methodology for Formulating National Food Security Programmes in Developing Countries', *IDS Bulletin* 21 (3).

Hussein, K. (2002) *Livelihoods Approaches Compared: A Multi-agency Review of Current Practice*. London: Overseas Development Institute.

Irz, X., Lin, L., Thirtle, C. and Wiggins, S. (2001) 'Agricultural Productivity Growth and Poverty Alleviation', *Development Policy Review* 19 (4): 449-66.

Joy, L. (1973) 'Food and Nutrition Planning', *Journal of Agricultural Economics* XXIV, January.

Kielman, A. A. et al. (1977) 'The Narangwal Nutrition Study: A Summary Review', Department of International Health, School of Hygiene and Public Health, Johns Hopkins University, Baltimore, MD (mimeo).

Killick, T. (2002) *Responding to Inequality*. Inequality Briefing No 3. London: Overseas Development Institute, March.

Lappé, F. M. and Collins, J. (1977) *Food First: A New Action Plan to Break the Famine Trap*. London: Abacus.

Leather, S. (1996) *The Making of Modern Malnutrition: An Overview of Food Poverty in the UK*. London: The Caroline Walker Trust.

Levinson, F. J. (1974) *'Morinda': An Economic Analysis of Malnutrition among Young Children in Rural India*. Nutrition Policy Series. Cambridge, MA: Cornell-MIT International.

Lipton, M. with Longhurst, R. (1989) *New Seeds and Poor People*. London: Unwin Hyman.

Maxwell, S. (1988) 'National Food Security Planning: First Thoughts from Sudan'. Paper presented to workshop on Food Security in Sudan, Institute of Development Studies at the University of Sussex.

Maxwell, S. (ed.) (1990) 'Food Security in Developing Countries', *IDS Bulletin* 21 (3): Special Issue.

Maxwell, S. (1991) 'National Food Security Planning: First Thought from Sudan', in S. Maxwell (ed.), *To Cure All Hunger: Food Policy and Food Security in Sudan*. London: Intermediate Technology Publications.

Maxwell, S. (1996) 'Food Security: A Post-Modern Perspective', *Food Policy* 21 (2).

Maxwell, S. (1997) 'Implementing the World Food Summit Plan of Action: Organizational Issues in Multi-sectoral Planning', *Food Policy* 22 (6): 515-31.

Maxwell, S. (1998a) 'Saucy with the Gods: Nutrition and Food Security Speak to Poverty', *Food Policy* 23 (3/4): 215-30.

Maxwell, S. (1998b) 'Comparison, Convergence and Connections: Development Studies in North and South', *IDS Bulletin* 29 (1).

Maxwell, S. (2001a) 'The Evolution of Thinking about Food Security', in S. Devereux and S. Maxwell (eds), *Food Security in Sub-Saharan Africa*. London: ITDG.

Maxwell, S. (2001b) 'Organisational Issue in Food Security Planning', in S. Devereux and S. Maxwell (eds), *Food Security in Sub-Saharan Africa*. London: ITDG.

McKay, A. (2002) *Defining and Measuring Inequality*. Inequality Briefing No 1. London: Overseas Development Institute, March.

Mellor, J. (1976) *The New Economics of Growth*. Ithaca, NY: Cornell University Press.

Millstone, E. and van Zwanenberg, P. (2002) 'The Evolution of Food Safety Policy-making Institutions in the UK, EU and Codex Alimentarius', *Social Policy and Administration* 36 (6): 593-609.

Morrissey, O. (ed.) (2002) 'WTO, Doha and Developing Countries', *Development Policy Review* 20 (1): Policy Symposium.

Naschold. F. (2002) *Why Inequality Matters for Poverty*. Inequality Briefing No 2. London: Overseas Development Institute, March.

Nestle, M. (2002) *Food Politics: How the Food Industry Influences Nutrition and Health*. Berkeley, CA: University of California Press.

Norwegian Ministry of Foreign Affairs (1993) *Evaluation of Development Assistance: Handbook for Evaluators and Managers*. Oslo: Royal Ministry of Foreign Affairs.

ODI (2001) *Economic Theory, Freedom and Human Rights: The Work of Amartya Sen*. ODI Briefing Paper. London: Overseas Development Institute, November.

ODI (2002) *The 'Water Crisis': Faultlines in Global Debates*. ODI Briefing Paper. London: Overseas Development Institute, July.

Oshaug, A. (1985) 'The Composite Concept of Food Security', in W. B. Edie et al. (eds), 'Introducing Nutritional Considerations into Rural Development Programmes with Focus on Agriculture: A Theoretical Contribution', *Development of Methodology for the Evaluation of Nutritional Impact of Development Programmes Report* 1, Institute of Nutrition Research, University of Oslo.

Page, S. (2003) *Developing Countries: Victims or Participants? Their Changing Roles in International Negotiations*. Globalisation and Poverty Programme. London: Overseas Development Institute.

Pretty, J. and Hine, R. (2000) *Feeding the World with Sustainable Agriculture: A Summary of New Evidence*. Final Report from the 'SAFE-World' Research Project, University of Essex.

Radimer, K. L., Olson, C. M., Green, J. C., Campbell, C. C. and Habicht, J. P. (1992) 'Understanding Hunger and Developing Indicators to Assess it in Women and Children', *Journal of Nutrition Education* 24 (1): 36S-46S.

Reardon, T. and Berdegué, J. A. (2002) 'The Rapid Rise of Supermarkets in Latin America: Challenges and Opportunities for Development', *Development Policy Review* 20 (4): 371-88.

Reardon, T., Berdegué, J. A. and Farrington, J. (2002) *Supermarkets and Farming in Latin America: Pointing Directions for Elsewhere?* Natural Resource Perspectives No. 81. London: Overseas Development Institute.

Reardon, T., Timmer, P. and Berdegué, J. A. (2003) 'The Rise of Supermarkets in Latin America and Asia: Implications for International Markets for Fruits and Vegetables', in A. Regmi and M. Gehlhar (eds), *Global Markets for High Value Food Products*. Agriculture Information Bulletin. Washington, DC: USADA-ERS.

Reutlinger, S. (1985) 'Food Security and Poverty in LDCs', *Finance and Development* 22 (4): 7-11.

Riches, G. (ed.) (1997) *First World Hunger: Food Security and Welfare Politics*. Basingstoke: Macmillan.

Schlosser, E. (2001) *Fast Food Nation: The Dark Side of the All-American Meal*. Boston, MA: Houghton Mifflin.

Sen, A. K. (1981) *Poverty and Famines: An Essay on Entitlement and Deprivation*. Oxford: Clarendon Press.

Tansey, G. and Worsley, T. (1995) *The Food System: A Guide*. London: Earthscan.

Timmer, C. P., Falcon, W. P. and Pearson, S. R. (1981) *Food Policy Analysis*. Baltimore, MD: Johns Hopkins University Press.

Tomlins, K. I., Johnson, P. N. T. and Myhara, B. (2001) 'Improving Street Food Vending in Accra: Problems and Prospects', in T. Sibanda and P. Hindmarsh (eds), *Food Safety in Crop Post-Harvest Systems*. Proceedings of an international workshop sponsored by the Crop Post-Harvest Programme of the UK Department for International Development, Harare, Zimbabwe, 20-1 September.

Townsend, P. (1979) *Poverty in the United Kingdom: A Survey of Household Resources and Standards of Living*. London: Penguin Books and Allen Lane.

Tudge, C. (1977) *The Famine Business*. Harmondsworth: Penguin.

UNDP (2003) *Human Development Report 2003: Millennium Development Goals: A Compact among Nations to End Human Poverty*. Oxford: Oxford University Press.

Weatherspoon, D. and Reardon, T. (2003) 'The Rise of Supermarkets in Africa: Implications for Agrifood Systems and the Rural Poor', *Development Policy Review* 21 (3): 333-55.

WHO-Europe (2000) *World Health Organisation Regional Committee for Europe. Resolution: The Impact of Food and Nutrition on Public Health*. 50th Session, EUR/RC50/R8, World Health Organisation, Copenhagen, 14 September,

World Bank (1986) *Poverty and Hunger: Issues and Options for Food Security in Developing Countries*. World Bank Policy Study. Washington, DC: World Bank.

Chapter 2

Ad-Brands (2003) Available at www.mind-advertising.com/us/index.html

Agrow (2002) 'Gap Narrows between Prospective Agrochemical Market Leaders', *AGROW World Crop Protection News* 397, 29 March, p.1.

Barling, D. and Lang, T. (2003a) 'A Reluctant Food Policy?', *Political Quarterly* 74 (1): 8-18.

Barlow, M. and Clarke, T. (2002) *Blue Gold: The Battle Against Corporate Theft of the World's Water*. Toronto: Stoddart.

Beveridge, W. (1928) *British Food Control*. Oxford: Oxford University Press.

Bickerton, I. (2003) 'New Scandal Hits Embattled Ahold', *Financial Times*, 27 May, p.22.

Brown, S. A. (1997) *Revolution at the Checkout Counter: the Explosion of the Bar Code*. Cambridge, MA: Harvard University Press.

Connor, J. (2003) 'The Changing Structure of Global Food Markets: Dimensions, Effects, and Policy Implications'. Paper presented at OECD Conference on Changing Dimensions of the Food Economy, The Hague, 6-7 February.

Curry, D. (2002) *Report of the Commission of Inquiry into the Future of Farming and Food*. London: Cabinet Office.

Dobson, P. (2003) 'Buyer Power in Food Retailing: the European Experience'. Paper presented at OECD Conference on Changing Dimensions of the Food Economy, The Hague, 6-7 February.

Gabriel, Y. and Lang, T. (1995). *The Unmanageable Consumer*. London: Sage.

Gold, M. (2003) *M-Eatless*. Petersfield, UK: Compassion in World Farming.

Grievink, J.-W. (2003) 'The Changing Face of the Global Food Supply Chain'. Paper presented at OECD Conference on Changing Dimensions of the Food Economy, The Hague, 6-7 February.

Hammond, R. J. (1950) *Food*. London: HMSO and Longmans.

Hendrickson, M., Heffernan, W. D., Howard, P. H. and Heffernan, J. B. (2001) *Consolidation in Food Retailing and Dairy: Implications for Farmers and Consumers in a Global System. Report to National Farmers Union (USA)*. Columbia, MO: Department of Rural Sociology, University of Missouri.

IGD (2001) *European Grocery Retailing: Now and in the Future*. Letchmore Heath: Institute of Grocery Distribution.

Kenkel, D. S. and Manning, W. (1999) 'Economic Evaluation of Nutrition Policy Or There's No Such Thing As a Free Lunch', *Food Policy* 24: 148.

Kinsey, J. (2003) 'Emerging Trends in the New Food Economy: Consumers, Firms and Science'. Paper presented at OECD Conference on Changing Dimensions of the Food Economy, The Hague, 6-7 February.

Lang, T. (1996) 'Going Public: Food Campaigns during the 1980s and 1990s', in David Smith (ed.), *Nutrition Scientists and Nutrition Policy in the 20th Century*. London: Routledge.

Lang, T. and Clutterbuck, C. (1991) *P is for Pesticides*. London: Ebury.

Le Gros Clark, F. and Titmus, R. M. (1939) *Our Food Problem and its Relation to Our National Defences*. Harmondsworth: Penguin.

Lobstein, T., Millstone, E., Lang, T. and van Zwanenberg, P. (2001) *The Lessons of Phillips: Questions the UK Government Should be Asking in Response to Lord Phillips' Inquiry into BSE*. A Discussion Paper. London: Food Commission/Centre for Food Policy/Science Policy Research Unit, University of Sussex.

Marketing (2002) 'Biggest Brands 2000: Top 50', *Marketing* (available at www.marketing.haynet.com/feature00/bigbrands00/top50.htm).

Marsden, T., Flynn, A. and Harrison, M. (2000) *Consuming Interests*. London: UCL Press.

Pretty, J., Griffin, M., Sellens, M. and Pretty, C. (2003). *Green Exercise: Complementary Roles of Nature, Exercise and Diet in Physical and Emotional Well-Being and Implications for Public Health Policy*. CES Occasional Paper 2003-1. Wivenhoe: University of Essex Centre for Environment and Society.

Santer, J. (1997) 'Speech by Jacques Santer, President of the European Commission at the Debate in the European Parliament on the report into BSE by the Committee of Enquiry of the European Parliament'. 18 February. Speech 97/39.

UNEP (2001) 'Climate Change: Billions Across The Tropics Face Hunger And Starvation As Big Drop In Crop Yields Forecast Soaring Temperatures Force Coffee and Tea Farmers to Abandon Traditional Plantations'. News Release 01/107, 8 November (available at www.unep.org/documents/default.asp? DocumentID=225&ArticleID=2952).

UNEP (2002) *Global Environment Outlook*. London: Earthscan and New York: United Nations Environment Programme.

Wanless, D. (2002) *Securing Our Future Health: Taking a Long-Term View. Final Report*. London: HM Treasury, April.

WHO (2003) *World Cancer Report*. Geneva: World Health Organization and International Agency for Research on Cancer.

WHO/FAO (2003) *Diet, Nutrition and the Prevention of Chronic Diseases*. Report of a consultation. Technical Series Report 916. Rome: Food and Agriculture Organization and Geneva: World Health Organization, 23 April.

Chapter 3

Abrams, F. (2002) *Below the Breadline: Living on the Minimum Wage*. London: Profile Books.

Acheson, D. (1998) *Independent Inquiry into Inequalities in Health Report*. London: HM Stationery Office.

Andrews, M., Nord, M., Bickel, G. and Carlson, S. (2000) *Household Food Security in the United States, 1999*. Food Assistance and Nutrition Research Report No. 8. (available at www.ers.usda.gov/publications/fanrr8/, accessed February 2002).

Barker, D. J. P. and Leon, D (1997) 'Prenatal Influences on Disease in Later Life', in Shetty and McPherson.

BBC (2003) news.bbc.co.uk/1/hi/health/2994275.stm (accessed 7 May 2003).

Beardsworth, A. and Keil, T. (1997) *Sociology on the Menu: An Invitation to the Study of Food and Society*. London: Routledge.

Berhman, J. (1988) *Nutrition and Incomes: Tightly Wedded or Loosely Meshed?* PEW/Cornell Lecture Series, Cornell Food and Nutrition Policy Program. Ithaca, NY: Cornell University Press.

Blair, A. (2003) *Developing a New Deal for Healthier Food in Greets Green*. Report for the Greets Green Partnership. West Bromwich: New Deal for Communities.

Brunner, E., Cohen, D. and Toon, L. (2001) 'Cost Effectiveness of Cardiovascular Disease Prevention Strategies: A Perspective on EU Food Based Dietary Guidelines', *Public Health Nutrition* 4 (2B): 711-15.

Callan, T., Nolan, B. and Whelan, C. T. (1993) 'Resources, Deprivation and the Measurement of Poverty', *Journal of Social Policy* 22 (2): 141-72.

Clarke, G., Eyre, H., and Guy, C. (2002) 'Deriving Indicators of Access to Food Retail Provision in British Cities: Studies of Cardiff, Leeds and Bradford', *Urban Studies* 39 (11): 2041-60.

Consumers' Association (1997) *The Food Divide: Eating on a Low Income*. Policy Paper. London: Consumers' Association, October.

Dallison, J. (1996) 'RDAs and DRVs: Scientific Constants or Social Constructs? The Case of Vitamin C'. PhD Thesis, University of Sussex (mimeo).

Davey Smith, G. and Brunner, E. (1997) 'Socio-economic Differentials in Health: The Role of Nutrition', *Proceedings of the Nutrition Society* 56: 75-90.

Department of Health (1999a) *Saving Lives: Our Healthier Nation*. Cm No. 4386. London: HM Stationery Office.

Department of Health (1999b) *Improving Shopping Access*. Policy Action Team 13. London: Department of Health (available from www.cabinet-office.gov.uk/seu/).

Department of Health (2000) *The NHS Plan*. Cmd No. 4818. London: HM Stationery Office.

Dibsdall, L. A., Lambert, N., Bobbin, R. F. and Frewer, L. J. (2003) 'Low-income Consumers' Attitudes and Behaviour Towards Access, Availability and Motivation to Eat Fruit and Vegetables', *Public Health Nutrition* 6 (2): 159-69.

Dobson, B., Beardsworth, A., Keil, T. and Walker, R. (1994) *Diet, Choice and Poverty: Social, Cultural and Nutritional Aspects of Food Consumption among Low Income Families*. London: Family Policy Studies Centre with the Joseph Rowntree Foundation.

Dowler, E. (2002) 'Food and Poverty in Britain: Rights and Responsibilities', *Social Policy and Administration* 36 (6): 698-717.

Dowler, Elizabeth and Calvert, Claire (1995) *Nutrition and Diet in Lone-Parent Families in London*. London: Family Policy Studies Centre with the Joseph Rowntree Foundation.

Dowler, E. and Caraher, M. (2003) 'Local Food Projects – The New Philanthropy?', *Political Quarterly* 74 (1): 57-65.

Dowler, E. and Dobson, B. (1997) 'Nutrition and Poverty in Europe: An Overview', *Proceedings of the Nutrition Society* 56 (1A): 51-62.

Dowler, E. and Leather, S. (2000) '"Spare Some Change for a Bite to Eat?" From Primary Poverty to Social Exclusion: The Role of Nutrition and Food', in J. Bradshaw and R. Sainsbury (eds), *Experiencing Poverty*. Aldershot: Ashgate.

Dowler, E., Turner, S. with Dobson, B. (2001a) *Poverty Bites: Food, Health and Poor Families*. London: Child Poverty Action Group.

Dowler, E., Blair, A., Rex, D. Donkin, A. and Grundy, C. (2001b) 'Mapping Access to Healthy Food in Sandwell'. Report to the Health Action Zone (available as pdf file from elizabeth.dowler@warwick.ac.uk).

FAO/WHO (2003) *Diet, Nutrition and the Prevention of Chronic Diseases*. Report of a Joint FAO/WHO Expert Consultation. WHO Technical Report Series 916. Geneva: World Health Organization.

Gepkens, A. and Gunning-Schepers, L. J. (1996) 'Interventions to Reduce Socio-economic Health Differences', *European Journal of Public Health* 6: 218-26.

Gordon, D. and Townsend, P. (eds) (2002) *Breadline Europe: The Measurement of Poverty.* Bristol: Policy Press.

Gordon, D., Adelman, L., Ashworth, K., Bradshaw, J., Levitas, R., Middleton, S., Pantazis, C., Patsios, D., Payne, S., Townsend, P. and Williams, J. (2000) *Poverty and Social Exclusion in Britain.* York: Joseph Rowntree Foundation.

Graham, H. (ed.) (2001) *Understanding Health Inequalties.* Buckingham: Open University Press.

Gundgaard, J., Nielsen, J. N., Olsen J. and Sørensen J. (2003) 'Increased Intake of Fruit and Vegetables: Estimation of Impact in Terms of Life Expectancy and Healthcare Costs', *Public Health Nutrition* 6 (1): 25-30.

Hawkes, C. and Webster, J. (2000) *Too Much and Too Little? Debates on Surplus food Redistribution.* London: Sustain.

Illsley, R. and Svensson, P.-G. (eds) (1990) 'Health Inequities in Europe, *Social Science and Medicine* 31 (3), Special Issue.

James, W. P. T., Nelson, M., Ralph, A. and Leather, S. (1997) 'The Contribution of Nutrition to Inequalities in Health', *British Medical Journal* 314: 1545-9.

Kunst, A. E., Groenhof, F., Machenbach, J. P. and EU Working Group on Socio-economic Inequalities in Health (1998) 'Mortality by Occupational Class Among Men 30-64 Years in 11 European Countries', *Social Science and Medicine* 46: 1459-76.

Lang, T. (1999) 'The Complexities of Globalization: The UK as a Case Study of Tensions within the Food System and the Challenge to Food Policy', *Agriculture and Human Values* 16: 169-85.

Lang, T., Barling, D., and Caraher, M. (2001) 'Food, Social Policy and the Environment: Towards a New Model', *Social Policy and Administration* 35 (5): 538-58.

Leon, D. and Walt, G. (eds) (2001) *Poverty, Inequality and Health: An International Perspective.* Oxford: Oxford University Press.

Mack, J. and Lansley, S. (1985) *Poor Britain.* London: George Allen and Unwin.

Marmot, M. and Wilkinson, R. G. (eds) (1999) *Social Determinants of Health.* Oxford: Oxford University Press.

Marsh, A. and McKay, S. (1994) *Poor Smokers.* London: Policy Studies Institute.

McMichael, P. (2001) 'The Impact of Globalisation, Free Trade and Technology on Food and Nutrition in the New Millennium', *Proceedings of the Nutrition Society* 60: 215-20.

Middleton, S. (2000) 'Agreeing Poverty Lines: The Development of Consensual Budget Standards Methodology', in J. Bradshaw and R. Sainsbury (eds), *Researching Poverty.* Aldershot: Ashgate.

Morris, J., Donkin, A., Wonderling, D., Wilkinson, P. and Dowler, E. (2000) 'A Minimum Income for Healthy Living', *Journal of Epidemiology and Community Health* 54: 885-9.

Mudur, G. (2003) 'Asia Grapples with Obesity Epidemic', *British Medical Journal* 325: 515.

Nicol, A. and Slaymaker, T. (2003) *Secure Water? Poverty, Livelihoods and Demand-Responsive Approaches.* ODI Water Policy Brief No. 4. London: Overseas Development Institute.

Office of National Statistics (2001) *Family Spending: A Report on the 1999-2001 Family Expenditure Survey.* London: HM Stationery Office.

Parker, H. with Nelson, M., Oldfield, N., Dallison, J., Hutton, S., Paterakis, S., Sutherland, H. and Thirlwart, M. (1998) *Low Cost but Acceptable: A Minimum Income Standard for the UK.* Bristol: Policy Press and Zacchaeus Trust for the Family Budget Unit.

Piachaud, D. and Webb, J. (1996) *The Price of Food: Missing Out on Mass Consumption.* London: STICERD, London School of Economics.

Power, C., Bartley, M., Davey Smith, G. and Blane, D. (1996) 'Transmission of Social and Biological Risk Across the Lifecourse', in D. Blane, E. Brunner and R. Wilkinson (eds), *Health and Social Organization.* London: Routledge.

Radimer, K. L., Olsen, C. M. and Campbell, C. C. (1990) 'Development of Indicators to Assess Hunger', *Journal of Nutrition* 120: 1544-8.

Riches, G. (1997) 'Hunger, Food Security and Welfare Policies: Issues and Debates in First World Societies', *Proceedings of the Nutrition Society* 56 (1a): 63-74.

Riches, G. (2002) 'Food Banks and Food Security: Welfare Reform, Human Rights and Social Policy. Lessons from Canada?', *Social Policy and Administration* 36 (6): 648-63.

Shetty, P. S. and McPherson, K. (eds) (1997) *Diet, Nutrition and Chronic Disease: Lessons from Contrasting Worlds*. Chichester: J. Wiley and Sons.

Social Exclusion Unit (1998) *Bringing Britain Together: A National Strategy for Neighbourhood Renewal*. London: HM Stationery Office.

Speak, S. and Graham, S. (2000) *Service Not Included: Social Implications of Private Sector Service Restructuring in Marginalised Neighbourhoods*. Bristol: The Policy Press for the Joseph Rowntree Foundation.

Steptoe, A., Perkins-Porras, L., McKay, C., Rink, E., Hilton, S. and Cappuccio, F. (2003) 'Behavioural Counselling to Increase Consumption of Fruit and Vegetables in Low Income Adults: A Randomised Trial', *British Medical Journal* 326: 855-60.

Sustain (2001) *TV Dinners: What's Being Served Up by the Advertisers?* London: Sustain.

Tansey, G. and Worsley, T. (1995) *The Food System: A Guide*. London: Earthscan.

Toynbee, P. (2003) *Hard Work: Life in Low-pay Britain*. London: Bloomsbury.

Travers, K. D. (1995) '"Do You Teach Them How to Budget?": Professional Discourse in the Construction of Nutritional Inequalities', in D. Maurer and J. Sobal (eds), *Eating Agendas: Food and Nutrition as Social Problems*. New York: Aldine de Gruyter.

Veit-Wilson, J. (1994) 'Condemned to Deprivation? Beveridge's Responsibility for the Invisibility of Poverty', in J. Hills, J. Ditch and H. Glennester (eds), *Beveridge and Social Security: An International Perspective/*. Oxford: Clarendon Press.

Wadsworth, M. (1999) 'Early Life', in Marmot and Wilkinson.

Wanless, D. (2002) *Securing our Future Health: Taking a Long-term View*. London: HM Treasury.

Whelan, A., Wrigley, N., Warm, D. and Cannings, E. (2002) 'Life in a "Food Desert"', *Urban Studies* 39 (11): 2083-100.

World Bank (2000) *World Development Report 2000/2001: Attacking Poverty*. New York: Oxford University Press for the World Bank.

World Health Organization (2000) *The Impact of Food and Nutrition on Public Health. Case for a Food and Nutrition Policy and Action Plan for the WHO European Region 2000-2005*. Food and Nutrition Policy Unit. Copenhagen: WHO Regional Office for Europe.

WHO (2002) *The World Health Report 2002 – Reducing Risks, Promoting Healthy Life*. Geneva: WHO.

Wrigley, N., Guy, C. and Lowe, M. (2002) 'Urban Regeneration, Social Inclusion and Large Store Development: The Seacroft Development in Context', *Urban Studies* 39 (11): 2101-14.

Chapter 4

Bell, A. C., Ge, K. and Popkin, B. M. (2002) 'The Road to Obesity or the Path to Prevention? Motorized Transportation and Obesity in China', *Obesity Research* 10: 277-83.

Bisgrove, E. and Popkin, B. M. (1996) 'Does Women's Work Improve Their Nutrition? Evidence from the Urban Philippines', *Social Science and Medicine* 43: 1475-88.

Bray, G. A. and Popkin, B. M. (1998) 'Dietary Fat Intake Does Affect Obesity', *American Journal of Clinical Nutrition* 68 (6): 1157-73.

Coitinho, D., Monteiro, C. A. and Popkin, B. M. (2002) 'What Brazil is Doing to Promote Healthy Diets and Active Life-Styles', *Public Health Nutrition* 5 (1A): 263-7.

Crimmins, E. M., Saito, Y. and Ingegneri, D. (1989) 'Changes in Life Expectancy and Disability-free Life Expectancy in the United States', *Population and Development Review* 15: 235-67.

Darmon, N., Ferguson, E. L. and Briend, A. (2002) 'A Cost Constraint Alone has Adverse Effects on Food Selection and Nutrient Density: An Analysis of Human Diets by Linear Programming', *Journal of Nutrition* 132: 3764-71.

Delgado, C. L. (forthcoming) 'A Food Revolution: Rising Consumption of Meat and Milk in Developing Countries, *Journal of Nutrition*.

Delgado, C., Rosegrant, M. and Meijer, S. (2001) 'Livestock to 2020: The Revolution Continues'. Paper presented at the annual meetings of the International Agricultural Trade Research Consortium (IATRC), Auckland, New Zealand, 18-19 January. Available at www.iatrcweb.org/publications/proceedings.

Delgado, C., Rosegrant, M., Steinfeld, H., Ehui, S. and Courbois, C. (1999) *Livestock to 2020: The Next Food Revolution*. Food, Agriculture, and the Environment Discussion Paper 28. Washington, DC: International Food Policy Research Institute.

Drewnowski, A. (1987) 'Sweetness and Obesity', in J. Dobbing (ed.), *Sweetness*. London: Springer-Verlag.

Drewnowski, A. (1989) 'Sensory Preferences for Fat and Sugar in Adolescence and in Adult Life', in C. Murphy, W. S. Cain and D. M Hegsted (eds), *Nutrition and the Chemical Senses in Aging*. Annals of the New York Academy of Sciences 561. New York: New York Academy of Sciences.

Drewnoswski, A. and Popkin, B. M. (1997) 'The Nutrition Transition: New Trends in the Global Diet', *Nutrition Reviews* 55: 31-43.

Du, S., Lu, B., Zhai, F. and Popkin, B. M. (2002) 'The Nutrition Transition in China: A New Stage of the Chinese Diet', in Benjamin Caballero and B.M. Popkin (eds), *The Nutrition Transition: Diet and Disease in the Developing World*. London: Academic Press.

Galloway, J. H. (2000) 'Sugar', in K. F. Kiple and K. C. Ornelas (eds), *The Cambridge World History of Food*. Vol. I. New York: Cambridge University Press.

Guo, X., Popkin, B. M., Mroz, T. A. and Zhai, F. (1999) 'Food Price Policy Can Favorably Alter Macronutrient Intake in China', *Journal of Nutrition* 129: 994-1001.

Guo, X., Mroz, T. A., Popkin, B. M. and Zhai, F. (2000) 'Structural Changes in the Impact of Income on Food Consumption in China, 1989-93', *Economic Development and Cultural Change* 48: 737-60.

Hodge, A. M., Dowse, G. K., Gareeboo, H., Tuomilehto, J., Alberti, K.G. M. M. and Zimmet, P. Z. (1996) 'Incidence, Increasing Prevalence, and Predictors of Change in Obesity and Fat Distribution over 5 years in the Rapidly Developing Population of Mauritius, *International Journal of Obesity* 20: 137-46.

Hodge, A. M., Dowse, G. K., Toelupe, P., Collins, V. R. and Zimmet, P. Z. (1997) 'The Association of Modernization with Dyslipidaemia and Changes in Lipid Levels in the Polynesian Population of Western Samoa', *International Journal of Epidemiology* 26: 297-306.

Horton, S. (1999) 'Opportunities for Investments in Nutrition in Low-income Asia', *Asian Development Review* 17: 246.

Jin, J. (ed.) (2000) *Feeding China's Little Emperors: Food, Children, and Social Change*. Palo Alto, CA: Stanford University Press.

King, H., Aubert, R. E. and Herman, W. H. (1998) 'Global Burden of Diabetes, 1995-2025: Prevalence, Numerical Estimates, and Projections', *Diabetes Care* 21: 1414-31.

Levitt, N. S., Katzenellenbogen, J. M., Bradshaw, D., Hoffman, M. N. and Bonnici, F. (1993) 'The Prevalence and Identification of Risk Factors for NIDDM in Urban Africans in Cape Town, South Africa', *Diabetes Care* 16: 601-7.

Manton, K. G. and Soldo, B. J. (1985) 'Dynamics of Health Changes in the Oldest Old: New Perspective and Evidence', *Milbank Memorial Fund Quarterly* 63: 206-85.

McGuire, J. and Popkin, B. M. (1989) 'Beating the Zero Sumgame: Women and Nutrition in the Third World', *Food and Nutrition Bulletin* 11 (4): 38-63; Part II 12 (1): 3-11.

Mintz, S. (1977) 'Time, Sugar, and Sweetness', in C. Counihan and P. Van Esterik (eds), *Food and Culture: A Reader*. New York: Routledge.

Monteiro, C. A., Conde, W. L., Lu, B. and Popkin, B. M. (2003) 'Is Obesity Fuelling Inequities in Health in the Developing World?' Chapel Hill, NC: Carolina Population Center (mimeo).

Murray, C. J. L. and Lopez, A. D. (1996) *The Global Burden of Disease*. Cambridge, MA: Harvard University Press.

Nielsen, S. J., Siega-Riz, A. M. and Popkin, B. M. (2002) 'Trends in Energy Intake in the US between 1977 and 1996: Similar Shifts Seen Across Agegroups', *Obesity Research* 10: 370-78.

Olshansky, S. J. and Ault, A. B. (1986) 'The Fourth Stage of the Epidemiologic Transition: The Age of Delayed Degenerative Diseases', *Milbank Memorial Fund Quarterly* 64: 355-91.

Omran, A. R. (1971) 'The Epidemiologic Transition: A Theory of the Epidemiology of Population Change', *Milbank Memorial Fund Quarterly* 49 (4, pt. 1): 509-38.

Panel on Macronutrients, Subcommittees on Upper Reference Levels of Nutrients and Interpretation and Uses of Reference Intakes, and the Standing Committee on the Scientific Evaluation of Dietary Reference Intakes (2002) *Dietary Reference Intakes for Energy, Carbohydrate, Fiber, Fat, Fatty Acids, Cholesterol, Protein, and Amino Acids (Macronutrients)*. Washington, DC: National Academy Press.

Popkin, B. M. (1999) 'Urbanization, Lifestyle Changes and the Nutrition Transition', *World Development* 27: 1905-16.

Popkin, B. M. (2002a) 'An Overview on the Nutrition Transition and Its Health Implications: The Bellagio Meeting', *Public Health Nutrition* 5 (1A): 93-103.

Popkin, B. M. (2002b) 'The Shift in Stages of the Nutrition Transition in the Developing World Differs from Past Experiences!', *Public Health Nutrition* 5 (1A): 205-14.

Popkin, B. M. and Bisgrove, E. (1988) 'Urbanization and Nutrition in Low-Income Countries', *Food and Nutrition Bulletin* 10 (1): 3-23.

Popkin, B. M. and Du, S. (forthcoming) 'Dynamics of the Nutrition Transition and their Implications for the Animal Foods Sector: A Worried Perspective', *Journal of Nutrition*.

Popkin, B. M., Ge, K., Zhai, F., Guo, X., Ma, H. and Zohoori, N. (1993) 'The Nutrition Transition in China: A Cross-sectional Analysis', *European Journal of Clinical Nutrition* 47: 333-46.

Popkin, B. M., Horton, S., Kim, S., Mahal, A. and Shuigao, J. (2001a) 'Trends in Diet, Nutritional Status and Diet-related Noncommunicable Diseases in China and India: The Economic Costs of the Nutrition Transition', *Nutrition Reviews* 59: 379-90.

Popkin, B. M., Horton, S. and Kim, S. (2001b) 'The Nutrition Transition and Prevention of Diet-related Chronic Diseases in Asia and the Pacific', *Food and Nutrition Bulletin* 22 (4): 1-58.

Popkin, B. M. and Nielsen, S. J. (forthcoming) *The Sweetening of the World's Diet*.

Puska, P., Pietinen, P. and Uusitalo, U. (2002) 'Influencing Public Nutrition for Noncommunicable Disease Prevention: From Community Intervention to National Programme: Experiences from Finland', *Public Health Nutrition* 5 (1A): 245-51.

Reardon, T. and Berdegué, J. A. (2002) 'The Rapid Rise of Supermarkets in Latin America: Challenges and Opportunities for Development', *Development Policy Review* 20 (4): 371-88.

Ross, J. and Horton, S. (1998) *Economic Consequences of Iron Deficiency*. Ottawa: The Micronutrient Initiative.

Solomons, N. W. and Gross, R. (1995) 'Urban Nutrition in Developing Countries', *Nutrition Reviews* 53: 90-5.

Tudor-Locke, C., Ainsworth, B. A., Adair, L. S. and Popkin, B. M. (2003) 'Physical Activity in Filipino Youth: The Cebu Longitudinal Health and Nutrition Survey', *International Journal of Obesity* 27: 181-90.

US Department of Agriculture (1997) 'World Agricultural Supply and Demand Estimates (WASDE-315)'. Table: Vegetable oil consumption balance sheets (in million metric tons), FAS Online. Washington, DC: USDA.

Watson, J. L. (ed.) (1997) *Golden Arches East: McDonald's in East Asia*. Palo Alto, CA: Stanford University Press.

WHO/FAO (2002) Expert Consultation on Diet, Nutrition and the Prevention of Chronic Diseases, 28 January-1 February Geneva.

Willett, W. C. (1998) 'Is Dietary Fat a Major Determinant of Body Fat?', *American Journal of Clinical Nutrition* 67(supplement): 556S-562S.

World Bank (1993) *World Development Report: Investing in Health*. Washington, DC: World Bank.

Zhai, F., Fu, D., Du, S.,ge, K., Chen, C. and Popkin, B. M. (2002) 'What is China Doing in Policy-making to Push Back the Negative Aspects of the Nutrition Transition?, *Public Health Nutrition* 5 (1A): 269-73.

Zimmet, P. Z. (1991) 'Kelly West Lecture: Challenges in Diabetes Epidemiology: From West to the Rest', *Diabetes Care* 15: 232-52.

Zimmet, P. Z., McCarty, D. J. and de Courten, M. P. (1997) 'The Global Epidemiology of Non-Insulin-Dependent Diabetes Mellitus and the Metabolic Syndrome', *Journal of Diabetic Complications* 11 (2): 60-8.

Chapter 5

Alderman, H. (1986) *The Effect of Food Price and Income Changes on the Acquisition of Food by Low-income Households*. Washington, DC: International Food Policy Research Institute.

Barker, D. J. (1998) 'In Utero Programming of Chronic Disease', *Clinical Science* 95 (2): 115-28.

Bisgrove, E. Z. and Popkin, B. M. (1996) 'Does Women's Work Improve their Nutrition? Evidence from the Urban Philippines', *Social Sciences and Medicine* 43 (10): 1475-88.

Brownell, K. D. (2002a) 'Public Policy and the Prevention of Obesity', in C. Fairburn and K. D. Brownell (eds), *Eating Disorders and Obesity: A Comprehensive Handbook*, 2nd edn. New York: Guilford.

Brownell, K. D. (2002b) 'The Environment and Obesity', in C. Fairburn and K. D. Brownell (eds), *Eating Disorders and Obesity: A Comprehensive Handbook*, 2nd edn. New York: Guilford.

Buse, K. and Walt, G. (2000a) 'Global Public-private Partnerships: Part 1 – A New Development in Health?', *Bulletin of the World Health Organization* 78 (4): 549-61.

Cogneau, D. and Robilliard, A. (2000) *Growth, Distribution and Poverty in Madagascar: Learning from a Microsimulation Model in a General Equilibrium Framework*. Trade and Macroeconomics Division Discussion Paper No. 61. Washington, DC: International Food Policy Research Institute.

Delgado, C., Rosegrant, M., Steinfeld, H., Ehui, S. and Courbois, C. (1999) *Livestock to 2020. The Next Food Revolution*. Food, Agriculture, and the Environment Discussion Paper No. 28. Washington, DC: International Food Policy Research Institute.

Doak, C. M. (2002) 'Large-scale Interventions and Programmes Addressing Nutrition-related Chronic Diseases and Obesity: Examples from 14 Countries', *Public Health Nutrition* 5 (1A): 275-7.

Fang, C. and Beghin, J. C. (2000) *Urban Demand for Edible Oils and Fats in China: Evidence from Household Survey Data*. Working Paper 00-WP-245. Ames, IA: Iowa State University.

FAOSTAT. www.fao.org.

Garrett, J. and Ruel, M. (2003) *Stunted Child-overweight Mother Pairs: An Emerging Policy Concern?* Food Consumption and Nutrition Division Discussion Paper No. 148. Washington, DC: International Food Policy Research Institute.

Guo, X., Popkin, B. M., Mroz, T. A, and Zhai, F. (1999) 'Food Price Policy Can Favorably Alter Macronutrient Intake in China', *Journal of Nutrition* 129: 994-1001.

Guo, X., Popkin, B. M. and Zhai, F. (2000a) 'Patterns of Change in Food Consumption and Dietary Fat Intake in Chinese Adults, 1989-93', *Food and Nutrition Bulletin* 20 (3): 344-53.

Guo, X., Mroz, T. A., Popkin, B. M. and Zhai, F. (2000b) 'Structural Change in the Impact of Income on Food Consumption in China, 1989-1993', *Economic Development and Cultural Change* 48 (4): 737-60.

Hawkes, C. (2002) 'Marketing Activities of Global Soft Drink and Fast Food Companies in Emerging Markets: A Review', in *Globalization, Diets and Noncommunicable Diseases*. Geneva: World Health Organization.

Huang, K. S. (1996) 'Nutrient Elasticities in a Complete Food Demand System', *American Journal of Agricultural Economics* 78 (February): 21-9.

Huang, J. and Bouis, H. (1996) *Structural Changes in the Demand for Food in Asia*. Food, Agriculture, and the Environment Discussion Paper No. 11. Washington, DC: International Food Policy Research Institute.

Kersh, R. and Morone, J. (2002) 'When the Personal Becomes Political: The Case of Obesity', Syracuse, NY: Syracuse University (mimeo).

Lakdawalla, D. and Philipson, T. J. (2002) *The Growth of Obesity and Technological Change: A Theoretical and Empirical Examination*. Working Paper No. 8946. Cambridge, MA: National Bureau of Economic Research.

Lin, B.-H., Guthrie, J. and Frazão, E. (2000) 'Nutrient Contribution of Food Away From Home', in *Nutrients Away From Home*. Washington, DC: Economic Research Service, US Department of Agriculture.

McCullough, M. L., Feskanich, D., Stampfer, M. J., Giovannucci, E. L., Rimm, E. B., Hu, F. B, Spiegelman, D., Hunter, D. J., Colditz, G. A. and Willett, W. C. (2002) 'Diet Quality and Major Chronic Disease Risk in Men and Women: Moving Toward Improved Dietary Guidance', *American Journal of Clinical Nutrition* 76: 1261-71.

Maxwell, D., Levin, C., Armar-Klemesu, M., Ruel, M., Morris, S. and Ahiadeke, C. (2000) *Urban Livelihoods and Food and Nutrition Security in Greater Accra, Ghana*. Research Report No. 112. Washington, DC: International Food Policy Research Institute in collaboration with the Noguchi Memorial Institute for Medical Research, Ghana, and the World Health Organization.

Nestle, M. (2002) *Food Politics*. Berkeley, CA: University of California Press.

Parsons, T. J., Power, C. and Manor, O. (2002) 'Fetal and Early Life Growth and Body Mass Index from Birth to Early Adulthood in 1958 British Cohort: Longitudinal Study', *British Medical Journal* 18 (1), March.

Philipson, T. J. and Posner, R. A. (1999) *The Long-run Growth in Obesity as a Function of Technological Change*. Working Paper No. 7423. Cambridge, MA: National Bureau of Economic Research.

Pitt, M. and Rosenzweig, M. (1986) 'Agricultural Prices, Food Consumption and the Health and Productivity of Indonesian Farmers', in I. Singh, L. Squire and J. Strauss, *Agricultural Household Models: Extensions, Applications and Policy*. Baltimore, MD: Johns Hopkins University Press for the World Bank.

Popkin, B. M. (1998) 'The Nutrition Transition and its Health Implications in Lower-income Countries', *Public Health Nutrition* 1 (1): 5-21.

Popkin, B. M. (2001) 'Nutrition in Transition: The Changing Global Nutrition Challenge', *Asia Pacific Journal of Clinical Nutrition* 10 (Supplement1): S13-S18.

Popkin, B. M., Horton, S. and Kim, S. (2001) 'The Nutrition Transition and Prevention of Diet-Related Chronic Diseases in Asia and the Pacific', *Nutrition and Development Series* 6: 58. Manila: Asian Development Bank.

Putnam, J. J. and Allshouse, J. E. (1999) 'Food Consumption, Prices, and Expenditures, 1970-97', *Statistical Bulletin* 965, Food and Rural Economics Division, Economic Research Services, US Department of Agriculture.

Ralston, K. (2000) 'How Government Policies and Regulations Can Affect Dietary Choices', in *Government Regulation and Food Choices*. Washington, DC: Economic Research Services, US Department of Agriculture.

Reardon, T. and Berdegué, J. A. (2002) 'The Rapid Rise of Supermarkets in Latin America: Challenges and Opportunities for Development', *Development Policy Review* 20 (4): 371-88.

Reardon, T. C., Timmer, P. Barrett, C. and Berdegué, J. (2003) 'The Rise of Supermarkets in Africa, Asia and Latin America', *American Journal of Agricultural Economics* 85 (5).

Regmi, A. (ed.) (2001) *Changing Structure of Global Food Consumption and Trade*. Agriculture and Trade Reports, WRS-01-1. Washington, DC: Market and Trade Economics Division, Economic Research Service, US Department of Agriculture.

Sims, L. S. (1998) *The Politics of Fat*. Armonk, NY: M. E. Sharpe Inc.

Tinker, I. (1997) *Street Foods: Urban Food and Employment in Developing Countries*. New York: Oxford University Press.

Verbeke, W. and Ward, R. (2001) 'A Fresh Meat Almost Ideal System Incorporating Negative TV Press and Advertising Impact', *Agricultural Economics* 25: 359-74.

Willett, W. and Stampfer, M. (2002) 'Rebuilding the Food Pyramid'. *Scientific American*, 17 December.

World Bank (1999) *Curbing the Epidemic: Governments and the Economics of Tobacco Control*. Washington, DC: World Bank.

WHO/FAO (2002) Expert Consultation on Diet, Nutrition and the Prevention of Chronic Diseases, 28 January-1 February, Geneva.

Chapter 6

Cadilhon, J.-J., Fearne, A., Hughes, D. and Moustier, P. (2003) *Wholesale Markets and Food Distribution in Europe: New Strategies for Old Functions*. Discussion Paper No. 2. London: Centre for Food Chain Research, Department of Agricultural Sciences, Imperial College, University of London.

Dolan, C. and Humphrey, J. (2001) 'Governance and Trade in Fresh Vegetables: The Impact of UK Supermarkets on the African Horticultural Industry', *Journal of Development Studies* 37 (2): 147-76.

Eurostat, Comext database.

Garcia, M. and Poole, N. (2002) 'The Impact of Private Safety and Quality Standards for Fresh Produce Exports from Mediterranean Countries'. London: Food Industry Management Unit, Department of Agricultural Sciences, Imperial College, University of London (mimeo).

Gereffi, G. (1994) 'The Organisation of Buyer-driven Global Commodity Chains: How US Retailers Shape Overseas Production Networks', in G. Gereffi and M. Korzeniewicz (eds), *Commodity Chains and Global Capitalism*. Westport, CT: Praeger.

Jaffee, S. (forthcoming) *From Challenge to Opportunity: The Transformation of the Kenyan Fresh Vegetable Trade in the Context of Emerging Food Safety and Other Standards*. Agricultural and Rural Development Working Paper. Washington, DC: World Bank.

Jensen, B. N. (2002) 'Standarder og markedskrav: implikationer for markedstruktur og markedsadgang, eksemplificeret ved Tanzanias eksport af groentsager til EU markedet'.

Master's thesis. Departments of Geography and International Development Studies, Roskilde University Centre.

Jensen, M. F. (2000) 'Standards and Smallholders: A Case Study from Kenyan Export Horticulture'. Department of Economics, Royal Danish Agricultural University (mimeo).

McCorriston, S. (2000) 'Market Structure Issues and the Evaluation of the EU Banana Regime', *The World Economy* 23 (7): 923-38.

Mather, C. and Greenberg, S. (2003) 'Market Liberalisation in Post-apartheid South Africa: The Restructuring of Citrus Exports after Deregulation', *Journal of Southern African Studies* 29 (2): 391-410.

mm.eurodata on www.eurodata.com

Rabobank (2001) *Fruit Traders in Trouble*. Industry Note 002-2001. Utrecht.

Reardon, T. and Berdegué, J. A. (2002) 'The Rapid Rise of Supermarkets in Latin America: Challenges and Opportunities for Development', *Development Policy Review* 20 (4): 371-88.

UK Competition Commission (2000) *Supermarkets: A Report on the Supply of Groceries from Multiple Stores in the United Kingdom*. London: Department of Trade and Industry.

Weatherspoon, D. and Reardon, T. (2003) 'The Role of Supermarkets in Africa: Implications for Agrifood Systems and the Rural Poor', *Development Policy Review* 21 (3): 333-55.

WTO (1997) *Report of the Panel on the EU Banana Regime Complaint*. Geneva: WTO.

Chapter 7

Alvarado, I. and Charmel, K. (2002) 'The Rapid Rise of Supermakets in Costa Rica: Impact on Horticultural Markets', *Development Policy Review* 20 (4): 473-85.

Andhra Pradesh Coalition in Defence of Diversity (2002) *Contract Farming: Burden on the Exchequer*. Dr Chowdry, Dr Prasada Rao, Dr Venkat and Dr Uma Shankari. Hyderabad: Deccan Development Society, July.

AP Department of Horticulture (nd) *Horticulture Statistics in Horticulture: Andhra Pradesh Action Plan, 2003-4*. (Available at www.aphorticulture.com/action_ index.html, accessed 21 May 2003.)

Department of Agriculture and Co-operation, Ministry of Agriculture, Government of India. Horticulture (nd) *Heralding a Golden Revolution*. (Available at www.agricoop.nic.in/hort/hortrevo2.htm, accessed 2 May 2003).

Dolan, C. and Humphrey, J. (2000) 'Governance and the Trade in Fresh Vegetables: The Impact of UK Supermarkets on the African Horticulture Industry', *Journal of Development Studies* 37 (2): 147-76.

Faiguenbaum, S., Berdegué, J. A. and Reardon, T. (2002) 'The Rapid Rise of Supermarkets in Chile: Effects on Dairy, Vegetable and Beef Chains', *Development Policy Review* 20 (4): 459-71.

FAO (1993) *Compendium of Food Consumption Statistics from Household Surveys in Developing Countries: Vol. 1, Asia*. Rome: FAO Statistics Division.

Gaull, G. and Goldberg, R. (1993) *The Emerging Global Food System: Public and Private Section Issues*. New York: Wiley.

Ghezan. G., Mateos, M. and Viteri, L. (2002) 'Impact of Supermarkets and Fast Food Chains on Horticulture Supply Chains in Argentina', *Development Policy Review* 20 (4): 389-408.

Government of Andhra Pradesh (1999) *Andhra Pradesh: Vision 2020*. (Available at www.aponline.gov.in/quick%20links/vision2020/o1.pdf, accessed 7 February 2003.)

Jaffee, S. and Morton, J. (eds) (1995) *Marketing Africa's High-Value Foods: Comparative Experiences of an Emergent Private Sector*. Washington, DC: World Bank.

Joshi, P. K., Gulati, A., Birthal, P. S and Tewari, L. (2002) 'Agricultural Diversification in South Asia and India'. Paper presented at the RGoB, MoA-NCAP-IFPRI Workshop on Agricultural Diversification in South Asia, Bhutan, 21-3 November.

Nair, G. K. (1999) 'Farmers Benefit from Kerala Horticulture Scheme', *Business Line*, 28 December.

NCAER (2001) *Projections on the Structure of the Indian Market*. New Delhi: National Council of Applied Economic Research.

Pricewaterhouse Coopers (2002) *Retail and Consumer from New Delhi to New Zealand*. London: Pricewaterhouse Coopers, October.

Rao, V. S. (2001) Statement by Minister of Agriculture (V. S. Rao) at a workshop on Post-harvest Handling and Technologies for Fresh Market Agricultural Produce, organised by the State Horticulture Department and BHC Agro (India) Pvt Limited. Reported in *The Hindu*, 1 August.

Rao, K. P. C., Lavanya, T. and Lakshminarayana, P. (n.d.) *An Evaluation Study of the Kuppam Agricultural Project*. Hyderabad: WTO Support Cell, Government of Andhra Pradesh.

Singh, G. and Haque, T (c.1997) *Potential of Agricultural Diversification Towards High Value Crops*. New Delhi: National Centre for Agricultural Economics and Policy.

Subrahmanyam, K. V. (1981) *Economics of Production and Marketing of Important Fruits and Vegetables in Karnataka, Andhra Pradesh and Tamil Nadu*. Final Report. Bangalore, UNDP Project, IIHR.

Suryanarayana, M. H. (2000) 'How Real is the Secular Decline in Rural Poverty?', *Economic and Political Weekly*, June 17, pp. 2129-40.

World Bank (1997) *India, Second National Dairy Project*. Implementation Completion Report 16218. Washington, DC: Rural Development and Agriculture Sector, Animal Resources Thematic Team, World Bank.

Chapter 8

Agriculture and Industry Survey (2000) 'Kerala Horticulture Development Programme: New Way to Help Farmers', November, pp. 23-34.

Bonaglia, Federico and Fukasaku, Kiichiro (2002) *Trading Competitively: Trade Capacity Building in Sub-Saharan Africa*. Paris: OECD.

Cafedirect (2002) *Cafedirect Company History* (available at www.cafedirect.co.uk/about/company.php).

Dearden, Peter, Greenhalgh, Peter and Havis, Eu (2002) 'Horticulture Exports from Ethiopia and EU Supermarket Sourcing: Report of a Scoping Study'. Report for DFID.

Dolan, Catherine and Humphrey, John (2000) 'Governance and Trade in Fresh Vegetables: The Impact of UK Supermarkets on the African Horticulture Industry', *Journal of Development Studies* 37(2): 147-76.

Dolan, Catherine and Humphrey, John (2001) 'Changing Governance Patterns in the Trade of Fresh Vegetables between Africa and the United Kingdom' (available at www.gapresearch.org/production/IFAMSubmission.pdf).

Humphrey, John, Lecler, Yveline and Salerno, Mario (eds) (2000) *Global Strategies, Local Realities: The Auto Industry in Emerging Markets*. Basingstoke: Macmillan.

IFAD (2002) *Report and Recommendation of the President* for the Rural Microenterprise Support Programme in Latin America and the Caribbean (PROMER) – Phase II. Executive Board – Seventy-Fifth Session, Rome, 22-3 April.

IFAT Africa (2002) 'Conference Report'. Africa Regional Conference, 28 April-4 May, Aburi, Ghana.

Jones, Richard, Freeman, H. Ade, and Lo Monaco, Gabriele (2002) *Improving the Access of Small Farmers in Eastern and Southern Africa to Global Pigeonpea Markets*. ODI Briefing Paper (AGREN) No. 120. London: Overseas Development Institute.

Keesing, Donald B. and Singer, Andrew (1990) *How Support Services Can Expand Manufactured Exports*. World Bank Policy, Research and External Affairs Working Papers No. WPS544. Washington, DC: World Bank.

Malins, Annabelle and Nelson, Valerie (2003) 'How Fair is Ethical Trade? A Look at Uganda's Organic Cotton Sector', ID21 website (available at www.id21.org/zinter/ id21zinter.exe?a=2&i=s7bam2g1&u=3e6f4c46).

Page, Sheila (1994) *Review of ODA/DECTA Core Services Grant*. Contract Reference: CNTR 93 1916A. London: Overseas Development Institute.

Page, Sheila (1998) 'South-North Investment by Developing Countries in the EC: A Sign of the Emergence of New Investors', in Bert G. Hickman and Lawrence Klein (eds), *LINK 1991-1992 Proceedings. Selected Papers from Meetings in Moscow, 1991 and Ankara, 1992*. London: World Scientific.

Page, Sheila (2003) 'Towards a Global Programme on Market Access: Opportunities and Options'. Report prepared for IFAD.

PROMER (2002) 'Qué es PROMER?' (available at www.promer.cl/ que_es_promer.html).

Quijandría, Benjamín, Monares, Aníbal and Ugarte de Peña Montenegro, Raquel (2001) *Assessment of Rural Poverty, Latin America and the Caribbean*. Santiago, Chile: IFAD.

Ramírez Farías, Leonel (2001) *Globalisation and Livelihood Diversification through non-Traditional Agricultural Products: the Mexico Case*. ODI Briefing Paper No. 67. London: Overseas Development Institute.

Ronchi, Lorraine (2002) *Monitoring Impact of Fairtrade Initiativies: A Case Study of Kuapa Kokoo and the Day Chocolate Company*. London: Twin, November.

Tripp, Robert (2001) 'Agricultural Technology Policies for Rural Development,' *Development Policy Review* 19 (4): 479-89.

Wadsworth, Jonathan (2002) 'Private Sector-Led Diversification among Indigenous Producers in Guatemala', London: DFID (mimeo).

World Trade Organization/OECD (1997) 'Note by OECD', *Survey of DAC Members' Co-operation for Capacity Development in Trade*. WT/LDC/HL/18, 21 October.

Zoomers, Annelies (1999) *Linking Livelihood Strategies to Development: Experiences from the Bolivian Andes*. Amsterdam: Royal Tropical Institute Center for Latin American Research and Documentation.

Chapter 9

Agriculture and Environment Biotechnology Commission (2001) *Crops on Trial*. London: AEBC (available at www.aebc.gov.uk/aebc/crops.pdf).

Commonwealth Science Council (forthcoming) *Review of Activities 2000-2003*. London: Commonwealth Science Council.

European Chemical Industry Council, Trans-Atlantic Business Dialogue. Brussels: European Chemical Industry Council (available at www.cefic.org).

European Commission (1999a) *Outcome of Discussions – Report on Public Health Aspects of the Use of Bovine Somatotrophin*. Scientific Committee on Veterinary Measures relating to Public Health, 15-16 March. Brussels: European Commission.

European Commission (1999b) *Report on Animal Welfare Aspects of the Use of Bovine Somatotrophin*. Scientific Committee on Animal Health and Animal Welfare, 10 March. Brussels: European Commission.

FSA (2002) *Annual Report and Accounts 2001-2002*. London: FSA (available at www.food.gov.uk/aboutus/publications/busreps).

Gaugitsch, H (ed.) (2002) *Evaluating Substantial Equivalence: A Step Towards Improving the Risk/Safety Evaluation of GMOs*. Vienna: UBA Austria.

Gupta, A. (2002) 'Advance Informed Agreement: A Shared Basis for Governing Trade in Genetically Modified Organisms?', *Indiana Journal of Global Legal Studies* 9 (2): 265-81.

Hilderbrand, M. E. and Grindle, M. S. (1994) *Building Sustainable Capacity: Challenges for the Public Sector*. Cambridge, MA: Harvard Institute for International Development.

Keeley, J. (forthcoming) *Regulating Biotechnology in China: The Politics of Biosafety*. Biotechnology Policy Series, Working Paper No. 7. Brighton: Institute of Development Studies at the University of Sussex.

Levidow, L. and Murphy, J. (2002) 'The Decline of Substantial Equivalence: How Civil Society Demoted a Risky Concept'. Paper for Conference on Science and Citizenship in a Global Context: Challenges from New Technologies, at the Institute of Development Studies, University of Sussex, 12-13 December (available at www.ids.ac.uk/ids/env/biotechpaperrev1Peter1.pdf).

Millstone, E. (2000) 'Analysing Biotechnology's Traumas', *New Genetics and Society* 19 (2): 117-32.

OECD (2000) *GM Food Safety: Facts, Uncertainties, and Assessment: Chairman's Report*. OECD Edinburgh Conference on the Scientific and Health Aspects of Genetically Modified Foods, 28 February-1 March (available at www.fao.org/ag/AGA/AGAP/FRG/Feedsafety/oecd-gmo.htm).

Royal Society of Canada (2001) *Elements of Precaution: Recommendations for the Regulation of Food Biotechnology in Canada*. An Expert Panel Report on the Future of Food Biotechnology prepared for Health Canada, Canadian Food Inspection Agency and Environment Canada. Ottawa: Royal Society of Canada, June.

Secretariat of the Convention on Biological Diversity (2000) *Cartagena Protocol on Biosafety to the Convention on Biological Diversity*. Montreal: SCBD, February (available at www.biodiv.org/doc/legal/cartagena-protocol-en.pdf).

UN Economic Commission for Europe (2003) Report of Working Party on Technical Harmonization and Standardization Policies (available at www.unece.org/trde/tips/wp6/wp6_start.htm).

WHO/Europe and Food Safety Authority of Ireland (2001) *Systems for Improved Coordination and Harmonization of National Food Safety Control Services*. Copenhagen: WHO and Dublin: Food Safety Authority of Ireland, June (available at www.who.dk/foodsafety/Assistance/20020418_4).

WTO (1997) *EC Measures Concerning Meat and Meat Products (Hormones) Complaint by the United States – Report of the Panel*. WT/DS26/R/USA, 18 August. Geneva: WTO.

Zarrilli, S. (2000) *International Trade in Genetically Modified Organisms and Multilateral Negotiations: A New Dilemma for Developing Countries*. UNCTD/DITC/TNCD/1, 5 July. Geneva: UNCTAD.

Chapter 10

Dolan, C., Humphrey, J. and Harris-Pascal, C. (1999) *Horticulture Commodity Chains: The Impact of the UK Market on the African Fresh Vegetable Industry*. Working Paper No. 96. Brighton: Institute of Development Studies at the University of Sussex, September.

McCulloch, N. and Ota, M. (2002) *Export Horticulture and Poverty in Kenya*. IDS Working Paper 174. Brighton: Institute of Development Studies at the University of Sussex.

McCulloch, N., Winters, L.A. and Cirera, X. (2001) *Trade Liberalization and Poverty: A Handbook*. London: Centre for Economic Policy Research.

Stevens, C. and Kennan, J. (2001) 'Food Aid and Trade', in S. Devereux and S. Maxwell (eds), *Food Security in Sub-Saharan Africa*. London: ITDG Publishing.

Stevens, C., Devereux, S. and Kennan, J. (2002) 'International Trade, Livelihoods and Food Security in Developing Countries' Brighton: Institute of Development Studies at the University of Sussex (mimeo).

Stevens, C., Greenhill, R., Kennan, J. and Devereux, S. (2000) *The WTO Agreement on Agriculture and Food Security*. Economic Paper 42. London: Commonwealth Secretariat.

WTO (2003) 'Negotiations on Agriculture: First Draft of Modalities for the Further Commitments (revision)', TN/AG/W/1/Rev.1, 18 March. Geneva: World Trade Organization, Committee on Agriculture.

Chapter 11

Dolan, C. and Humphrey, J. (2001) 'Governance and Trade in Fresh Vegetables: The Impact of UK Supermarkets on the African Horticultural Industry', *Journal of Development Studies* 37 (2): 147-76.

Dowler, E., Turner, S. and Dobson, B. (2001) *Poverty Bites: Food, Health and Poor Families*. London: Child Poverty Action Group.

FAO (1997) 'Street Foods', *Food and Nutrition Bulletin* 63. Rome: FAO.

FAO (2002a) *World Agriculture towards 2015/2030*. Rome: FAO.

FAO (2002b) 'Anti-Hunger Programme: Reducing Hunger through Sustainable Agricultural and Rural Development and Wider Access to Food'. Second Draft. Rome: FAO.

FAO (2002c) *The State of Food Insecurity in the World 2002*. Rome: FAO.

FAO (2002d) *FAO Factsheet on Biotechnology and Food Security*. Rome: FAO.

FAO (2002e) *FAO Factsheet on Food Quality and Safety*. Rome: FAO.

FAO (2002f) *FAO Factsheet on Feeding the Cities*. Rome: FAO.

FAO (2003) 'Codex Alimentarius Commission Adopts More Than 50 New Food Standards: New Guidelines on Genetically Modified and Irradiated Food'. FAO Newsroom (available at www.fao.org/english/newsroom/news/2003/20363-en.html, accessed 9 July 2003).

Gustafsson, U. (2002) 'School Meals Policy: The Problem with Governing Children', *Social Policy and Administration* 36 (6): 685-97.

Horton, S. (2002) 'Dietary Changes', in IFPRI, *Sustainable Food Security for All by 2020*. Proceedings of an International Conference, 4-6 September 2001. Washington, DC: International Food Policy Research Institute.

Hussain, S. (2002) 'Food Security: Rights, Livelihoods and the World Food Summit – Five Years Later', *Social Policy and Administration* 36 (6): 626-47.

Maxwell, D. (1999) 'The Political Economy of Urban Food Security in Sub-Saharan Africa', *World Development* 27 (11): 1939-54.

Maxwell, D., Levin, C., Armar-Klemesu, M., Ahiadeke, C., Ruel, M. and Morris, S. (1998) *Urban Livelihoods, Food and Nutrition Security in Greater Accra*. Research Report. Washington, DC: International Food Policy Research Institute.

Pingali, P. L. (1997) 'From Subsistence to Commercial Production Systems: The Transformation of Asian Agriculture', *American Journal of Agricultural Economics* 79: 628-34.

Pingali, P. L. and Rosegrant, M. (1995) 'Agricultural Commercialisation and Diversification: Processes and Policies', *Food Policy* 20 (3): 171-85.

Popkin, B. M. (1999) 'Urbanization, Lifestyle Changes and the Nutrition Transition', *World Development* 27 (11): 1905-16.

Reardon, T. and Berdegué, J. A. (eds) (2002a) 'Supermarkets and Agrifood Systems: Latin American Challenges', *Development Policy Review* 20 (4): Theme Issue.

Reardon, T. and Berdegué, J. A. (2002b) 'The Rapid Rise of Supermarkets in Latin America: Challenges and Opportunities for Development', *Development Policy Review* 20 (4): 371-88.

Reardon, T., Berdegué, J. A. and Farrington, J. (2002) *Supermarkets and Farming in Latin America: Pointing Directions for Elsewhere?*. Natural Resource Perspectives No. 81. London: Overseas Development Institute.

Reardon, T., Timmer, P. and Berdegué, J. A. (2003) 'The Rise of Supermarkets in Latin America and Asia: Implications for International Markets for Fruits and Vegetables', in A. Regmi and M. Gehlhar (eds), *Global Markets for High Value Food Products*. Agriculture Information Bulletin. Washington, DC: Economic Research Service, US Department of Agriculture.

Ruel, M. T., Garrett, J. L., Morris S. M., Maxwell, D., Oshaug, A., Engle, P., Purima, M., Slack, A. and Haddad, L. (1998) *Urban Challenges to Food and Nutrition Security: A Review of Food Security, Health and Caregiving in the Cities*. IFPRI FCND Discussion Paper No. 51. Washington, DC: International Food Policy Research Institute, October.

United Nations (2001) *World Urbanization Prospects: The 2001 Revision*. New York: United Nations.

UN Habitat (2001) *The State of the World's Cities 2001*. Nairobi: UN Habitat.

Chapter 12

AusAid (1997) *Report of the Committee of Review on Australian Overseas Aid Program*. The Simons Report. Canberra: AusAid.

Barrett, C. B. (2001) 'Does Food Aid Stabilize Food Availability?', *Economic Development and Cultural Change* 49 (2): 335-49.

Barrett, C. B. and Heisey, K. C. (2002) 'How Effectively Does Multilateral Food Aid Respond to Fluctuating Needs?', *Food Policy* 27 (5-6): 477-92.

Benson, C. (2000) 'The Food Aid Convention: An Effective Safety Net?', in Clay and Stokke.

Benson, C. and Clay, Edward J. (1998) 'Additionality and Diversion: Agricultural Credits and Food Aid to Eastern Europe and the Former Soviet Republics', *World Development* 26 (1): 31-44.

Canadian International Development Agency (CIDA) (1997) *Food Aid Strategy*. Quebec: CIDA, March.

Christian Michelsen Institute (CMI) (1993) *Evaluation of the World Food Programme. Final Report*. Bergen: CMI, December.

Clay, Edward J. (1995) 'Conditionality and Programme Food Aid: From the Marshall Plan to Structural Adjustment', in Olav Stokke (ed.), *Aid and Political Conditionality*. EADI Book Series 16. London: Frank Cass.

Clay, Edward J. and Benson, C. (1993) *Food Aid Programmes of the European Community and its Member States: A Comparative Statistical Analysis*. Working Paper No. 72. London: Overseas Development Institute, June.

Clay, Edward J., Dhiri, Sanjay and Benson, C. (1996) *Joint Evaluation of European Union Programme Food Aid. Synthesis Report*. London: Overseas Development Institute.

Clay, Edward J., Pillai, Nita and Benson, C. (1998a) *The Future of Food Aid: A Policy Review*. London: Overseas Development Institute.

Clay, Edward J., Pillai, Nita and Benson, C. (1998b) *Food Aid and Food Security in the 1990s: Performance and Effectiveness*. Working Paper No. 113. London: Overseas Development Institute.

Clay, Edward J. and Singer, Hans W. (1985) *Food Aid and Development: Issues and Evidence*. WFP Occasional Paper No. 3. Rome: World Food Programme, September.

Clay, Edward J. and Stokke, Olav (eds) (1991) *Food Aid Reconsidered: Assessing the Impact on Third World Countries*. EADI Book Series 11. London: Frank Cass.

Clay, Edward J. and Stokke, Olav (eds) (2000) *Food Aid and Human Security*. EADI Book Series 24. London: Frank Cass.

Doornbos, Martin (2000) 'Revisiting the Food Aid Debate: Taking a Closer Look at the Institutional Factor', in Clay and Stokke.

European Commission (1996) *Programme communautaire de sécurité et d'aide alimentaire.* Brussels: Directorate General for Development, Food Security and Food Aid Unit, April.

European Council (1996) 'Council Regulation (EC) No. 1292/96 of 27 June 1996 on Food Aid Policy and Food Aid Management and Special Operations in Support of Food Security', *Official Journal L* 166. Brussels, 5 July.

European Court of Auditors (1997) 'Special Report No 2/97 Concerning Humanitarian Aid from the European Union between 1992 and 1995 together with the Commission's Replies', *Official Journal* C143. Brussels, 12 May.

Faaland, Just, McLean, Diana and Norbye, Ole David Kot (2000) 'The World Food Programme and International Food Aid', in Clay and Stokke.

Food and Agriculture Organisation (FAO) (1996) *Food Security and Food Assistance.* Technical background document 13, World Food Summit, Rome, 13-17 November.

FAO (2002) *The State of Food Insecurity in the World 2001.* Rome: FAO.

FAO, IFAD and WFP (2002) 'Reducing Poverty and Hunger: The Critical Role of Financing for Food, Agriculture and Rural Development'. Paper prepared for the International Conference on Financing for Development, Monterrey, Mexico, 18-22 March.

IDC (2003) *The Humanitarian Crisis is Southern Africa.* House of Commons, Session 2002-3, Third Report, together with the Proceedings of the Committee, Evidence and Appendices. London, 4 March.

Jackson, Tony (1982) *Against the Grain: The Dilemma of Project Food Aid.* Oxford: Oxfam.

Marchione, T. (2002) 'Foods Provided through US Government Emergency Food Aid Programmes: Policies and Customs Governing their Formulation, Selection and Distribution', *Journal of Nutrition* 132: 2104S-2111S.

Maxwell, Simon (1991) 'The Disincentive Effect of Food Aid: A Pragmatic Approach', in Clay and Stokke.

Overseas Development Institute (2000) *Time to Grasp the Nettle.* ODI Briefing Paper No. 1. London: Overseas Development Institute.

Shaw, D. John (2001) *The UN World Food Programme and the Development of Food Aid.* Basingstoke and New York: Palgrave.

Shaw, D. John and Clay, Edward J. (1994) *World Food Aid.* London: James Currey.

Shaw, D. John and Clay, Edward J. (1998) 'Global Hunger and Food Security after the World Food Summit', *Canadian Journal of Development Studies* 39: 55-76, Special Issue.

Stevens, Christopher (1979) *Food Aid and the Developing World.* London: Croom Helm.

USAID (2002) *US International Food Assistance Report 2001.* Washington, DC: United States Agency for International Development.

WFP (1996) *Tackling Hunger in a World Full of Food: Tasks Ahead for Food Aid.* Rome: WFP.

WFP (1999) *Enabling Development.* Executive Board Annual Session 17-20 May. Agenda Item 4. WFP/EB.A/99/4-A. Rome: WFP.

Index

CPSIA information can be obtained at www.ICGtesting.com
Printed in the USA
BVOW04s0745260416

445575BV00005B/6/P

9 781405 126021